SEBEI LAW

The late Y. M. Chemonges, member of the Uganda Legislative Council, talking to the oldest living son of the prophet Matui at the ceremony to release Matui's spirit, November, 1962.

WALTER GOLDSCHMIDT

SEBEI LAW

Berkeley and Los Angeles
UNIVERSITY OF CALIFORNIA PRESS
1967

University of California Press
Berkeley and Los Angeles, California
Cambridge University Press
London, England

Designed by Jorn Jorgensen
Printed in the United States of America

To the
KIRWOKIK OF SEBEI
both ancient and modern
and to the memory of
Y. M. CHEMONGES

Acknowledgments

An ethnographic work has been in so many ways helped by so many people that it is impossible to give direct thanks to all.

The first and outstanding debt is owed to the Sebei themselves, the officials, the informants, and the many citizens who helped to shape my image of Sebei customs. I hope this record of their legal system repays them somewhat for their patience and friendship. Among the leaders whose help I would like particularly to mention are the late Y. M. Chemonges, member of the Uganda Legislature and creative leader of the Sebei; Aloni Muzungyo, saza chief of Sebei for many years and latterly of the Saza of Bukwa; Yunusu Wandera, the first saza chief of Sebei; A. S. Ngokit, chairman of the District Council; Stanley Salimu, for many years Saza judge; the members of the District Council, the district and county officials, and the chiefs of Sebei.

A particular debt is owed to my two interpreters and good friends, whose patience and skill were necessary to the performance of their essential task, Richard Bomet and Y. A. Chemtai.

Many officials have helped to make the research both pleasurable and useful: Sir Andrew Cohen, governor of Uganda at the time of my first visit; Dr. Audrey Richards, formerly director of the East African Institute of Social Research, Kampala; Mr. R. F. J. Lindsell and Mr. M. G. Johnson, district commissioners of Mbale District in 1954 and 1961, respectively; and many others in Mbale.

For particular help in organizing and sitting in on the Law Conference, I want to express my gratitude to Mr. James Fleming, then head of the Uganda Law School at Entebbe, and to Mr. Peter Hunt, then Courts Advisor, Eastern Region, Uganda.

The Sebei who participated in this conference, listed in Appendix C, likewise deserve my sincerest appreciation.

My colleagues in the field in conjunction with the Culture and Ecology in East Africa Project, Francis P. Conant of Hunter University, Robert B. Edgerton of the Neuropsychiatric Institute, University of California, Los Angeles, Symmes C. Oliver of the University of Texas, Philip W. Porter of the University of Minnesota, and Edgar V. Winans of the University of Washington, have been helpful and supportive in many ways; they have read the manuscript and given me generously and widely of their advice. Others who examined an earlier draft manuscript and gave me help were Paul Mishkin of the University of Pennsylvania Law School, Laura Nader of the Department of Anthropology, University of California, Berkeley, Murray Schwartz of the UCLA Law School, and Mr. Peter Hunt. The constructive criticisms by Professor Herbert Morris of the UCLA Department of Philosophy and School of Law significantly improved the final draft. Dr. Christine Montgomery was helpful in working out the orthography and in providing numerous etymologies. Mary Schaeffer's secretarial and editorial functions were performed beyond the normal call of duty, for which again my thanks are most happily expressed. I also express appreciation to the Cartographic Laboratory of the Department of Geography, University of Minnesota, for drawing the maps and charts.

The fieldwork in 1954 was supported by a Fulbright Research Scholarship, a Wenner-Gren Postdoctoral Fellowship, and a grant-in-aid from the Social Science Research Council. The Culture and Ecology Project, under which the 1961–62 fieldwork was supported, was made possible by a grant from the National Science Foundation and by a United States Public Health Service grant from the National Institute of Mental Health.

The first draft of this manuscript was prepared while I was a Fellow of the Center for Advanced Study in the Behavioral Sciences. I have had an opportunity to express my gratitude to that institution before, and it is a pleasure to say again how much the staff contributed to my productive effort during that year by placing its facilities and its talents at my disposal, and how much I gained by the stimulation of the Fellows assembled there.

My wife Gale, who participated in all phases of the research, helped me not only in this material way but also in giving me the benefit of her insight; for her companionship in the field no expression of appreciation is adequate.

W. G.

Contents

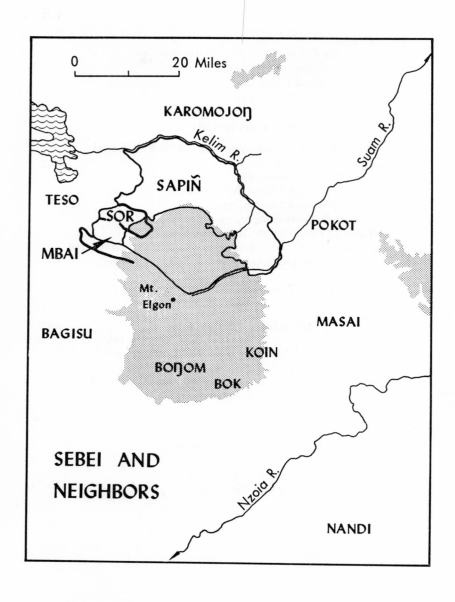

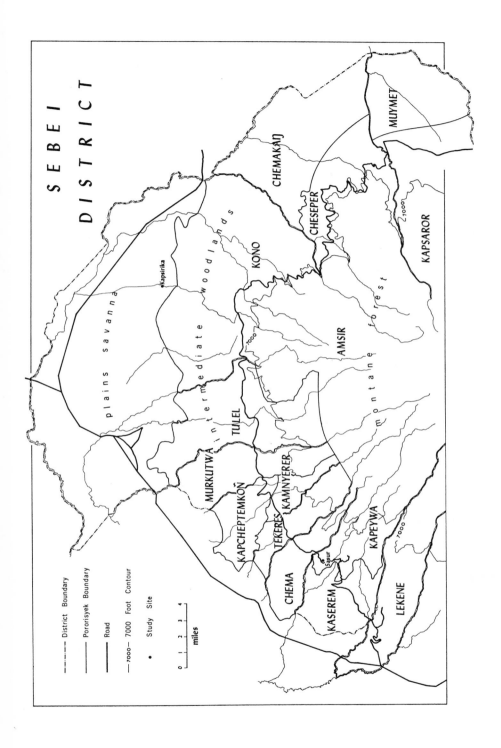

S E B E I
D I S T R I C T

District Boundary
Pororisyek Boundary
Road
─7000─ 7000 Foot Contour
• Study Site

0 1 2 3 4
miles

MUYMET

CHEMAKAŊ

CHESEPER

KAPSAROR

KONO

•Kapsirika

plains savanna

woodlands

intermediate

7000

AMSIR

montane forest

7000

MURKUTWA

TULEL

KAMNYERER

KAPCHEPTEMKOŇ

TEKERES

KAPEYWA

CHEMA

Sasur

KASEREM

LEKENE

7000

Theoretical Orientation

In this book I endeavor to delineate the rules that regulate
formal interpersonal relationships among a people of Uganda
and, where relevant, the methods by which these rules are enforced and their transgressors punished. In brief, it is a treatise
on Sebei law. Although primarily interested in pre-
Europeanized Sebei law, I give attention to the dynamic historic
changes that have taken place both prior to and during the
Baganda-European influences of the past half century. I have
sought to make this substantive record as accurate and as detailed as possible. Furthermore, I have tried to be explicit about
my sources of information, quoting both informants' statements
and key legal cases, so as to enable the reader to understand the
basis upon which my generalizations rest. In this I hope to make
a substantive contribution to ethnography and aid administra-
tors to apply, with such modifications as are necessary and wise,
the time-honored regulations of old Sebei.

My initial purpose was the innocent one of describing the
corpus of laws of the Sebei, without concern either for any
theory as to what the law is nor, for that matter, expecting to
make any contribution (beyond providing substantive information) to the general theory of jurisprudence. I find—as students
of customary law have generally found—that one cannot entirely avoid the former problem, and I think that the Sebei data
do, in fact, offer some important contributions to the latter. I
shall not here discuss these contributions, which are the subject
matter of my two concluding chapters, other than to say they
derive entirely from the data on Sebei, I having made no at-

tempt at comparisons to other societies nor reviewed the literature on the theory of primitive law.

The theoretical position I have taken here has been expressed
in broad terms in my *Comparative Functionalism*.[1] In that essay
I argued that the endeavor to establish transcultural entities is a
false reification of concepts; that it is a bootless enterprise to try
to define the family, government, or other institutional activities in universal terms. The same applies to the law. What we
must do, instead, is to focus upon the universal demands of
social systems, the requisite *functions,* and to seek out in each
culture the institutional means by which these functions are
performed. Thus I have not tried to apply a universal definition
of law to delimit my subject of discourse.

One means that has been used to avoid the problem of universal definition has been to examine behavior entirely in terms
of the native terminologies, that is, to discover what the native
people would consider the law and follow through the subject
matter as they would describe it. I find this procedure objection-
able for two reasons. The first is the question as to whether the
subjects of study have a conceptual scheme that is applicable, a
native conception of what is legal and what is not. Insofar as I
can tell, with respect to the Sebei, I think that in some ways they
do, and in some they do not, have such a scheme. They seem to
distinguish both morality and etiquette from that which they
treat as legal, for instance. On the other hand, they have no
special term for the law, no truly separate legal institutions, no
specialists in the law. My second objection is that if we examined each society in terms of what it considered to be the law,
we could not engage in comparative studies, as (unless they all
turn out to be coterminous, which would make the procedure
unnecessary) there would be no consensus as to the subject of
comparison.

What I have in fact done is to examine those facets of Sebei
behavior which are the counterpart to those we, in our everyday
use of English, call law, without consideration as to whether the

[1] Walter Goldschmidt, *Comparative Functionalism: An Essay on Anthropological Theory* (Berkeley and Los Angeles: University of California
Press, 1966) .

same things would also be called law among the Sebei, or whether they are actions that take place in the context of primarily "legal" institutions. That is, I assert that we recognize loosely a realm of law, as distinct from other areas of consideration such as religion or economics or even the more closely associated categories of government, morality, and etiquette. I do not think this realm of law to be a transcultural entity, but rather a somewhat coherent subject of discourse. I do not think we can verbalize precisely a set of criteria, such as the application of sanctions or the existence of certain types of institutions, which mark off what is law in our society from what is not law. I do think that despite these deficiencies most of us have a reasonably clear idea as to what are legal matters and what are not, with considerable fuzziness at the edges. We know that there is a distinction between law and etiquette even though we would be hard put to verbalize it, and would not be surprised to learn that today's etiquette may have been yesterday's law. We make a distinction between law and morality despite the fact that in our society a good deal of "morality" is reinforced by legislation. The Sebei also, as it happens, treat matters of etiquette and matters of morality differently from matters of law, and while things we consider to be in one category might among the Sebei be considered to be in the other, the problem does not plague us in fact. My program calls for examining, insofar as possible, the realm of behavior among the Sebei which is the counterpart to our everyday conception of the realm of law among ourselves.

Fundamentally, this mode of operation has led to a focus on what may best be called law jobs—the functional requisites within the realm of law. Just as I believe it is proper to focus on governance as a process rather than on government as an institution, on procreation and child-rearing as an activity rather than on marriage and family as institutions, so it seems to me it is proper to focus upon the requisite tasks in the realm of law rather than on the institutional devices by which these are undertaken. The fact of Sebei life is that matters of law are not exclusively or even primarily operative under institutions devoted to legal activities; on the contrary, diverse institutions—familial, religious, economic—concern themselves with the performance of law jobs. Some institutions do exist (the local moots, the institutionalized role of certain elders) which may be viewed as primarily legal institutions, but had we focused upon them we would never have come to an understanding of Sebei legal action.

We focus, then, on law jobs. These law jobs are the definition of the rights and obligations of persons and groups to one another and to the things that constitute the resources and equipment from which they gain their livelihood and their satisfactions, the enforcement and reaffirmation of such rights and obligations, and the resolution of conflicts as they arise as a result of the transgression of these rights and obligations.

If my analysis of the materials reported here is correct, the interesting fact is that, though there is no distinction of the legal from the nonlegal, either conceptually or institutionally, Sebei legal behavior does have an internal ideational unity. But such unity cannot be seen merely at the level of legal action or of jural rules; it relates to the cultural presuppositions and the metaphysical assumptions that lie deep in Sebei ideology. This does not necessarily mean that the law is an institutional reality distinct from other institutional realities. It means, rather, that when we examine the manner in which the Sebei function with respect to a related set of tasks, without regard to the institutional unities, we find that the underlying consistency of Sebei culture gives a coherence to the whole. This discovery is the more surprising in view of the fact that the Sebei are diversified areally and have undergone, as we shall see, considerable cultural modification.

I have found it meaningful to discuss the legal institutions of the Sebei under three major categories of action, which I have called the Law of Affiliation, the Law of Violence, and the Law of Property. The Law of Violence is essentially clan law; that is, the treatment of breaches involving physical harm inflicted by one person on another are treated as acts between corporate groups for which group responsibility is demanded. The Law of Property is essentially individual law; an act involving the "things" of Sebeiland (whether it be theft or contract) is an act between two individuals and must be so treated in the adjudication of interests. The Law of Affiliation is close to what is usually called Family Law and it offers us an understanding of the way the two other forms of law articulate; for, quite clearly, the pattern of social identification and the character of property transfers relate the individual to his broader community both through ties of sentiment and the nexus of economic goods.

I have generally avoided legal terminology, in part because I have no legal training and the use of such terminology has many pitfalls, but more because such terms (which have often developed a high degree of precision in the growth of our own jurisprudence) do not accord with Sebei practices. There are exceptions—words of wide currency in English, like "murder" and "contract"; in these instances I have given as explicitly as possible the Sebei definitions. For many terms I have regularly used the Sebei word, for the nearest English equivalent (even when defined) is misleading; however, I have tried to keep these Sebei words to a minimum. Where possible I have sought the Sebei terminological distinctions, as, for instance, in the kinds of property delicts, the kinds of cattle and work contracts, and the kinds of witchcraft. It is a well-established ethnographic principle that where such terminology exists and has clear and consistent meaning it offers a key to understanding the under-lying sentiments and attitudes. On the other hand, I am not convinced that we could develop a picture of the legal actions of the Sebei by an examination of their legal terminology, as some recent students of law would have us believe.

We must remember that the Sebei not only do not have a delineated set of legal institutions, they do not have lawyers or students of jurisprudence, and only with some falsification can they be said to have had judges. This suggests that they do not have their own theories of the law nor a closed body of doctrine with respect to the law; they have only statements about what the law holds with respect to this matter or that, based on what is normally done or what has in fact been done in this or that instance. Perhaps my task has thereby been made easier, for I had less opportunity to be confused by a native jurisprudence and therefore more freedom in letting the cumulative data lead me to the analysis herein rendered. What is important is that, for better or worse, it is my systematization, not that of Sebei jurists. I do not mean that Sebei elders cannot make generalizations as to what the rules are with respect to this or that matter, and how a particular case should be decided, or the relevance of precedent. What I do mean is that the total picture, the interconnectedness of diverse elements, and the principles that underlie legal action were not formulated by Sebei informants. Nor do I believe they could have been.

I have found it necessary to use certain words with respect to the kinds of sanctions applied against persons who have been found guilty of a delict. These sanctions may be applied by the community or by the adversary in a legal conflict; they may be in the form of a property demand or a physical retaliation against his person or his property. I have used the term *fine* when the community demands a payment that is shared rather than given to the adversary; *compensation* when a payment is demanded, either by the community or the adversary, to be given to the adversary. I have used the term *vengeance* when the sanction is a physical act applied with impunity by the adversary (normally killing a clansman of the murderer by a clansman of his victim) and *punishment* when the hurt is inflicted by the community. In many instances the only demand is the *restitution* of the property that has been stolen or falsely taken.

One of the dangers inherent in discussions of legal systems of unlettered peoples is that the description may take on a false precision. It is after all one of the culture traits in Western law that words are given very exact meanings, and the nicety of verbal distinctions is the hallmark of good reporting. But legal action, among the Sebei at least, is rarely very precise. Even in the cattle contracts, which are the most developed aspect of Sebei law, one can be guilty of trying to force too closely the limits of legal demand. The Sebei themselves recognize the existence of conditions that are not enforceable, but which would be honored under the proper circumstances—a twilight zone at the edges of legal obligations. This is not merely a disagreement over details (though that occurs too), but a consensus that a person really ought to do things he is not obligated to do.

This situation, which I assume to be general, is exacerbated among the Sebei by the fact of their internal differentiation, and more important, by the fact that they had in the century or so prior to European contact shifted their economy from predominantly cattle-keeping, with only ancillary hoe-farming, to one that in most areas is predominantly (and in some almost exclusively) hoe-farming of an intensive kind. The theoretical implications of this shift, the evidence of certain adaptations in Sebei legal behavior, and the broader significance of this adaptation are dealt with in the final chapter of this book.

Who the Sebei Are

The word *Sebei* refers to a group of formerly independent but closely interrelated tribes living on the northern and northwestern slopes of Mount Elgon (and on the plains below) in Eastern Uganda. The term has come into use in modern administration parlance and these people now identify themselves as Sebei. Etymologically, *Sebei* (variously *Sabei, Sapei,* etc.) is a corruption of *Sapiñ,* the name of one of the tribes that constitute modern Sebei. Their territory was curtailed by the formation of the Kenya-Uganda border, for Sapiñ formerly extended into modern Kenya on the eastern side of the mountain and on to the Uasin Gisu Plateau. The Sebei speak a language of the Nandi cluster of the family of languages now generally called Kalenjin; they are most closely affiliated in language and culture to the Kalenjin-speaking peoples on the southern slopes of Elgon. The Kalenjin cluster constitutes the southern group of Nilotic languages, which belong to the Eastern Sudanic branch of Chari-Nile in Greenberg's Nilo-Saharan language family.[2]

The history of the Sebei remains to be established. Ethnographic data are ambiguous; there is some mythic suggestion that the Sebei originated on Mount Elgon, but the evidence indicates an origin from the east and north, and at least many of the clans recently migrated from the Elgeyo district across the high plains to the east. The original Sebei economy appears to have rested chiefly on cattle-keeping, with ancillary use of goats

---

[2] Joseph H. Greenberg, "The Languages of Africa," *International Journal of American Linguistics* (Bloomington, Ind.), vol. 29, no. 1 (1963).

and sheep, and with a secondary involvement in shifting hoe cultivation of millet and sorghum. Comparative evidence and ethnographic data collected suggest that the Sebei moved around the mountain two or more centuries ago and occupied the whole of it until early in the nineteenth century, when they were forced out of the southwest sector by Bantu peoples,[3] from whom they obtained plantains. This late nineteenth-century Gisu pressure caused an internal movement in which these now plantain-growing Sebei pushed into the relatively sparsely populated north escarpment, bringing a more sedentary mode of life and more intensive use of land into an area that until then had only secondary involvement with agriculture.

The Sebei share age-sets with their related tribesmen, and there is some indication of age-grade encampments or manyattas at one time, but settlement is now in scattered homesteads within explicitly delimited but undemarcated minor territorial entities. These age-sets, which form so important a role in the organization of the more predominantly pastoral linguistic and cultural relatives of the Sebei, play virtually no part in the legal machinery of Sebei itself. Indeed, except for the strong rule against marriage between a man and the daughters of an age-set mate, I believe one could describe Sebei law in all its details without reference to age-sets, though the still important initiation ceremonies of both men and women define adult status. In keeping with the developing agriculture from which Sebei derive most of their sustenance today, the locality has taken on greater importance as the age-set declined. But this is getting us too deep too soon into the details of Sebei law, which will be developed at the appropriate place.

Overview of Sebei Culture

It may help the reader to have a brief overview of Sebei culture; however, as a comprehensive monograph on Sebei life is in preparation, I will not enter into detail. Sebeiland today consists of the northern slope of Mount Elgon, extending northward

---

[3] J. S. LaFontaine, "The Gisu of Uganda," in *Ethnographic Survey of Africa,* ed. C. D. Forde, East Central Africa, Part X (London: International African Institute, 1959) , p. 11.

from the summit in a fan shape and down to the Karamoja plain as far as the Greek River, which flows westward a few miles north of Elgon. Sebei territory is readily divided into three zones: (*a*) a highland area above the forest line, extending from about the 9,000-foot contour to as far up the summit as habitation is feasible; (*b*) the escarpment, on which most of the 35,000 Sebei dwell, which lies between the 5,000- and 7,000-foot contours; and (*c*) the strip of dry plains, lying at 4,000 feet above sea level.

The first zone is the habitation for but a few hundred; remote from roads and outside influence, it remains culturally conservative. The economy consists chiefly of cattle-grazing on the grassy downs and the cultivation of small gardens in which the potato is now the chief crop. Honey is an important resource. The rectangular flat-roofed houses are beginning to be replaced with rondevals.

Most Sebei live along the escarpment, which has been heavily infiltrated by Bagisu, their Bantu-speaking neighbors to the west. A road now runs along the escarpment, connecting the towns of Mbale, in Uganda, and Kitale, of the Trans-Nzoia district in Kenya. This zone varies as one moves from west to east; on the western border the land is overwhelmingly devoted to plantains, which gradually thin out, giving way as one moves eastward to a higher ratio of grain cultivation, and this in turn to larger amounts of open grazing land, so that the central and eastern sections are rugged, largely pastoral country. As one rounds the mountain and comes to the eastern Kenya border the land is again more heavily cultivated, but now largely in maize. This eastern, Bukwa, region is influenced by Europeans of Kenya, and fences, plows, and even one or two tractors are to be found.

The plains are sparsely populated, but they are gradually filling up as roads improve, wild herbivores disappear, and use of the plow increases to make possible a new (for the Sebei) kind of agriculture. Though Sebei territory, this lowland was depopulated in the nineteenth century through the force of aggressive military predators (Karamojong, Pokot, Nandi, Masai), and used only sporadically until about 1914 when establishment of a police post on the Greek River encouraged resettlement.

The economy of the Sebei has varied both regionally and temporally, but regularly consists of a mixture, in differing proportions, of the herding of cattle, sheep, and goats; the cultivation of plantains, maize, millet, various root crops, sorghum (which has virtually disappeared), and manioc (which, like maize, is a European introduction); the gathering of wild products, of which honey is the most important; and the hunting of game. Neither of the last two activities is proportionately very important, though they have supplemented the economy in varying degrees. Livestock is grazed and not stall-fed. Cultivation is with the short iron-bladed hoe (formerly bone blades), and nowadays there is increasing use of the ox-drawn plow, mainly in Bukwa and on the plains, but also, when feasible, on the western escarpment. Coffee, which was introduced into Sebeiland at least as early as 1920, is the principal cash crop of the escarpment area; it is of excellent quality, but cultivation practices are not considered up to standard. Cattle and grain are the chief sources of cash on the plains and in Bukwa.

Daily life is lived in the context of a household. Marriage is polygynous, and usually the wife moves to the area of the husband and takes over land previously cultivated by her mother-in-law. Normally each wife has her own house, which is her kitchen and living quarters; the man may have his own house, but more often does not. Usually these huts are close together, and wives, though they have their own plots, are expected to collaborate on cultivation. The cattle are kraaled in a small enclosure near the houses; the whole may be circumscribed by a brush fence on the plains. The women do most of the garden work, cook food, make beer, milk the cows, seek wild foods, mud the walls and floors of their houses, and nowadays often market produce. Men clear bush, look after cattle, occasionally help the women in cultivation, do such hunting of game as occurs, gather honey, and tend the coffee. Much cultivation, building, and the like is done in work groups, for which beer is provided, and the beer party is the central feature of the daily social life of Sebei. Beer is made of maize, plantains, or honey, in descending order of frequency.

The native social organization was dominated by three kinds of social units: a system of spatial entities; a system of agnatic kin groups; and a system of age-sets. As these are necessarily described in the section on affiliation, we need not go into detail here. The Sebei recognized a series of acephalous tribes, each with a name and a defined territory (usually extending from the mountain to the plain). These tribes were loosely amalgamated into a larger entity—a sensed commonality without formal organization—which was essentially coterminous with present-day Sebeiland. Only ceremonial action and adherence to common supratribal prophets or seers gave unity to this larger entity. The effective spatial unit was a territory called *pororyet* (*pororisyek*, pl.), of which about fifteen existed throughout Sebeiland, and within which masculine affiliation was formalized. These territories were divided into smaller named spatial units called *sangta* (*songmwek*, pl.), which I shall call villages. Though clearly delimited, the houses are not clustered but scattered over the land, so the boundaries (either physical or social) are not obvious to the casual observer.

The essential kin group was the *aret* (*arosyek*, pl.), a named exogamous patrilineal descent group without totemic or ceremonial reinforcement and without control of property. These clans were subdivided into lineages (*kota; korik,* pl.), the descendants of the presumed sons of the founder of the aret. Formal affiliations were with the larger entity, but the smaller (usually less scattered in residence) was more intimately concerned with daily family affairs. I refer to the larger groups as clans, the lesser as lineages. Clans were occasionally linked in groups of two to four; marriage was then forbidden between their members, but the groups were not named, nor was there any other evidence of corporate behavior.

Each man is initiated at about the age of eighteen (though when much older in earlier days) in an elaborate ritual involving circumcision, and by means of which he enters into an age-set (*pinta*). These age-sets form a cycle of named groups, each of which formerly spanned about a twenty-year period and was divided into three subsets made up of coinitiates. Initiation formerly took place every five to seven years, but nowadays takes place every second year. Women also are initiated (involving an operation in which the clitoris and labia minora are removed) at age sixteen to eighteen, and are inducted into age-sets with counterpart names, though otherwise not unified with the male groups. Initiation for girls now takes place annually. The initiation marks majority status for both sexes, and women are normally married shortly after the initiation cycle is completed. The age-sets evoke a measure of protocol in interpersonal relationships, but they do not, as in other closely related tribes, form functional groups such as warriors, elders, and the like, nor do they display any evidence of corporate responsibility.

The Sebei aboriginally had little formalized office, and, except for the prophets, nobody whose sole work was other than farming or stockkeeping. Informally recognized special statuses included elders or judges (*kirwokintet; kirwokik,* pl.) , and military leaders (*aletarion*) . These persons attained such roles through the demonstration of talents for persuasive discourse and military prowess, respectively; they did not inherit the status nor were they specifically appointed, but acquired the positions gradually through public recognition. The kirwokik might be of greater or lesser stature; a dozen or so were known throughout Sebeiland and were called upon to help adjudicate difficult matters, particularly where separate regions were involved, while the lesser ones seem to have served to adjudicate only localized and unimportant disputes. Each clan recognized the most senior man of the most senior line (from age-order of the siblings who formed the lineages, and so on) as a headman who would be expected to take leadership in clan matters, pour libations to the spirits on ceremonial or social occasions, and lead any discussion of clan matters. Each lineage similarly had such a headman; other than the prestige that derived from his seniority, he seems to have had no explicit powers, title, or special privileges.

Each social unit—sangta, pororyet, aret, or kota—might hold

hearings or councils, called *kokwet*. These were informal or semiformalized affairs, in which either the kirwokik or clan heads would lead the discussion. The prophets (*workoyontet, workoyik*) were persons who had the capacity to foresee events and were consulted by the citizenry to determine the propitious time and course of action on diverse matters. They had no direct secular power but exerted considerable influence. This institution served to hold together loosely the several tribes and pororisyek of Sebeiland. The role of prophet was limited to certain families, the spirit of the deceased entering into one of his descendants.

Warfare was largely defensive, and was engaged in by all active men. There was no age-set definition of a warrior category. Each pororyet (region) was an independent unit, though collaboration was frequent. The Sebei rarely initiated raids, but did mount retaliatory raids against the more aggressive cattle-keepers and defended (with limited success) against the encroachment of the Bagisu and other Bantu peoples to the west. Both spears and bows were used.

Sebei native handicraft is limited. Smiths forge weapons and tools of scrap iron; they formerly knew the smelting of iron from ore. Smithing is an art limited to certain clans, the smith enjoying a measure of special respect. Baskets and mats (chiefly of split bamboo) are woven in the highland area and exchanged for food. Gourds are used for milk and water containers. Some crude pottery could earlier be found in Sebeiland, but it is no longer made there. Leatherwork has largely disappeared with the acquisition of imported cloth, though buffalo-hide shields and a few other articles are made by individuals with special talents. The material culture of the Sebei was never rich; with the rapid acceptance of European clothes and utensils it has become further impoverished.

In addition to the initiation rites, which remain a focal point in Sebei ritual activities, there were ceremonial reinforcements through periodic rituals of purification. The more important of these were performed by the pororyet, while those dealing with mere domestic matters were performed by each village individually. The former were initiated by the prophet and coordinated by the custom of orderly progression of rituals from east to west across Sebeiland.

Verbalization regarding religious belief is sparse, and there is no evidence that Sebei are either speculative or engrossed by cosmological matters or supernatural events. Two elements in the belief system are particularly relevant for a discussion of Sebei law. The first is the concept that each person has a spirit (*onantet; oyik,* pl.) which leaves his body to dwell in an underworld of spirits, that these oyik may be (or do) good or evil, that they must be placated with libations of beer and offerings of food at all ceremonial occasions, and above all that they may harm men for faults committed, including the failure to propitiate them. Oyik bring harm only to their own clan descendants, except that the mother's spirit (or her clansmen's spirits?) may harm her children. There is, as we shall see, a close spiritual bond between clansmen. Second, there is a pervasive fear of witchcraft; the use of sorcery is a conscious effort to do harm. Other beliefs, such as the determination of future events through divination and omens, fear of the evil eye, and the belief in inherited clan characteristics, may also be mentioned; the prophet's powers were occult, as well as secular.

The Sebei are today influenced in varying and increasing degrees by Western culture and alien attitudes and customs imported from the Bagisu and other neighboring tribes. They are least affected, perhaps, in the highland zone, where many have seen no whites other than an occasional mountain-climbing party. But even here European dress is regularly used, iron neck and arm rings of native manufacture are infrequently worn, potatos are a major crop, taxes must be paid, and influences of European attitudes may be found. On the escarpment there are some who have been off to wars in foreign lands (the first appointed Sebei chief served in the 1914–1918 war), while others have never been to the nearby town of Mbale. All require money and purchase clothes, ornaments, household goods, and implements; an increasing number have bicycles, corrugated iron roofs, and other Western items of practical or prestige value. There has long been a Catholic mission at Sipi and another at Bukwa, and many schools were originally established by the Native Anglican Church.

Sebeiland has increasingly been brought into the bureaucratic system established by the British and now taken over by the Uganda government (our fieldwork was largely finished before the establishment of Uganda's independence). Sebeiland was first brought into the administration through the action of a Muganda general, Kakunguru, who established military control over much of eastern Uganda with the quiet support of the British.[4] This control was a harsh one, and the establishment of British authority came as a relief. Yet for most of its subsequent history Sebeiland was dominated by the Bagisu, their erstwhile enemies, who lived in the area where governmental offices were established and who outnumbered the Sebei nearly tenfold. Sebei became a separate county (Saza) in 1934 with a Sebei chief named Yunusu Wandera. He was superseded by Aloni Muzungyo, who served until the county was made a separate district in 1962. The period after World War II saw increased administrative concern with the area and increased devolution of responsibility upon local peoples. The Saza was divided into subcounties and smaller groups, with hierarchies of appointed chiefs supported by local councils. This bureaucracy was charged with administering governmental directives, collecting taxes from local households, and serving as a court system. Formation of the Sebei District was accomplished in 1962 through actions initiated by young educated leaders who chafed under Bagisu bureaucratic domination. Increased use of democratic processes has also created a number of elective posts as well as appointive ones, and the Sebei elected their first member to the Uganda legislative body in 1961.

A cadre of educated elite, literate in Luganda and sometimes in English, has developed with the growth of government. Most of these hold the major offices or serve as schoolteachers, or both; a few shop owners and tradesmen may also be influential. This group is increasingly concerned with Western values; a few have cars, sack suits, permanent houses, and are at home in

[4] See H. B. Thomas, "Capax Imperii: The Story of Semei Kakunguru," *Uganda Journal*, VI (Jan., 1937), 125–136.

Kampala or even Nairobi. Except for service in the army (until recently the King's Africa Rifles) or the police, few have left Sebeiland, and of those that do, fewer still return.

Sources of Information

Research among the Sebei was carried out in two separate expeditions. The first, extending from January to July, 1954, was sponsored by a Fulbright research grant to the United Kingdom, a Social Science Research Council grant, and a postdoctoral fellowship from the Wenner-Gren Foundation. The second, from July, 1961, to November, 1962, was made in the context of the Culture and Ecology in East Africa Project,[5] for which I served as director as well as member of the research team. This latter had as its central purpose the analysis of the adaptation of cultural institutions to ecologic demands in four East African tribes.[6] While the present analysis owes a good deal to the conceptual apparatus developed for that program, and particularly to an increased awareness of the dynamics of cultural adaptation, it does not utilize the specific apparatus of that research, but only the general ethnographic information obtained. A full description of Sebei culture, with special reference to spatial and temporal variation, is in preparation.

The data upon which the document rests are of two basic kinds: (1) statements made by Sebei informants about matters pertaining to what we here call law, and (2) actual instances of legal action, which I call law cases. The latter may again be divided into two categories: (a) those told to me as having been observed or learned about by informants, and (b) those to which I was, in part at least, a participant observer. The former

[5] The Culture and Ecology in East Africa Project was sponsored by the University of California, Los Angeles, and supported by a grant, G-11713, from the National Science Foundation, and by a United States Public Health Service grant, MH-04097, from the National Institute of Mental Health.

[6] The research program has been described in some detail in a symposium presented to the American Anthropological Association (see Walter Goldschmidt, Philip W. Porter, Symmes C. Oliver, Francis P. Conant, Edgar V. Winans, and Robert B. Edgerton, "Variation and Adaptability of Culture: A Symposium," American Anthropologist, 67 [April, 1965], 400–447).

generally, though not in every instance, relate to the pre-European or early historical periods in Sebei life; the latter, usually recorded while taking place, obviously were current. These observed cases again fall into two categories; they were either actual court cases (in which instance both procedure and substance have been influenced by the Baganda and European bureaucracies) or disputes handled outside the regular governmental channels more or less in accordance with old Sebei procedures. Modern local courts, manned by Sebei leaders, demonstrate a good deal of consistency with old legal norms, though we shall have to take note of certain adaptations of old law to modern circumstances. Certain kinds of cases (notably cases involving loss of life or European principals) did not come before the local courts but were heard by the "subordinate courts" with appeal to the High Court.

I mean by a legal case any instance in which the rights and obligations of one or more specific individuals or groups came to public notice and were subject to question and determination. The public notice may have been a clan conflict, a major hearing, a local beer-party dispute, or a hearing before a modern court. It may have been decided or left open; it may have been the subject of a major retaliatory action or have come to ready agreement between the parties. It differs from an informant's statement about legal action in that, however much it might be cited as precedent, it represents a specific instance in which the parties involved are identified. This is, of course, a much broader definition than is normally used; it might have been better to call them legal encounters, but it would have been awkward. In my field notes I have more than 250 separate legal cases, classified by source and character in Appendix B.

There is no legal action that I observed from beginning to end, and no case was narrated to me in full detail. Each case is, in fact, a fragment, but the sum gives us a picture of legal behavior and expectations among the Sebei, with some appreciation of the manner in which these vary both in time and in space. There remain many uncertainties in detail; one would like to know how precedents are used and when they are disregarded, the manner in which decisions were reached in the days when important kirwokik were called in, the uses of both evidence and oath in their procedural aspects, and many other things. But we might very well be carried away by false details. The evidence from direct observation indicates that Sebei legal action involved neither niceties of procedure nor (except in certain areas) specificity of distinctions. We must also remember that informants narrating cases from the depth of their memory supply only the details they consider important, even though they elide matters we feel have much greater significance.

In discussing legal matters I frequently worked with two or more informants at one time, a method that often gives a measure of check against individual bias. The most important such instance, and the one from which much general information and some eighty-five cases derived, was the Law Conference I held for ten days (July 31–August 9, 1962) at Kapchorwa, the district center of Sebeiland. Additional details of this activity are presented in Appendix C, but its general character should be described here.

An agenda of questions was drawn up (but not publicized) in advance, with the aid of Mr. James Fleming and Mr. Peter Hunt, both of them legal experts with the Uganda government. Upon the advice of modern leaders, a group of about ten knowledgeable senior men and women were paid to spend the period of time in Kapchorwa. In addition, a number of officials, particularly Aloni Muzungyo, then the Saza Chief, and Stanley Salimu, the chief judge of Sebei, sat in on the hearings. Mr. Y. Chemtai served as interpreter, aided by Mr. Richard Bomet, both of whom were always present. The questions were generally put by me, but either Fleming or Hunt was present at each session, and they, my wife, and occasionally Sebei also asked questions. A running account of the discourse was recorded, with speakers identified. Sessions generally ran uninterrupted (except when rain on the tin roof drowned our words) until about 2:00 P.M., after which my wife and I would transcribe the day's record. It was found that the participants were very keen about the matter, maintained their own discipline, and hewed to the mark. All persons, including the two women, participated freely in the discussions. They were specifically instructed to cite cases in support of their general statements, which they regularly did, and these were nearly always in point. Only rarely was there disagreement; the presence of two or more English-speaking Sebei served as some check on interpretation. The full transcript runs over 200 typewritten pages.

Another important source of data was the informal hearings that regularly take place in conjunction with the funeral rites for Sebei men. Five or six such hearings were observed, and four were recorded in detail. These hearings involved two matters of law: (1) the allocation of property and wives of the deceased to the appropriate heirs, which gives us the best data on actual inheritance practices; and (2) claims against the estate of a man who dies, which must be made public at the time of his funeral on penalty of forfeit. The family of the deceased may also bring forth claims against others. Since such claims involve the diverse contractual arrangements the deceased has made which are still unfulfilled, this is a primary source of data on the nature of such agreements. In my records there are more than forty separate items adjudicated at funeral moots, not counting matters of inheritance.

One such hearing for a man of considerable wealth was extended over a period of several weeks. The full record of the hearings, as these were transcribed in the process, is being prepared for publication concurrently, and will appear under the title *Kambuya's Cattle: The Legacy of an African Herdsman.*[7]

Such funeral hearings are most informal. The senior member of the clan or of the kota presides; the heirs and relatives of the deceased are expected to be present; and the neighbors and friends participate in the discussion. But the whole is so informally conducted that, except as major disputes arise, it is not easy to see that anything important is being discussed. Individual claims are taken up as persons in the group raise them, and they are summarily disposed of by a kind of consensus appar-

[7] In preparation, University of California Press, Berkeley and Los Angeles.

ently dominated by the family member best in control of the information. No votes are taken. In modern times a disappointed claimant may walk off muttering a threat to take the matter to the formal courts; we may assume that similar threats were made in earlier times—threats to appeal to force or retaliation, or perhaps to the use of curses or sorcery. Indeed, we heard one such threat of sorcery in a family hearing, though not in direct conjunction with a funeral moot.

Many modern disputes do not enter the formal courts today but are taken care of by informal moots, similar in character to funeral moots, called for some special situation. Those disputes I learned of were frequently associated with accusations of sorcery or efforts to remove curses—the kind of thing the modern court is not capable of handling. In the chapter on witchcraft I present in detail one such hearing held in response to accusations between two co-wives, and in conjunction with a ceremonial effort to appease the spirits. I have presented in still greater detail the hearings—again of witchcraft accusation involving co-wives—of such a family kokwet in *Kambuya's Cattle*.

I also attended numerous court cases administered by the local chiefs at different levels under the Uganda Protectorate organization. For such cases there are numerous innovations brought by the British colonial officers, many being adaptations of old Buganda procedure. Such courts were generally held in the official headquarters of the (then) county office or its local subdivisions, though some were held out in the field. These courts are presided over by the local chief; there is a court clerk and a group of assessors. Both plaintiff and defendant stand before the court, and each presents his case in turn; after both have been heard, each brings forward his witnesses. The court endeavors to find the crucial issue that the testimony of the witnesses is to determine. Each assessor then states his opinion, with recommendations for action, including magnitude of penalty when a sentence or fine has been suggested. The chief makes the final determination. While this procedure is certainly alien to Sebei aboriginal practice, the court nevertheless frequently applies the regulations and reinforces the values of the

Sebei in assessing cases, so that such records do give us some knowledge of old Sebei law as well as of current practice.

On the whole, however, these court cases are the least satisfactory of my data, not only because it is difficult to assess the influence of other cultures on actions taken, but because they were always fragmentary. Most cases, after elaborate discussion, are put over to another day for want of a witness, while others (having previously been heard) are difficult to understand. Sometimes—even without a decision—the issue is clearly set forth. Such cases have occasionally been used in this analysis, for they demonstrate current usage and often are manifestly a product of Sebei attitudes uncontaminated by governmental demands; however, I find that court cases are relatively unimportant to the analysis, and I have used them with caution.

My own assessment of the data on which this study is based is that they reflect with a reasonable degree of accuracy the actual policies and programs for adjudication and the diverse regulations that are applicable to Sebei interpersonal relationships, but that they are lacking in detail, both with respect to manner of redress and refinements in legal theory. I suspect, from my general knowledge of Sebei, that this failing also reflects a reality; that the Sebei rules were neither intricate nor sharply delineated, that much was left to ad hoc decisions and the gamesmanship of everyday life. Yet certainly the shared legal understanding of the Sebei was more detailed than the present account suggests; if I had had more direct observation or if the informants had been less terse, a fuller account could have been rendered. So far as they go, and based upon internal evidence, the data do seem to be accurate, for the following reasons: (1) In several instances a case was recorded at different times, and such records, though they stress different details, do not demonstrate any inconsistencies. (2) There are few important differences between the generalized statements made at different times by diverse informants and actual cases on record; where such uncertainties exist, they are reflected in my presentation. (3) Much of the generalization was recorded in group sessions. The most important of these was the Law Conference, but at other times I worked with two or more informants jointly, and

I was particularly sensitive to internal disagreements.[8] In the Law Conference not only did I endeavor to get expression of disagreement, which occasionally was found, but also exemplification with respect to specific cases—a point of view clearly understood by the participants, who recognized precedent as a basis for rendering decisions. (4) I observed enough legal process outside the context of modern courts—in informal family moots—to feel certain that in those matters thus handled the general rules here developed are substantially as indicated, including, incidentally, the lack of subtle detail that characterizes more professional legal controversy. (5) Finally, through the good offices of Dr. Christine Montgomery who was in the field in 1965 obtaining linguistic data, a draft of this manuscript was carefully examined by both Bomet and Chemtai; their few corrections and suggestions have been incorporated.

It must be stated that in recording Sebei data I worked entirely through interpreters. There is no doubt in my mind that it would have been better had I had a full command of Sebei so as to enable me to understand more detail and avoid the filter of interpretation. This lack I tried to minimize by using several interpreters (there were several English-speaking Sebei present throughout the Law Conference, and they did not hesitate to question interpretation) and by seeking native terms and their semantic boundaries. I believe that the disadvantage in the use of interpreters can, however, be overemphasized, and that they are in fact better for this kind of material than anything less than a full command of the native language of a kind that I, at least, cannot achieve in a short time.

More basic than this consideration is the fact that a legal system is not merely a matter of verbalization; it is a pattern of action. The analysis rests, to be sure, on verbal records, but ultimately we are concerned with the actions, the actual cases, which these describe. With the Sebei (and I presume the same thing would be true in any homogeneous, nonliterate commu-

---

[8] Indeed, inasmuch as our research was directed toward differential adaptation of institutions to economy, I rather sought evidence of diverse opinion. Less came to light than I expected, though some is reflected in the data, as we shall see.

nity) a great deal of what goes on is structured by implicit assumptions rather than by explicit and verbalized regulations. Many of these implicit assumptions are outside the awareness of the participants themselves, so that it is essentially a false enterprise either to limit oneself to what informants can verbalize or to force a verbalization of attitudes that are not naturally in the discussion pattern of native speakers. It seems to me quite likely that an overconcern with native terms can lead us to a false specificity of a kind that is as serious a distortion as is the interpreters' contamination. The analysis of actions, even when seen largely through verbalizations of actions, strikes me as more reliable.

Ultimately, my sense of security in the detail rests upon internal consistency, the ability to "make sense" out of underlying patterns of behavior, and the relationship between the legal events described here and the events in other departments of culture. At the same time, it seems important that the reader should have as much data as possible against which to check my generalizations; for this reason I have quoted cases as illustrations and I maintain a file of all cases recorded; I have quoted informants' statements copiously, and have even occasionally reproduced some of the record from the Law Conference.

The fact that Sebei legal behavior and attitude patterns have been subject to adaptation, that some of these have remained constant while others have changed, and the further fact that in this analysis I am particularly concerned with the adaptive process and hence with the temporal dimension of Sebei legal behavior, have all created a particularly vexing problem in writing: the matter of tense. It would have been possible to cast the whole essay in the past tense, but aside from the soporific effect of such writing, it would have created a spurious impression that none of what is here described remains operative. I have chosen, instead, to write in the "ethnographic present" when dealing with generalities, using the past tense either when describing a specific past event or discussing an early epoch in Sebei history.

The whole spirit under which the research was undertaken—the Culture and Ecology Project was focused on

institutional adaptation—made me very concerned with both
the temporal and spatial aspects of the actions analyzed in the
present work, though I was not always successful in establishing
these. We have tried to indicate the time of action in each
instance. For this purpose, the existence of age-sets has been of
value, for the Sebei will speak of "Maina times" as that period
of approximately twenty years during which this group was
initiated but before the next was circumcised. We allocate cases
(where we can) to the following time periods:

1. Prior to direct European influence (*ca.* 1907)
   a. Ñongki times (*ca.* 1865–1885)
   b. Maina times (*ca.* 1885–1905)
2. Period of Baganda overrule (*ca.* 1906–1919)
3. Period of British overrule
   a. *Ca.* 1920–1953
   b. Current (observed cases)

The reader, however, should have some sense of what is
today's Sebei law and what has now gone out of fashion or has
been superseded by the institutions provided by the British, the
Baganda, and the modern Uganda government. I deal briefly
with the broad influences of modernization in Appendix D, but
a few generalizations will be useful at the outset. By and large,
the underlying pattern of attitudes and assumptions remains
operative both as the source of legal dispute and the appropri-
ateness of fair settlement. Furthermore, a good deal of family
and contractual negotiations are relatively unaffected by modernization, and legal action on a private basis concerning such
matters continues to take place. The uses of sorcery and the
action of clans continue surreptitiously but not without effec-
tiveness in many matters under dispute. On the other hand, the
earlier formal legal apparatus—the kirwokik and formal councils, the oath and ordeal, the resort to feud—have all been
superseded by the governmental court system. Local courts
operate chiefly with respect to land disputes, marital strife,
and petty theft. Witnesses and signed statements have superseded the use of the oath as the chief source of evidence.

PART ONE: The Law
of Affiliation

CHAPTER 2 *Affiliation*

General Considerations

By law of affiliation I mean the rules defining membership, the
bases by which a person's belonging is established, and the rights
and obligations inherent in such membership. We thus are talking about what is usually discussed by anthropologists under the
rubric "social organization," and what in jurisprudence is
largely discussed under the rubric "family law." But I deal here
only with the legalistic aspects of social organization, and I also
deal with memberships other than the familial; therefore I have
coined the phrase that is the title of Part One of this discussion
of Sebei legal institutions. I deal with it first because one cannot
appreciate the character of Sebei law-ways without an understanding of the manner in which the individual relates to the
groups in his society.

Every adult Sebei man belongs to three sets of enduring institutionalized social groups which define the basic parameters of
his statuses and roles in the community. The first set of groups
is the familial: he is a member of a *kota*, or lineage, which is a
subdivision of an *aret* or clan, and these clans may be linked in
groups of two or three into loosely defined superclans. The
second set of groups is the spatial: he is a member of a *sangta*
(village), which is a geographically delimited section of a delimited region called *pororyet*, which in turn is part of a tribe
and a supertribe. The third set of groups is one based on his
initiation at puberty in a manner that creates a finite and delimited series of age-sets: he is a member of a group initiated
together during the same period; the units thus formed are in
turn clustered in threes to form a *pinta* or age-set, of which

there are eight, which repeat themselves in long historical cycles. The character of these groupings is set out below.

Each person is also a member of a household, a group of coresidents normally comprising a man, his wives, and their children living together in a group of houses and sharing the tasks of daily life and the rewards of their labors. This group is a transitory unit, existing only for the duration of the marriage; it constitutes what is essentially a family in our legal sense.

Every adult woman has these affiliations as well, but they are not quite so clearly defined in Sebei law and her role in them is less clearly marked; to make these affiliations easier to follow, our generalizations in this chapter are made applicable only to men, and then the relationship of women to these generalizations is examined. The present chapter concerns the familial, spatial, and age-based groupings, dealt with in reverse order to make for easier exposition. The next chapter deals with the household, in the sense that it examines rules pertaining to marriage, divorce, internal responsibility, and inheritance.

The Age-Set

In the introduction I said it would be possible, except for one rule, to discuss the legal institutions and judicial behavior of the Sebei without reference to the age-sets. It is necessary, however, to understand what age-sets are and what they mean to the individual if we are to appreciate the fabric of life in which the Sebei laws operate, and particularly if we are to appreciate the dynamics of legal adaptation—one of our main themes.

The most important ritual event of the Sebei is their periodic initiation of young men and women. This takes place when boys are about age eighteen (girls somewhat younger), though at one time, informants say, boys' initiation took place much later in the life cycle. For men this initiation involves a circumcision; for women, the removal of the clitoris and labia minora, for which there is no appropriate simple English term, and which (in accordance with local and Sebei usage) I will call female circumcision. To the European this is the most dramatic aspect of the initiation ritual, and it is certainly an ordeal that dramatizes the ceremony for the Sebei. But it is only part of a ceremonial cycle that lasts over a period of as much as six months, culminating in a highly secret rite in which the neophytes are given instruction in the magical practices of everyday life and are admitted into their age-set.

Circumcisions (*mutisyet,* from the verb *mut,* "to cut") take place every year for girls, every second year for boys, and at present the subdivision of the age-set is established in this two-year group. In the old days the initiation took place every five to seven years, so that a pinta subdivision comprised youths over a wider range of years, and a pinta (the cluster of three subdivisions) constituted roughly a twenty-year span. The span of years was gradually reduced between about 1910 and 1930, and is now standardized by governmental ruling. Boys and girls are circumcised in separate ceremonies, though I saw one instance in which they went through their preliminary activities together, separating at the time of cutting and remaining apart for all subsequent ceremonial activity.

In Sebei law the initiation redefines completely the social status of the individual: before circumcision the individual is just a boy; after circumcision he is a man. Before circumcision a girl is not marriageable; after circumcision she may become married, and normally does so within the year. The circumcision ritual, then, has the legal function of defining adult status and legal competence to engage in the affairs of the society. (When initiation was delayed, men could fight in wars but still could not get married, though in some parts of Sebeiland they did participate in public discussions or engage in contractual arrangements.) It also has the function of placing the individual, as a member of a particular age-set, in an affiliation that remains throughout life.

When we look at other societies closely related in language and culture to the Sebei, we find that the age-set system has important legal functions, often defining a set of warriors or elders and giving them specified rights and duties. It is not reasonable to doubt that this was once true of the Sebei. But it is not true today; and what is more important, it has not been true of Sebei for any period of time for which directly relevant data can be obtained from living informants. In some of the neighboring societies, age-grade encampments were established, and an ongoing conflict over power manifested itself between age-grades. I have evidence that there were such "manyattas" in parts of Sebei in the past, but they were not noted by the earliest travelers (1890–1900), and now there is no sense of direct, corporate age-set conflict whatsoever. The fact is that age-grades as social entities—as groups with a corporate interest—are not an important part of the Sebei social organization; what we find is a pattern of social observances that are unimportant and relatively empty relics from the time when age-grades were important: a demand to be polite in greeting one's age-mate, an expectation that he feed you, the recognition that beer is available for an age-mate, and so forth. The only regulation of broader significance coming out of this system is that a man must not marry the daughter of his age-mate; it is a strict rule, though examples of its breach can be found. The Nandi and some other neighbors extended hospitality to the sharing of wives. This was not done among the Sebei, though the practice would render meaningful the urgent restriction against marriage with an age-mate's daughter.

In my opinion the age-set system declined in Sebei as a result of the increased involvement with agriculture, the attendant decline of aggressive raiding and warfare, the greater concern with defensive and protective measures—all of which required a fundamentally territorially based military operation under the control of the pororyet. These matters are given further consideration in chapter 13.

The women's initiation inducts them into age-sets having the same names as those of their male contemporaries. These entities have even less function than do the men's, for a woman comes to be concerned with her husband's age-mates, for whom she must prepare food, provide beer, and show politeness, rather than with her own age-mates. Some women do not remember exactly to what age-set they belong. The initiation must be viewed much more as a coming into womanhood, not only in the sense of a transition from childhood into marriageableness, but also in the sense of womanhood as against the world of men.

For certainly at least one thing the woman learns during her initiation is the magical formulas to be used against men.

There is one aspect of the age-set system which relates to social control, if not to law itself. The distinction between man and boy is very far-reaching; not only is the latter denied legal competence, he is also subject to social controls by his elders. Any man may chastise any boy for misbehavior. This recognized right is supported by the magical power, learned at initiation, by which a person may be made to cry or to bleed excessively during circumcision—a terrible consequence for persons of either sex. It is also an effective means of preventing rudeness on the part of youth against age. The pattern extends to a general expectation of deference toward older persons; matters of precedence, arrangements around the beer pot, and the like are governed (at least among polite and tradition-minded Sebei) by considerations of age-grade. While not wanting to be drawn into a discussion of the nice line between law and custom, I nevertheless consider these merely matters of propriety and etiquette, and outside the scope of this work.

Spatial Affiliations

The Sebei are not nomads; hence each person is resident in a location. The spatial units to which he belongs are important to his social interactions and his legal rights and responsibilities. The progressive sedentarization of the Sebei over the past century or more has been a major dynamic; it has required the readjustment and realignment of many of the Sebei institutions, including those dealing with matters of law. In this section I examine the kinds of spatial groups and the role they play.

The Sebei have no special set of institutions that perform the functions of government; they are an acephalous tribe, in which matters of governance are handled through other institutional means. The Sebei tribes were loosely aggregated by sentiment into a unity; they maintained an amity that enabled a person ordinarily to go throughout Sebeiland without fear of being killed. When Sebei did fight, it was an internal fight, and a man could not claim the honorific shoulder scarification for killing another Sebei person as he could for killing a Pokot, a Karamojong, or a member of any of the other neighboring tribes. The eastern limits of this entity were not clearly and precisely drawn. The tribes in what is now Kenya—the Bok, Koin, and Bongom—speak the same language, intermarry, and share the same customs, but their relationship was otherwise somewhat ambiguous. I return to this in the discussion of the law of violence.

This loose unity was supported and maintained by the existence of prophets. The prophet (*workoyontet*) was a man who could foresee events; he also determined when certain major ceremonies, such as the periodic circumcisions, were propitious; he advised men on diverse group activities, from hunts to wars, as well as upon lesser, personal matters. He had no power other than his prophecy, but as his word was sought and followed, it was inevitable that he should have considerable influence on secular matters. He did not function as a judge nor as a peacemaker for ongoing conflicts, though he was responsible for initiating the *ntarastit*, which will later engage our attention.

There apparently were several prophets working contemporaneously in Sebeiland. There is no indication of how they related to one another, whether they rose to importance at different times, or if they were in direct conflict. The prophets came from certain clans; they attained their position through a spiritual force that entered them and manifested itself in their behavior. False prophets might be killed (Case 35). The prophet Matui was the last to be active; he was outlawed by the British and ceased to be effective after about 1910, but he is much admired for his influence for peace. It was he who ordered the ntarastit ceremony; some informants said he invented it, others that he reinstituted it.

Sebei-wide unity is also supported by the ceremonial system, for all the major ceremonies are coordinated. The ntarastit ceremony, the annual harvest ceremony, the ceremonies of purification, and the circumcisions—which all used to be ordered to begin by the prophet—each start at the eastern end of Sebeiland and continue, pororyet by pororyet, until they reach the southeastern border. But while this coordination characterizes the program, it is very important to appreciate that each of these ceremonial forms is a pororyet function; they are engaged in separately, each in its own place within the respective pororisyek, each with its own leaders, its own slaughtered animals, and its own personnel. If, as I believe, they are to be seen as rites of intensification, the community they primarily serve is the pororyet. But, secondarily, they also serve to reinforce that sense of Sebei-wide unity that we might call a federation of separate and (in a limited sense) sovereign pororisyek.

Significantly, the ceremonies do not serve the tribe at all. Indeed, though the Sebei informants consistently referred to tribes, as already defined, I can discover nothing in which they are the operative unit—no function, no symbolic expression, no organization. Perhaps at a more remote era they did offer some unity, but no evidence, other than names, boundaries, and a vague sentiment of loyalty and mutual opposition, remains.

It is the pororyet that is the focus of the spatially based social divisions. It is the pororyet that acts independently in war, in the sense that no pororyet is automatically committed to aiding another (except for one pair, Kapcheptemkoñ and Kamnyerer). If a major conflict involving several pororisyek arises, each is under its own military leaders.[1] It is the pororyet that holds the ntarastit, initiation, and other ceremonies that evoke loyalties. It is the pororyet that has a kokwet, and leading kirwokik are spoken of as being those of the pororyet.

Most important, both for its general and its legalistic implications, is the fact that it is only the pororyet for which a person's membership is formalized. A man belongs to the pororyet of his birth. (There are no rules with respect to marriage regarding spatial units; wives may be of the same village or an entirely different pororyet. Residence is normally patrilocal though there are no rules of exogamy with respect to spatial groupings.) A man may change his affiliation, but he does not do so

[1] I am not certain how soldiers were recruited; presumably every able-bodied man was expected to help protect his land and kindred, while aggressive action was individually recruited and sponsored. There are remnants of a set of social values attendant upon military prowess, but even these have completely disappeared in the predominantly farming areas of modern Sebei.

lightly. He may wish to transfer his allegiance either because of developing enmity with others in his home, or because a series of deaths or other disasters has made him feel a need to change his fortune. A proper person making such a change gives a beer party, announces his departure, and makes his farewell. "If he fails to do this, the pororyet people may send bad words after him and he will find bad luck where he goes and will have to return to the pororyet and beg forgiveness." A person may also be ostracized, though no cases were given. Some time after he has taken up residence in a new pororyet, he is expected to slaughter a bull and invite the members of the adopted pororyet. He is also expected to marry a woman of this pororyet.

When a clan moves into a new area, the ceremonial demands appear to be greater. When the Kapsumpata clan moved from Mbai into the Chema pororyet (probably in Nongki times), a three-day feast was held. The pororyet furnished two bulls, the Kapsumpata elders furnished two bulls and many rams, and the entire pororyet gathered in a ritual of peace and amity. (See Case 194, p. 54.)

A person is also resident in a sangta, and the sangta has its kokwet, its meeting place, and its own kirwokik. It also holds an annual ceremony to prevent the influence of the evil eye and domestic magic, but this is in no way as important as the pororyet ceremonies. Nor are there any formalities with respect to residence or membership, and a man may have residence in more than one village.

We may summarize the legal implications of these spatial entities as follows. Every man has a kind of citizenship in one pororyet, and to this group he owes continued allegiance and support. It is this unit that (when ntarastit is effective) punishes him for his misdeeds; it is this group that endeavors to protect itself from outside attack; it is this group that hears disputes and decides cases of an important nature. As a result of such membership the individual is also aligned to the unity of the Sebei as a whole, but this is not his primary allegiance. Within the pororyet he is a member also of a village. This smaller community of coresidents concerns itself chiefly with domestic matters, handling the disputes of a minor kind arising locally, particularly cases of domestic quarrels. Significantly, its ceremonial is concerned with domestic matters.

The spatial affiliation of women is that of their husbands.

Kin Groups

Clans (*aret, arosyek*) are patrilineal, exogamous, named social units. Every person is born into a clan, and, except as noted below, cannot change that affiliation. We will see in the discussion of the law of violence the great importance clan membership has to each individual—an importance relating not only to his physical protection, but also to his psychic well-being through the operation of oaths, curses, and other magical actions. Clan membership stands side by side in importance with pororyet citizenship; it presumably had more importance in the past, though because of the magical beliefs it retains a good deal of its hold upon the Sebei. No person can be indifferent to the welfare or the behavior of his clansmen, however much he may be in personal conflict with them.

A man belongs to the clan of his father, and by this the Sebei mean his biological father, his genitor rather than his pater.

If a woman becomes pregnant when her husband is missing, her husband's clan members won't like it because the child belongs to the aret of his [biological] father, and not to their clan. This applies to a boy child, not to a girl, because when she becomes a woman she gets married anyhow and joins that aret. Outsiders may come to be part of an aret when a divorced woman with children goes back to her own clan or when a woman has a child from an adulterous relationship. In the latter case she will be asked who the child's father is when he is about four or five years old, and the son will be returned to his genitor's aret. If the boy should stay in the aret until he is full grown and is allowed to join in the funeral ceremony as a member of the aret, or if a cow is slaughtered and he is given a piece of the heart to eat, it means that the original members of that aret will die out, that he will become the outstanding member of that group, and his descendants will prosper. I have seen that happen in Kenya, when rich men who had no sons bought other men's children. These children are now remaining as heads of their clans and are rich. [Field notes]

Nevertheless, as indicated above, adoptions do occur.

Chemonges Kapsunku had a wife who died when she gave birth, but the child lived. Her sister, married to Aramunyo [of another aret, in accordance with regulations], took care of the child. Chemonges offered a cow to Aramunyo for food. The boy grew to circumcision age and Aramunyo arranged the circumcision feast. The cattle given by the father multiplied, so the boy was able to pay a bride-price from them. Aramunyo's wife had no children and when Aramunyo died the boy looked after her and treated her as his own mother. The old woman died recently and the boy is rich and has two children. [Case 234]

The clan is perceived as an agnatic descent line from the (usually patronymic) founder. It is normally divided into several lineages, also named, who are each presumed to be the descendants of one of the sons of the founder. Thus we have a partial segmentary lineage system. Further evidence of this kind of organization lies in the fact that some clans are linked together and mutual intermarriage is forbidden, though no real sodality is created. Though it may be useful to consider this as a truncated segmentary system, and though it may in fact have derived from such a system historically, I do not think such categorization helps us to understand Sebei social life. What, rather, is the essential fact of this system is the recognition that each man has a strong sense of personal identification with his clan and is—or was—highly dependent upon his clansmen for the preservation of his welfare. Sorcery operates on the clan, and any wrong of a clansman may harm him, just as any difficulty he might get into will require the aid of his clan. Furthermore, though there is no trace of totemistic belief (in the form of animal associations or otherwise), there is a strong sense of spiritual unity. The spirits (oyik) of the dead are clan spirits; they work good and evil only on their own clansmen; contrariwise, it is the clan descendants who are responsible for preserving the postmortem spiritual welfare of the dead. In all this, in the private ceremonials (as distinct from the public, pororyet matters), it is the clan that is the focus of attention.

But modern Sebeiland has increased in population, clans are widespread, there has been much moving about of the people, and a man will not normally have all his clan kin within calling distance. For the usual events of everyday life, and for the more intimate life crises, it is the kota, rather than the clan, which is the de facto operating unit. The members of a kota will more frequently be coresidents in an area, will have stronger bonds of kinship reinforced by actual social intercourse, and will therefore be more immediately concerned with the marriages, divorces, and inheritances that mark off the events of the life cycle. For this reason it is fair to say that the kota is to the clan as the sangta is to the pororyet; the individual has a subsidiary and in a sense derivative membership, more relevant to everyday matters but less so to the more dramatic and public events.

It is, however, possible for a kota to break off from the clan. This is done by mutual agreement through a ceremony of renunciation. The breach destroys the sense of mutual responsibility, and presumably the supernatural ties, but leaves a sense of relatedness which apparently is responsible for the existence of linked clans. When a man and his sons move a long distance and settle down in another area, the kota is effectively if not legally a separate clan; this appears to have taken place repeatedly according to clan histories and migrations recorded.

Though a man's affiliations are agnatic, he retains ties with his mother's clan, propitiates their oyik, recognizes certain moral responsibilities toward its members, is restricted from marrying their daughters, and may (in the event of a quarrel) serve as a link between his paternal and maternal clans. Similarly, there is some responsibility to his father's maternal clan, but these details are not significant for legal action.

The clan is not formally organized, but the senior member of the clan is viewed informally as its head, is responsible for ceremonial leadership in any clan ritual, and leads any family discussion. Seniority does not go to the oldest person, but to the most senior member of the senior line, reckoned in terms of relative sibling age of ancestors. There is a head person for each kota, likewise based on lineal seniority.

Women are said to take the clan affiliation of their husbands; but their position must be viewed as ambiguous, for there is no formal ritual that specifies this fact. It is merely an evaluation of the social actions. Where clans tend to have residential contiguity, a woman is living among her husband's clansmen and working land that her mother-in-law had worked, derived from her father-in-law. More telling is the role she plays in funerals, which are highly symbolic of clan affiliation. If a man dies, those who should be ceremonially shaved and bathed include his brothers and sons, whether married or not; his father and father's brothers; his wife, his mother, his brother's wife, and his son's wife; but his daughter and his sister only if they are unmarried, not if they are married. In short, after marriage women engage in the mourning ceremonies of their husband's clansmen, but not in those of their natal clansmen. Furthermore, while there is marked concern over having an illegitimate son become part of a clan, the same distress is not caused by a daughter, for she is not considered in the same sense to belong to the clan, and need not participate in clan ceremonies. Yet I was told at the Law Conference (but without any support in cases) that a woman retains the group responsibility of her natal clan in case of murder. Should a woman commit murder, vengeance or compensation is exacted from her father's clan, not her husband's, and, conversely, she is liable to be avenged against for a crime committed by a man or woman of her natal clan. If a woman has difficulties with her husband, she ultimately seeks support from her natal clansmen. Also, her clan spirits will have influence on the affairs of her children, and she will be propitiated by these children after she dies. It must be said that in Sebei eyes—at least in those of the men, but I believe women would agree—the matter of a woman's affiliation is relatively insignificant.

In final analysis, clan affiliation in Sebei has significance in the realm of mutual protection against personal physical injury, which is the affair of the men. This legal-political role is the major function, manifest or latent, which the clans perform. If the clan is to perform this function, however, it must be a closely felt entity, for each man may be called upon to take up arms for his fellow clansmen, or to provide cattle in order to avoid such dangers. The Sebei do not, in fact, give much public ceremony to reinforce this all-important unity; however, the spiritual unity, in the literal sense of the word, provides a strong centripetal tendency. The belief in clan spirits and the fear of clan-involved sorcery reinforce the pattern of necessary self-sacrificing acts to maintain the system. It might be said that this centralizing force is a requisite in order to overcome the tendency to personal self-interest and the intense sibling hostility that Sebei culture, in its nonlegal aspects, generates.

The Character of the Sebei Household

Each individual in Sebei articulates to the larger society through his household. It is the smallest and most intimate unit in Sebei society; it belongs in one way to the sangta and pororyet of which it is a part; in another way it articulates through the male head to the kota and aret. In earlier times the houses were grouped together to form a kind of neighborhood, but nowadays they are scattered upon the land, each located at a distance from all others—undoubtedly a response to the elimination of raids as a major threat to personal safety. (An increase of raiding has brought about the reestablishment of manyattas in the past few years in some locations on the plains.)

When a man marries he soon builds a separate house for his wife, and thus a new household is created. As time goes on and he acquires other wives, the household becomes a compound family, normally with each wife having her own house. These houses are situated close to one another around a loosely formed central court. A household thus may be expected to continue—though houses will be replaced—until the man dies and his wives have grown old. Unlike the kota and aret, the household is a transient unit, tied to the lives of its incumbents.

The compound household is the ideal type, but most men have but one wife nowadays, for land is relatively scarce and the elimination of war has reduced the ratio of women to men. Each marriage contract involves only the husband and wife; their relationship is essentially dyadic as expressed in the accompanying diagram. The wives' obligations to one another are legally only to respect one another's rights; they have no positive mutual obligations. Each wife has the right to expect the use of a portion of the land and livestock belonging to her husband, and the right of regular sexual relations with him. The husband has the right to expect work and food from his wives, and the right of sexual access. He also has the right to add to his number of wives at any time. The senior wife, who is always the first woman he marries (except that an inherited wife, even if a man's first, never acts as senior wife), has certain obligations to instruct her younger co-wives, but beyond this there seem to be no demands of one upon another. She is spoken of as being like a mother to the young bride. The senior is also the wife who is to succor the husband in illness, and to whose

H U	S B A	N D
First	Second	N^{th}
wife	wife	wife
and her	and her	and her
children	children	children

house he is taken for funeral rites when he dies; she has a more important status than the other wives.

Marital Restrictions

The Sebei are polygynous; there are no restrictions upon the number of wives a man may have. In point of fact, most men have only one wife, and very few have more than three concurrent wives.

A man may not marry:

1) A woman of his own clan or of a clan linked with his clan.
2) A woman of his mother's clan.
3) A woman of his mother's mother's mother's clan. (However, he may marry into the clan of his maternal grandmother. If he

does so he must clip a bit off the woman's ear and throw it into a running stream to prevent a barren union.)

4) A member of the clan of any living wife, or the true sister of a deceased wife. (This is apparently no longer strictly ad-hered to.)

5) Any woman of a clan of a prior wife's mother, or of a brother's wife's mother.

6) The daughter of any man who belongs to his age-set (pinta).

These rules, given to me by men, are expressed from the mascu-line point of view. It was said that a woman may not marry into the clan of her sister's husband; this was expressed as a rule, but it is now no longer adhered to. She cannot, of course, marry her sister's son.

Marriage as a Contractual Arrangement

We are not here concerned with the details of marital proce-dures, which may be by capture, elopement, or prearrangement. Legally a couple is married when a bride-price has been agreed upon and certain ceremonial obligations have been fulfilled. We are concerned only with the legal aspects of the relationship, and these are the same whatever the character of the wedding procedure. They involve a contractual arrangement that is be-tween either the father of the groom or the groom himself and the father of the bride. The Sebei formerly did not recognize that a woman had any right to determine whom she would marry; she had to abide by a choice that was fundamentally her father's to make. Nowadays there is increased recognition of her will, and the native local courts tend to put some restraints on a father who would force his daughter into a marriage against her will.

Whether the couple gets together by prearrangement, elope-ment, or capture, their marriage is legally established through the payment of a bride-price consisting of cattle, sheep and goats, and various chattels, the precise amount arrived at by mutual agreement in a somewhat ritualized bargaining session called "breaking the sticks" (*kiriketik ap koyeyto;* from *kiri,* "to break"; *ketik,* "sticks"; *ap,* "of"; *koyeyto,* "bride-price").[1]

[1] This phrase has reference to the use of tallies, about 6 inches in length, cut from stems of the *ankurwet* bush, or banana frond rib, or some

When a young man takes his first wife, his principal [2] in the bargaining process is his father (or guardian), who has the legal responsibility for providing the necessary goods; in all subsequent marriages the husband himself performs this role, as the father's legal obligation has been discharged. The principal on the bride's side is her father (or guardian).

We need not here go into the economics of the wife-payment system, but a few points should be noted. First, the amount is basically standard at any one time but has gradually increased over the last sixty or so years. It was quite low at the turn of the century as a result of disease and famines which decimated the herds. Precedent is used as a basis for both demand and refusal. Theoretically, it is of no importance to the final outcome whether or not the couple are already living together, nor is it relevant whether the bride comes (or came) to her husband a virgin. If she was previously married, the session is informal ("sticks are not broken") and there is less total payment.

I have the feeling that today, as well as formerly, it is preferred that the arrangements for marriages be made in advance, but frequently they are not, and were not. In earlier days men captured their wives by force, aided by a group of friends who carried the girl and watched her to prevent escape ("I had to stay with her night and day until she became pregnant, and that was her handcuff" [Case 78]). Some of these captures were connived, some were really distasteful to the girl, and some apparently were fought by the family. Nowadays it appears that most marriages start with an "elopement," the interpreter's

---

substitute plant, or in the Bukwa area, dried cow dung. The tallies, kept by the bride's father, once served as a kind of evidence of contractual agreement. They were put in the roof thatch in the area of the house in which goats and calves are kept, and a tally was returned to the groom's people as each item was paid off. I do not think this practice is followed now; there is a growing tendency to make a written record of the agreements.

[2] By principals I mean the persons basically responsible for delivering and receiving the obligations and rights of the contract: seeing that the cattle and other goods are furnished, assuring that the wife will perform her tasks, etc. The bargaining itself is done by others, and certain persons (as indicated below) receive some of the goods.

term for living together prior to making arrangements. There is no stigma attached to such a procedure.

The bargaining session is arranged in advance (ideally at a small beer party by which the prospective son-in-law "opens the house"). The bride's side is normally attended by the following persons (others may be present, but do not take part) :

1) The father (or guardian) of the bride.
2) The neighbor (*latyet*) of the bride's father, who is the one who conducts the bargaining for that side.
3) The bride's mother's brothers.
4) One or more aret brothers of the bride.
5) The mother of the bride, or the father's mother, if she is alive.

The groom's side is normally attended either by his father or one or more brothers, or by a close personal friend. The groom himself is not normally present during the bargaining, nor does he, or his father, do the actual talking, which is usually done by a brother, friend, or neighbor. The session traditionally takes place in the house of the girl's mother.

Though the persons may be closely acquainted, the session has an air of formality, and both parties are apt to be quite concerned about the outcome. After the purpose of the visit (though well known to all) is formally stated, a member of the bride's family is sent to prepare the sticks that are used as tallies. The negotiations are opened first with a demand by the bride's family spokesman, which is then discussed by the groom's, until agreement is reached. The tally sticks are placed on the ground, and may be pushed away and shoved back several times before the matter is settled. First the number of cattle are specified, next the goats and sheep, then the money, and finally the personal goods.[3] The animals go to the girl's father, except that

[3] In order to give a sense of the involvement, I list the following payments made at one session I attended. There appears to be nothing unusual in the amount or kind of goods involved.

Cattle:	3 heifers, 1 cow with calf, 1 bull, and 1 bull for the girl's mother's brother.
Goats and sheep:	5 she-goats and 1 he-goat, and 1 she-goat for girl's mother.
Chattels:	3 blankets—one each for father, mother, and father's father (or father's mother).
	2 cloths for women's dresses (one for visiting and one for working in the field).

usually one bull, one goat, about 10 percent of the money, and some of the hens go to the girl's mother's brother; one goat goes to the girl's mother; and some of the chattels are for specified relatives.[4] All but the last of these are clearly established and universally recognized rights of the persons involved. The girl's maternal uncles may be numerous; the mother's uterine brothers have precedence over her half brothers, and these over more remote "brothers." The first payment to uncles from a family goes to the oldest uncle, and as subsequent daughters of the house marry, other uncles receive their payment in turn. Beyond this, there is no recognized demand right for any of these animals on the part of any clansman. The animals may be used to pay the bride-price of the girl's brothers.

A son has a moral and legal demand on his father to provide him with the cattle and other goods necessary for the acquisition of his first wife. Should the father refuse, the matter may be taken to clan elders who may order the younger clansmen to seize the animals from the father's kraal. A father has no further obligation, but is expected to furnish cattle if he is rich and does not have too many sons. He has an interest in providing for his sons' wives, as they increase his descendants and therefore his postmortem welfare, as well as strengthening his clan and thereby its importance. A man (either the groom or his father)

---

	1 mosquito net ("not to be counted as part of the bride-price, but as a free gift").
	1 large aluminum pot (sufaria).
	1 iron bracelet (for which now 2 shillings is substituted).
	1 iron hoe (for which now 3 shillings is substituted).
Hens:	30, plus 5 for girl's mother's brother.
Tobacco:	1 5-gallon tin (or a calabash) valued at 30 shillings.
Beer:	2 sacks of dried beer with sprouted millet for fermentation, plus 1 sack for mother's brother.

The bride's family had asked for 2 more cattle, 1 more goat, 100 shillings more. In another session, the bride's father refused to request as much as his agent originally asked and took much less than the groom's people were prepared to pay. He may have been so undemanding because of the ethnographers' presence.

[4] The bull, sheep, and chickens to the mother's brother are called, respectively, *yeytaphamama, kechiryet ap kamama* and *nkokok ap kamama*. The payment to the girl's mother is called *cherewontet,* from *rewo,* "dew." It repays the mother for the dew on her feet from seeking medicines at dawn for her infant, now grown to womanhood.

may request help of his kinsmen and either be given or loaned animals for such payment, but there is no clear line of moral obligation and certainly no legal claim against any relative (other than the father himself) to assist in a marriage. Inasmuch as the Sebei recognize in all their transactions the right to defer payment, the absence of livestock is no bar to making the agreement; payment is frequently long deferred. Both the obligation of the father and the delay in payment are illustrated in the following case:

My father owes my brother-in-law an ox. In 1929 when my older brother wanted to marry, the brother of my brother's wife demanded an ox instead of money. As we had none in the herd, my father obtained one from my sister's husband. We paid a heifer for it, but she died, and the debt remains. My older brother [i.e., the man for whom the bride was obtained] cannot pay that. Any debt that is incurred when a man marries his first wife cannot be paid by that man himself. (But the marriage debt of his second wife is upon him.) I cannot now pay that debt because the heifers I have are all descendants of that cow that he paid on the dowry and it is a law that we cannot pay him back with such cows. Also, in '38, '39, and '41 our cattle nearly died off and I have no spare calves. He asks for it but I explain that only the very young ones are not descendants of his own cows. This debt must be paid from my herd because it is one with my father's herd. I couldn't pay a heifer out of the ration I was given. But since I have taken over my father's cows, I can be responsible for this and the man goes to my father first and then afterward comes to me. [Case 9]

It is also worthwhile to note some attendant attitudes. The girl's father will be quite explicit about what he expects (as for instance a particular kind of coat), and, if the groom's people say his demand is beyond the cost of a normal item, may offer to pay the extra cost; that is, there is an explicit view that the economic considerations are just that, and are not merely bonds of sentiment. In one or two instances it was noted that certain things were not part of the bride-price, but were viewed as a gift (as, for instance, the mosquito net in the list set forth in n. 3, above).

The bargaining session does, however, establish bonds of mutual social obligation and sentiment between the two families.

They expect mutual entertainment; one consideration in the acceptance of a suitor is whether he will be willing and able to provide beer. In the old days the affinal tie served as a potential link for the resolution of feud. The presumption of friendship thus underlies the session; a man will want to make the tie with persons for whom he has an established amity. Mutuality is indicated by the fact that the bride's family should, if the cattle increase in their kraals, give one animal to their daughter's son, in a payment called *put*. (See Case 201, p. 166.)

The underlying friendship leads, in turn, to another element in the bargaining session: a need to cleanse the air of enmity resulting from old conflicts. Thus, potentially in every bargaining session and actually in many the bride's parents will raise some ancient harm done by the groom's family against them and demand compensation for it, perhaps an added cow or a money payment. Such a penalty is called *ropsyet*, derived from the verb *rop*, to weave or to join together. In one session I observed, the bride's father demanded his daughter's school fees from her husband, as he had eloped with her in midyear and prevented her from obtaining a school certificate by which she might have supported him in his old age. One man was "fined" 120 shillings for the fact that his father had once threatened the life of a member of his bride's family; another was fined because of refusal to pay compensation for a bull that was killed in a fight with a bull of the groom's family. Thus a marriage offers an opportunity to clear up minor delicts involving insults or personal injuries, contractual obligations, and the like. It is only the bride's people that can raise such issues and make demands; the groom's people cannot raise any family issues.

Issues raised on old quarrels between the families are not taken up until after the bride-price negotiations have been concluded. The delay is of no significance, however, for the contract is not yet binding on either party, even if (as in many modern instances) reduced to writing and signed by both parties. The marriage contract becomes binding only at the time of the "exchange of bracelets" ceremony, which takes place some time after the couple has been living together. At this time "it is known that she is married." The girl's father, however, cannot break the agreement he has made because some other suitor has offered more. Indeed, protocol is quite clear on the point: one determines to what suitor one wishes to give precedence (in accordance with whatever considerations the girl's father chooses, but nowadays supposedly on the basis of the girl's preference) and reaches an agreement with him; only if these negotiations break down would the father allow another suitor to enter into a bargaining session. No man is expected to bid against another.

Either party, however, can withdraw from the agreement for proper reasons, one of which would certainly be failure to meet the demand for compensation of the kinds indicated above. Other appropriate reasons are discovery that the clan of the other party has certain "inherent" diseases; discovery of kinship between the parties which would make the marriage improper; discovery of an uncompensated murder that involved the two clans; discovery that the groom's clan had earlier refused one of its daughters to a bride's clansman; a subsequent quarrel be-tween the boy's aret and either the girl's clan or her mother's clan, or an earlier one that had not come to the attention of the bride's parents prior to the bargaining (though such matters could themselves be subject to negotiation) .

I made arrangements to marry Kapkemin's daughter. I eloped with her and when I brought her home my grandmother said that the girl belong to one of the "bad birds" clans so I had to send her back. She went back and was married by a man; she was his first wife and he died soon afterward without having any children. [Case 225]

But these issues must all be resolved before the ceremony of the bracelets. If a couple separates at a later date, the separation is appropriately regarded as a divorce.

The ceremonial cycle for the wedding is a long one, and need not detain us here; however, a few matters are relevant to the legal aspect of every marriage in Sebeiland. On at least two occasions presents must be distributed to the relatives of the bride. There may be discussion of the propriety of the amount of such gifts, which are part of the moral obligation but not part of the bride-price. Gifts are also given by the bride's people to the husband's. At the last ceremonial of the cycle, the girl's relatives may adduce complaints regarding the treatment she receives from her in-laws (among whom she dwells). These complaints are not actionable, but their presentation does constitute a public hearing on domestic matters that might later endanger the relationship. They also express the continuing interest of the woman's clansmen in their daughter's welfare.

The marriage contract is an enforceable one, and every divorce complaint may be viewed as an effort to enforce compliance; furthermore, the kokwets attached to funerals and any later efforts to marry between the clans would certainly be used to reopen matters. The potential of sorcery lies behind each agreement.

Psiwa had a daughter who was married to a man of Ragon. The bride-price was bargained and cows were given, but unfortunately these cows died. The husband had had many sons by Psiwa's daughter and Psiwa went to the father of the groom and asked for a replacement of the cows. The man refused, saying that it wasn't his affair but Psiwa's mistake, so Psiwa bewitched him and now the man is very fat and sick. I know this happened because Psiwa said in front of the people, "I see you have built a nice mbati house [corrugated iron roof], but you won't live in that; my sons will, because you will have died as I am going to kill you." [Case 99]

This case, incidentally, makes it quite clear that the bride-price cattle must be replaced should they die. I have no measure of how long after marriage this obligation remains operative, but in this instance Psiwa's daughter had had several children. I suspect it depends a good deal upon how strong a character the father-in-law is; Psiwa was a member of one of the clans that could practice *kankanet* sorcery.

At this juncture it seems advisable to review some of the general implications of marriage as a contract. First, I have chosen to use the term "bride-price" because I feel it is semantically closest to the actual sentiment involved. The goods transferred are bargained; the Sebei distinguish them from gifts (which are also transferred), and they themselves (when they use English) use this gloss. The goods transferred represent a substantial sum to both parties, and many chance and side remarks imply that economic considerations are important, if not paramount. On the other hand, I think it irrelevant to discuss whether the transaction is a "purchase" in our sense of the term; such a discussion would merely lead us into useless concern with semantics in cross-cultural perspective. Marriage is, however, a contract, with a recognized obligation that both parties must perform; the obligation is continuous, and its breach leads to recognizable forms of legal redress.[5] The contract is an agreement between the groom's father (in a first marriage) or the groom (in subsequent ones), and the bride's father. Even in modern court action, a woman is not given a divorce by Sebei assessors without their first inquiring into the attitude of her father (see Case 2, p. 56). The groom's side agrees to payment of a fixed sum of wealth and to the performance of obligations of a Sebei husband [6] in exchange for a woman, with her obligations as a Sebei wife and mother. What these obligations are is spelled out in the discussion of divorce, for clearly they are precisely the things that give recognized grounds for divorce.

It has been customary to view these contracts in African societies as agreements between the respective clans; this is undoubtedly true elsewhere, but the data do not support such a formulation for the Sebei. We shall see, again, that in divorce proceedings the community is involved in the decision to dissolve a marriage; it is not a clan matter. The important point is that the cattle are not contributed (per obligation) by the clan or the kota, nor are they distributed widely to the clansmen of the bride's father; indeed, the only specified redistribution is to certain of her mother's clansmen. To say that marriage is a contract (which of course it is in our society as well) is not to suggest that it is merely a legal quid pro quo involving the principals. It is also a tie of sentiment between husband and wife and between their respective families.

[5] In an interesting instance (Case 242), a boy's father was anxious to obtain a particular girl for his son and did not make arrangements in a formal contractual manner. The girl's father took advantage of this situation by keeping some oxen he had borrowed as part of the "bride-price."

[6] The woman may complain of the husband's failure to have intercourse with her, saying, "My house has leaked for a long time; I have been wet all the time in my home" (referring to the regular menstrual flow), or "It has been a long time since my husband has had a meal in my house."

The Household as Economic Entity

In this section I want briefly to review the allocation of rights within the household. Like people everywhere, the Sebei have standard divisions of labor between the sexes and among the age-groups. Sebei men are expected to herd the cattle and clear the bush for farming, to frame and thatch houses, and to engage in public affairs, such as wars, raids, and kokwets. The women are expected to cultivate the gardens, to milk the cattle, to prepare all food and beer (except roasting meat), and to mud the walls and floors of houses. Daughters usually assist their mothers; young children herd the goats, and nowadays (with the decline of raiding), often the cattle as well. None of the work is particularly onerous; certainly it is far less so for the men than for the women. Nowadays men help in some aspects of fieldwork, particularly in the use of plows and the cultivation of plantains and predominantly in the growing of coffee, the major commercial crop.

When a man marries, his father pays the bride-price and normally allocates some land and cattle to him. The character of property and the rights adhering to ownership are dealt with in detail in Part III, on the law of property. The rules regarding transfer of property are dealt with in the next section. The groom allocates some property to his wife: the cattle in a formal ceremonial manner, the land in a less formal way. Some he holds back (if there is adequate land) for subsequent wives or (in the case of cattle) for his own use. The cattle given to a wife are called by diverse terms: *toka che kichengothi korket* (*toka,* "cattle"; *che,* "which"; *kiche,* "have been"; *ngot,* "marked"; *hi,* "for"; *korket,* "women"); *teta nye kicheyilwo* (*teta,* "cow"; *nye,* "which"; *kiche,* "has been"; *yil,* "anointed"; *wo,* "for me"—presumably woman speaking); or *teta nye kichengotwo* ("cow which has been marked for me"). The cattle retained by the husband are called *tokapsoy.* I have no term for land given to wives nor any evidence of a ceremonial allocation, but Sebei give a parallel term to *tokapsoy,* namely *tengek ap soy* (*tengek,* "land").

Subsequently acquired wives are similarly given stock to milk and land to work. Each wife thus has her own land to work and her own cows to milk, and with these she feeds her own children and perhaps even sells produce in order to buy minor personal things, or perhaps to build up her own herd. Ideally, the property, like the household itself, is divided in accordance with the accompanying diagram (a counterpart to the household itself), which applies specifically to the cattle but also to land and to small stock.[7]

| T   O   K   A   P   S   O   Y |||
(allocated for milking to wives)		
Anointed cattle belonging to First Wife (go to her sons)	Anointed cattle belonging to Second Wife (go to her sons)	Anointed cattle belonging to N^{th} wife (go to her sons)

The cows retained by the husband as tokapsoy will also be allocated to the several wives for milking. Each wife has the power to determine the use of the animals "belonging" to her (i.e., not tokapsoy); if a bullock is exchanged, the return animal comes to her holdings. Her property may be augmented by gifts to her or to her sons, and the progeny of her cows continue as part of her herd; thus a fortunate or industrious wife (or a favored one) may come to have many more animals than her co-wives. These animals not only increase her own and her children's well-being, but also assure bride-price and thus marriage for her sons; in fact, they are held for that purpose, as a man cannot use the cattle of his mother's co-wives for a bride-price. A received bride-price, however, does not go to the mother of the girl (except for the goat that is paid explicitly to her), but becomes part of the father's cattle, which he may hold as tokapsoy or assign to any of his wives.

[7] Unfortunately we must make a choice in what is presented first; for the meaning and legal implications of ownership, see the chapter on property (pp. 143–161).

The land is similarly controlled. Because the husband has less direct involvement with land than with cattle, the concept of his holding some back as tengek ap soy is not so clearly formulated. Furthermore, he may apparently take land from an earlier wife and reassign it to a new bride, though the former's sons may raise objections.

As each son marries and sets up a household, he is given his share of livestock and land, both from among those allocated to his mother and from the tokapsoy. I discuss this aspect in conjunction with matters of inheritance. We might note at this point, however, that there are exceptional instances in which land is transferred to a daughter. Inasmuch as this procedure has implications for the rules and practices with respect to residence, it deserves our attention despite the fact that it does not occur often.

A man may choose to give his daughter some land. When he does, an unusual condition of matrilocal residence is created, and we are not surprised to learn that each instance is in the area of intensified farming, rather than in a predominantly cattle-keeping area. The first two cases involve the transfer of land to the descendants of a clan daughter, rather than directly to the daughter; the third is a direct gift by a man to his daughter.

Arapsiker came to join the Kapsumbata people because the Kapsumbata are his father's uncles (i.e., clan of father's mother's brother). They provided land to him. He is now living among them, but meanwhile their sons and daughters have married. He did not have to buy the land. [Case 81]

Psatey of Kapketon aret came to live with Mwoko of Kapsumbata aret; the latter is a man he calls nephew. He was provided land. He didn't buy it. Some of the Kapsumbata people left their land to Psatey's sons, who looked after the land. Psatey is a Ñongki age-set man who came here when he was a young man. They own the land; nobody can take it from them. There are twelve grandsons now living on it. They can sell the land because now it has become theirs. They have established boundary divisions on it. But Psatey never paid for that land. [Case 82]

My grandfather, Lelbel, lived near Kamatui. He had three sons and two daughters. Lelbel loved his elder daughter very much and provided her with whatever she needed and gave her land on which she planted bananas. Her husband had no land. The land Lelbel gave her has never been taken back by his sons. [Case 233]

The following case, on the other hand, took place in an area that, at the time, was devoted chiefly to pastoral pursuits. Here we see that it is the incoming man who furnished the wives and that the land continued in the name of the original clan owners.

Kapyatya migrated from Kaserem to Kapcheptemkoñ and came to live with Kony of Kapchemandan aret. There was no relationship; they were just friends. When he arrived, he brewed beer and killed a cow and was declared a member of the pororyet. The food and beer were enjoyed by the whole pororyet. Kapyatya had three girls of marriageable age. Kony married one and at the same time gave land to his father-in-law. Kapyatya lived there a long time and became rich. Later, however, he returned to his former pororyet, after which the land went back to the former owners. [Case 194]

I observed one case where two sisters, both without husbands, were purchasing land (Case 120). Their right to do so was not questioned; however, both their father and a younger brother tried to insist that the brother's name be placed on the document, which the quite independent and willful sisters did not want. They admitted that the land would go to their brother's children rather than their own, but claimed they feared that if the brother's name was on the paper he would take the land from them while they were still alive. The incident demonstrates the tensions that arise between siblings in the farming area where land is scarce and where men claim possession of all land while it is the women who work it.

Divorce

The grounds for divorce reveal the elements of expectation in the marriage contract. A man may divorce his wife for the following reasons (as adumbrated in the Law Conference):

1) Laziness (*puronet*).

My father had two wives. The second wife was lazy and my father had to buy granaries each year. She stayed home idle and would not even sweep her own house. My father used to stay in the house with the first wife. He had been married to the second wife for three years and she had only one child. She didn't have more because my father would not sleep with her, as he thought that if she had more children she would not be able to feed them. So he sent this second wife back to her parents and then he asked his neighbors to accompany him to her father's house. When my father arrived there his father-in-law said to him: "I have seen your wife here; what is wrong?" My father said: "Your daughter is too lazy. Have you ever enjoyed beer in her house? Ask my neighbors and they will tell you that she does nothing. Even when her relatives visit, she does not cook food for them." The father-in-law said it was up to my father, who said: "I want my cattle back." When they were holding a kokwet at the house of the father-in-law, his neighbors said to him: "You have nothing to say; you must return the cows." My father said he would leave now but be back in three days; and on the third day he took his cows. From that time, no one would marry her as she had a reputation for laziness. Later, when the Maina famine occurred, she died of hunger. My father married another woman who was hardworking. [Case 230]

2) Repeated adultery. There is no general term for adultery, but a married woman who chases after many men is called *chemorunyontet,* from *morun,* men. A single instance would not be regarded as grounds for divorce, though when I asked if adultery with two men would be grounds, the reply was, "Two are many men."

3) Refusal to have intercourse with husband (which would be presumptive evidence that a woman is regularly engaging in adultery).

4) If a wife refuses to cook or if she abuses or curses her husband because he is annoyed.

5) If she either engages in *ntoyenik,* the magic that weakens a man, or prevents him from taking or loving another wife (Case 19, p. 121).

6) "If she has children three times and each time she kills them."

7) If she uses a weapon against her husband.

8) If she murders somebody, or attacks the neighbors in such a way as to bring disrepute to her husband, or if she is a thief.

9) "If her vagina is black," a fact that is discovered during delivery by the midwife.

10) If for some reason she is unable to have intercourse with

her husband (though this inability would normally be known prior to the conclusion of the marriage contract) .

11) If she belongs to a clan that is *kasaña* (from *kasan,* "to carry on back," with reference to grandchild) to the husband's aret, and the fact was not known prior to marriage. This means that the children of the marriage will all die.

My mother was married to a member of the Kapsaro aret and was a *kasañantet* of that aret. She had five children who all died, so they decided that they should find out the reason for the death and they found out that she was kasañantet of this aret and that she should marry somebody else, so she married my father. [Case 226]

Childlessness is not grounds for divorce among the Sebei. Nor can a man divorce a wife who has become mad; on the contrary, he is expected to help her be cured. There was disagreement as to whether a man could divorce a wife who practiced witchcraft, other than against the husband himself.

A woman may initiate a divorce also:

1) If the husband mistreats her "by beating her too much when she has done nothing wrong." The following case is from a local governmental court.

Plaintiff claims husband beats her daily, that this is the second case brought against him, and is supported in the matter by her father who acted as witness. Medical testimony in the form of a dispensary chit is brought forward as well. Defendant denies these charges and insists he will demand return of the bride-price if a divorce is granted. The court granted the divorce. [Case 2]

2) If the husband does not provide enough cleared land so she can cultivate it and feed her family.

3) If her husband is impotent or sterile, or refuses to sleep with her, preferring other wives or adulterous unions. But this does not mean that adultery is grounds for divorce, only sexual neglect.[8]

4) If the man engages in "unnatural" sex relations (sodomy) with her.

---

[8] I was told that in the old days if a husband was sterile the wife could seek out a clan brother (but not the true brother) and have intercourse with him in order to have a child.

5) If her husband is mad (unless she has grown sons with whom she can live).

6) If her husband curses her or spreads evil rumors about her.

We may summarize by saying that the two partners are expected to perform their respective economic and sexual roles as a part of the contract; that in addition the husband must not apply the rod too strongly in chastising the wife, while the wife must be submissive to her husband.

Quarrels between husband and wife are common, and it is expected that a man will beat his wife for cause. It was said, however, that a man does not beat his wife on a first offense, but mentally "breaks the sticks"—keeps a tally on her misbehavior—and then accuses her the fourth time. We may take this as a kind of model for behavior with respect to marital relations and divorce procedures. A single offense does not constitute just cause; a person must build up a case by making it public that his partner has repeatedly given offense. We have seen that this applies with respect to women's adultery; it is also applicable to other grounds for divorce.

A serious quarrel is initiated by the husband's beating the wife, after which "she must run to the home of her own father, nobody else's." Then the husband, together with neighbors or a friend, calls on the father-in-law and, with members of the latter's sangta, holds a kokwet. The woman is allowed to express herself, and the group will indicate who is in the right. If the kokwet finds the woman to have been misbehaving, her brothers will whip her on the thighs with a small walking stick and scold her. If the husband is found to be in the wrong, the brother-in-law or father-in-law will warn him that he may lose his wife. A man is expected to be respectful in front of his father-in-law, and if he (by word or act) insults the latter, he may be made to pay a goat or a heifer; this presumably puts some restraint upon his behavior.

It is only upon the repetition of complaints that a divorce is seen as the appropriate solution. According to one statement, members of the pororyet, in addition to the sangta, are called in, but the procedure is not entirely clear. It is clear, however, that the hearings are always at the village of the girl's father, though the husband brings his neighbors, whose witness regarding repetitive behavior is necessary to the determination of fault. The kokwet represents the community; it is neither a clan affair nor an interclan confrontation. The father of the woman has a vested interest in preserving the marriage, as he must return the bride-price irrespective of fault; but neutral community members will put pressure on him to agree to a divorce if his daughter's life is endangered by the husband's cruelty.

The kokwet is also concerned with the return of the bride-price. It is expected that the same cattle that were given should be returned, together with their issue; if some of the animals have died, the loss is the husband's. If the cattle have been exchanged, the woman's father is expected to try to get them back. Cattle (at the appropriate ratio) may be given instead of sheep and goats, but not the other way around. Nowadays money is acceptable in lieu of cattle.

There is a rough sliding scale of the amount of bride-price returned in case of divorce, in inverse (but not precise) ratio to the number of children produced. If the marriage is childless, the whole is returned.

A woman who had been married in Binyinyi lost her husband through death. She went to Sipi to marry but had no children by her second husband and returned to Binyinyi. Now the second husband wants his bride-price back. The woman's father agreed to pay back the cattle if the woman didn't have any children there. [Case 12]

If there is one child, then at least one animal is left with the father-in-law, "or he can curse you." One informant said, "You leave a bullock for a boy, a heifer for a girl." There are exceptions, however:

I had a wife who had one son. We quarreled and I divorced her. She married someone else and I demanded my property and I got everything but the goat. The son is now married. [Case 227]

If there are more children, then a larger amount—or even the total amount—may be left. The following cases show the diversity of the application of this rule.

Chemonges Arumi married a girl named Cherotmoi and had two boys and one girl. She divorced and Chemonges claimed the bride-price back. By this time there were five cows [presumably referring not to the payment but to the total number including payment and descendants still living after the not inconsiderable passage of time]. He decided to leave one cow with his father-in-law because his aret members told him that if he did not, their clan would get a bad reputation. People would say that members of this clan claimed *all* their property back. So they left one cow and three small stock and brought home four cows and three goats and sheep. [Case 229]

I had a wife from whom I had three sons. She left me and married somebody else. I had paid two cows, five goats, and 50 shillings, and when I demanded my property I was paid one cow, but all the rest was kept by my father-in-law. I thought that was fair because of the three sons. [Case 228]

The children, of course, belong to the husband's clan and will live with him; a suckling child is taken care of by the mother until he is old enough to herd goats, at which time he will be returned to the father's custody. The mother retains her rights in the children, and obligations to them. When they are circumcised, she must provide the beer and anoint them; when her daughter marries, she gets the goat and other things specified for the mother, and the bargaining takes place in her house.

Livestock and cattle belong to the man. A divorced woman takes with her only those personal things that are viewed as hers: clothes, personal ornaments, cowry belt, knife, pipe, hoe, drinking gourd, cooking pots, and such things as may have been given her by her own parents. The animals allocated to her (and even any given to her by her parents) will be given to the surrogate mother of her children (co-wife or husband's sister), who will use them for feeding the children. Her sons will retain the subsidiary right to the cattle that were anointed for her, just as if she were not divorced. The sons also retain the right to the use of their mother's land. The only case evidence for this is an instance in which the sons of a deceased first wife took over land that had been cultivated by the second wife after their mother's death, when they themselves married (Case 238); I understand that the sons would have had this right had their mother been divorced, rather than having died.

Inheritance

The circumstances of a household are changed by the death of the husband or wife, and in this section we deal with the legal consequences of such an occurrence—broadly speaking, the rules regarding inheritance.

If a woman dies without children the husband is not liable to pay the bride-price unless his actions have caused her death. Death in pregnancy is so viewed (see Cases 152 and 154, p. 94). If he has had children by her, presumably the bride-price is not reclaimed. I believe that the wife's clan may substitute another daughter, but in the only recorded instance of such substitution the bride refused to accept the husband. As already noted, any sons of a deceased wife retain her subsidiary rights to both cattle and land.

In order to understand the practices surrounding inheritance upon the death of a man, we must return to some aspects of the household. We recall the diagram of the compound household, in which each wife has her own rights, and these devolve upon her sons. The father is legally responsible for having the children circumcised, and for obtaining the necessary cattle for bride-price, in the sense that ultimately the community would force him to do so. Some time after a son marries he is given land and cattle, which constitute his heritage; the father has "chased him out of the house" (*kichepchuyta*),[9] and he has (with some exceptions to be noted) no further legal claim against his father's estate. Each son is thus treated in turn, leaving the youngest son to care for his father's old age, which means also to care for his herds (*tewet nye makwek kontintet;* "last child / who / will be / heir"). Indeed, he is residual legatee of the animals, and youngest sons of old fathers often speak of this herd as their own (cf. Case 9, p. 46). The nature of the pattern of inheritance depends, therefore, on the state of the family cycle when a man dies.

Further complications arise from the fact that there may be

[9] Dr. Christine Montgomery derives this from the verb *pcuwu*, "to serve from a dish" or "give out," plus the suffix *te* denoting movement away; hence, "he has been given away."

several wives, and that the cattle anointed for each wife and the fields assigned to her remain with her own sons. Furthermore, the son who is caring for the father may not be the youngest, but merely the youngest married one; those who are still uncircumcised also retain a right in the residual herd. The basic inheritance rules are as follows:

1) Land, livestock, and wives go together.

2) When a man inherits a wife he takes the land and animals to which she has subsidiary rights in trust for her junior sons. (Junior sons for this purpose are those who, whether married or not, have not been given their share of the parental estate and "chased out of the house.")

3) The last son to have become married at the time of his father's death is normally acting as his herdsman. He becomes the residual legatee of his mother's land and herd, but must hold in trust and share the estate with any junior sons of that mother.

4) This son also acts as residual legatee for the tokapsoy of the father, and inherits all of them, holding them too in trust for junior members of any other.

5) If all the sons from one mother have established independent households, these brothers share the land and cattle remaining to their mother. One son (by one of the wives) is the recognized residual legatee for the tokapsoy.

6) Aside from the bull of the herd (*kintet*), which is slaughtered at the death of the owner, and the *cheporir* ("cow of tears"), given to the brother (or alternate relative) who "buries the father," the residual legatee is expected to share his heritage with his older brothers as follows: one cow each if the herd is large; one cow to be shared by them if the herd is small. (I do not know how "large" and "small" are defined; I believe this depends upon the number of brothers, their sentiments and attitudes, and other local and idiosyncratic factors.) There may also be moral obligations that are recognized by men who have many cattle. In one instance the estate gave the shilling equivalent of a good cow to an age-mate of the deceased.

7) If a man dies without sons, his cows are inherited by his brothers, with the ones nearest him in age, and especially the

next younger, getting most of them. If he has only daughters, his brothers still inherit the cows, but the daughters receive a "cow for crying." If he has only young sons, the man who inherits the wives takes their land and cattle in trust.

8) No claim on the herd or the land may be made by the mother's brother of the deceased ("he may be given some hens"), or by a daughter's husband, except (as we see in Case 201, p. 166) when the bride-price cattle have prospered; but this matter is not associated with inheritance.

9) There is nothing comparable to a will, except as animals or land are given prior to the man's death. A man can let a favored son know about a debt owed him and thus prevent other sons from inheriting the animal. A wife has no say over how the animals in her herd are to be divided, beyond the assurance that they go to her own sons.

The foregoing are the general rules. We will turn shortly to the case material on inheritance which shows their more specific operations.

On the third or fourth day after a man dies a kokwet is held. This funeral kokwet is presided over by the senior member of the kota of the deceased. Not only are all family members present, but also the people from the deceased's village and other persons who wish either to express their respects for the dead man or to voice a claim against the estate.

The kokwet and attendant ceremonials are designed to perform the following functions:

1) Determine who shall inherit the widows of the deceased and hence be the guardian of any minor children.

2) Assign the livestock and presumably, if there is a question, the land to the proper heirs.

3) Anoint the personal possessions of the deceased so they may be taken by the heirs.

4) Have a public hearing on all claims against the estate and any claims by the estate against others.

The kokwet is informally conducted; the decisions are reached by mutual consent after debate. Neutral persons serve as referees, and also act as witnesses to the claims of the parties concerned. I reproduce part of such a kokwet discussion later in this section (pp. 71–73). Manifestly, the variety of circumstances is such that no general rules can be formulated which will apply to every case; in fact the degree of freedom allows for considerable manipulation of events by persons of strong character.[10] Legal details and areas of negotiation and interpretation can best be seen by examining specific cases.

A very rich man who died sometime before 1910 had six sons, all initiated; none of them, contrary to custom, had established an independent household.

Koñ, a rich man, died at a very old age, when I was a boy. He had eight wives, and six sons were living with him. The oldest son buried him and received 100 head of cattle; the remaining five each received 25. As all the wives were old, they were taken care of by their sons rather than inherited. The oldest son also took the shield and spear of his father. Though some of Koñ's sons were married, they were all living with him and had not been sent away from the house. [Case 61]

This case, incidentally, shows that the oldest son has a favored position. He is, of course, senior in the relation with the broader society, enjoys the psychological advantage of earlier initiation and the demands of deference, and in a very real sense may be in charge of the kota or even the clan. This position may lead to a kind of noblessee oblige, as indicated in the following case, which took place on the plains in about 1920.

When my grandfather died, my father (Kambuya) was the eldest of three sons, and when dividing the cows he gave fourteen to his next brother, Musani, but the younger brother, Mangusyo, was too young. Kambuya kept only four and became Mangusyo's guardian. When Mangusyo grew up and got married, Kambuya went to Musani for cows, but he refused to give them. So my father gave Mangusyo twelve cows descended from the original four, and kept only three. Later Musani found that Kambuya had many more cows and he said my father had hidden some, and asked to be given some more. My father refused, and Musani took a case against him. My father won the case, even when it was appealed to Budadiri, which was then the saza headquarters. Musani admitted he had been given fourteen and my father had retained four, and so the court ordered

[10] In the detailed presentation of an extensive kokwet dealing with the estate of one rich cattleman, given in *Kambuya's Cattle: The Legacy of an African Herdsman,* the nature of such manipulation becomes manifest.

Musani to return five to him. My father said he was pleased with the court decision but not only refused these cows but when he returned said: "You are crying for cows. Here, take these." And he gave him a bull and a heifer. [Case 263]

The pattern of sibling hostility continues, as seen in a brief summary of a case heard in Gombolola Court in 1954:

Plaintiff, Seberya Muneria, claims that his brother (by a different mother), Eria Kwalya, failed to share dowry received in 1930 for one of their sisters, despite the fact that the cattle had increased to ten, of which seven are now remaining. Defendant states that plaintiff was given heifer and that also he had given two heifers when plaintiff married his second wife; and furthermore that at different times he had given a total of fourteen cattle to his brother. The court supported the defendant. [Case 52]

The case of Psiwa Kaptyemesyegin of Sasur, a man rich in both land and cattle, with two wives and ten sons, is not an inheritance case, for Psiwa is very much alive. It does, however, indicate the pattern of disposition of his livestock holdings and attendant attitudes. When I knew Psiwa in 1962, his youngest son by his first wife was acting as his herdsman. Three sons by the first wife and two by the second had been given their share of the cattle, as well as one son (now deceased) whose wives had been inherited by two of the brothers. I have details only for the first wife's family. Psiwa gave fourteen cattle to the first son (having paid five head each as bride-price for two women), eight to the second, fourteen to the third (who died), eight to the fourth, seven to the fifth, and five (for his bride-price) to the youngest who is his herdsman. The explanation for the differential is presumably that neither the second nor the fourth son had taken a second wife. Psiwa said that in the event of his death his herdsman might "be kind enough to give one or two cows" to his next older brother (because he "follows his back"), and that the older sons could not even make such a request.

The material from Case 10 gives us some insight into the inheritance pattern, though it is not so detailed as one might like. The data were obtained from Barteka, a man circumcised in 1920, some years after his father had died. The genealogical relationships are shown in the accompanying diagram.

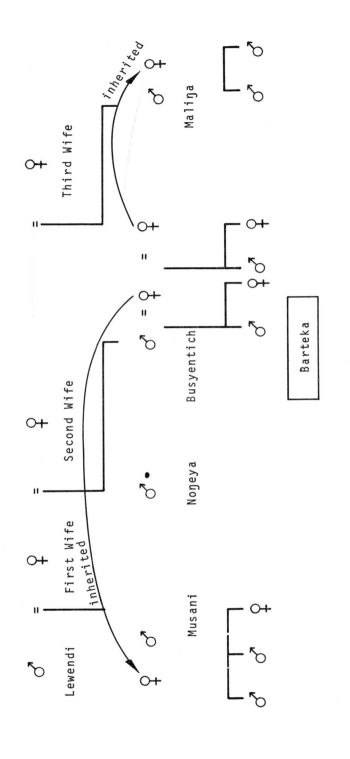

Busyentich's true brother had died by the time Busyentich died (which was about 1910) ; thus his half brothers each inherited one wife, and each had additional children by them. Busyentich had ten cattle when he died. I took five and the son of his other wife took three. The "bull of the herd" was slaughtered at the feast; the "cow of tears" was given to Malinga, who was a poor man without any animals. Musani was given no cows. [The mother of Malinga had been married and divorced before she came to Lewendi, the implication being that this reduced her status and that of her son in the eyes of the family.] By 1914 all but three of my cows had died, and my brother had only two left. After the rinderpest, the cattle multiplied and my mother showed me the debts owed to my father. By 1920 when I was initiated the cows that I collected had multiplied to nineteen. Two of the debts I collected were for granaries and two were *namanya* exchanges for slaughtered bullocks.[11] I paid two debts when the owners reported them and my mother agreed. As I was the older, I represented my father and everyone came to see me about the debts. I became as the father; if my brother wanted anything, he had to ask me. He was circumcised in 1926. By 1925 the namanya cattle had released themselves and I had enough animals to marry my first wife. Out of those cattle I married five wives. I gave my brother one cow out of the namanisyek heifers, and one to my father's brother [Musani?].

There were four sheep and five goats. I shared two goats and one sheep with my brother, because my father would have shared them.

There were three fields. I gave one to my brother, and one went to Musani, whose sons shared that. None went to Malinga. [Case 10]

The following case, heard in Gombolola Court in 1954, involves the recognition that a father's herd belongs by right to the younger son even before the father dies, if the older brothers have already received their inheritance. Though the case was not decided, it is clear that it hinges on whether the animal had been slaughtered by the son for his own purposes, or had died of natural causes, or had been slaughtered by the father for his purposes.

The two men in the docket were brothers by different wives. The younger was complaining against the elder that in 1923 the elder had slaughtered a bull belonging to their father (who was then still alive) . This elder brother was then already married, had left home and been given his share of the cattle. The younger brother claimed

[11] The nature of such exchanges is fully discussed under contracts (pp. 192–206) .

that at the time of the event in question, the elder brother returned
home and asked his father for a bull to slaughter (for some ceremonial purpose). The plaintiff also claimed that at the time he asked
his older brother for a namanya heifer to make up his share of the
bull, but that the brother had said to wait, as he did not at that time
have a heifer, and thus put him off for some time. Then the plaintiff
went to Kenya for a period of many years, and since it was a matter
between brothers did not feel he should press his claim.

COURT: Who was present at the slaughter of the bull?
PLAINTIFF: Two witnesses—Koñ Kusombo of Bukwa, the father's
    brother, and Tumbu, a man who married our sister.
COURT: If your witnesses say that it was the father who slaughtered
    the cow and not your brother, what will you say that means?
PLAINTIFF: That means that I have lost the case.
COURT: Have you brought witnesses?
PAINTIFF: I brought them last time, but they did not come this
    time.
COURT: Any questions from assessors?
ASSESSOR: No. Only if there are witnesses.
COURT (to Defendant): Have you any witnesses that you did not get
    a bull from your father?
DEFENDANT: Yes, I have witnesses; only one, as the others have died.
    He is Busyentich Kapchesir, a neighbor in those days.
COURT: What does your witness know?
DEFENDANT: He knows that the bull died, that my father ate the
    meat of the bull, and it was not given to me by my father to
    slaughter. [Pause] The witness of my brother [Koñ] shared a
    piece of the dead cow, as he is our father's brother. He had the
    hind leg of that bull.
COURT: So you think that Koñ will support you?
DEFENDANT: Yes, he will surely say so. He even took the hide of the
    bull and paid a he-goat for it.
ASSESSOR: If your father's brother comes and says that you were given
    the bull to slaughter, against whom is the judgment to go?
DEFENDANT: Against me.
COURT: Have you brought your witnesses?
DEFENDANT: No, he will come next Tuesday to confirm what I have
    spoken to be true.
(The case was held over pending availability of witnesses.) [Case 1]

Land inheritance follows a similar pattern. We may use the
heritage of Psiwa Cherop of Sipi (a densely farmed area) as an
indication of the pattern (Case 69). The numbers in the geneal-
ogy shown here refer to the fields received by the person; if

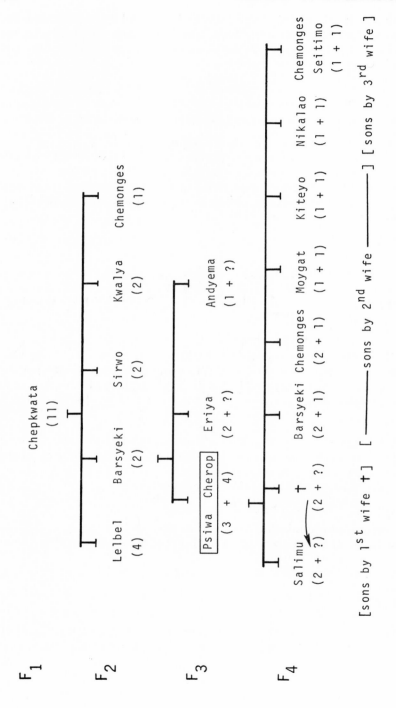

there are two numbers, the first refers to plantain fields and the second to open fields or bush. The distinction was not made in the first two generations. Sons are in the order of age from left to right.

This case extends from the 1850's, when Chepkwata was a young adult, to 1954 when the data were obtained from Psiwa Cherop, who had been initiated about 1906. During this time the amount of land in bush was reduced through increased pressure on the land. Chepkwata had eleven fields in two separate locations. When the sons were given their land for use, the eldest received more than the others. The eleventh field was given to Chemonges, as residual legatee, when his father died. Our informant, again, inherited more than either of his two younger brothers (the increase in number represents the transformation of bush into plantain fields) .

Psiwa had eight sons. He allocated all the plantains he inherited to his first wife, and these were to go to her two sons; but, as the second son died, all four fields went to Salimu. In addition to creating fields out of his open land, Psiwa purchased land from a clan brother of his second wife, an outright purchase of open land for 80 rupees (160 shillings) in 1910–1915. Concerning these matters, Psiwa said: "Kiteyo will inherit the other field remaining to his mother, who has left me and is living with her sons. The two plantain fields I have belong to Nikalao's mother. When I die, Chemonges Seitimo will inherit them but if he is kind enough he will share with his brother Nikalao. This is because he is the last son. It is just as with cattle." The more important elements in this case history are: (1) the senior son is given favored treatment, (2) the junior son is residual legatee, and (3) the land allocated to a wife goes to her own sons.[12]

As indicated earlier, widows of the deceased are inherited if they are still of childbearing age. If they are old and have grown

---

[12] Sons are jealous to protect against reallocation of land that has been assigned to their mother. A son may (when he is grown) claim back the land of his deceased mother:

Steven had three wives and the first wife died. She had had two plantain fields. After she died, I used that land, but when her sons grew up, they took back the plantain fields that had belonged to their mother. [Case 238]

sons, they will live with these sons. The order of preference in heirs to the widows is:

1. Next younger full brother
2. Next older full brother
3. Older full brothers in reverse order of their seniority
4. Younger (adult) full brothers in order of seniority
5. Half brothers
6. Kota brothers
7. Clan brothers

The expectation is that the wives will remain together, but it seems they rarely do. Many considerations intervene. One is the widow's own preference. Though theoretically she has no say in the matter, she may have enough force or reason on her side so that her wish is followed.

Kiberin was the richest of the sons of Pyechonge. He had only one wife. He quarreled with his brother over a land boundary. Subsequently this brother died and the other brothers accused Kiberin of wizardry, though there had been only quarreling and not fighting. The brothers held a large beer party to which they invited Kiberin and asked him to remain to enjoy an extra pot after the others had gone. After the others had left they held him down and pressed his testicles between two sticks until it killed him.

The woman did not like these men and at the funeral ceremony selected a man of a different kota to inherit her. She announced that if her husband had really caused his brother's death by wizardry, nothing would happen; but that if he had not done so, the brothers had murdered her husband for nothing and that "something will hurt them." Her position with respect to inheritance was supported by the pororyet. The brothers all died in a similar way. [Case 11]

Forbidden relationships may intervene, for no man can inherit a wife he might not have married on his own. He may not marry a widow if she belongs to the clan of his mother, to the clan of any of his existing wives,[13] or to the clan of any of his wives' mothers, or if the widow's mother belongs to the clan of any of his wives. In Case 10 (p. 66), the two wives of a deceased man were inherited by separate half brothers of the deceased. Other special factors may intervene, such as having

[13] It was said that the reason a man must not marry into the same clan as his brother was because he then could not inherit that brother's wife. The rule is frequently broken and not strongly felt, but is a consideration.

twins, but I do not know all the special regulations. One of Psiwa Kapchemesyekin's sons (see p. 64) had died, and the two widows were inherited by the youngest full brother (there were three intervening ones) and the oldest half brother. I have no explanation of this inheritance.

The inheritance of widows may evoke considerable feeling on the part of the wife and the potential heirs. The following discourse took place in 1962 in the kokwet of the funeral for Stanley Seswet:

After the shaving ceremony, a council was held among the assembled family members and neighbors present. Mustafa Chemwok acted as a kind of chairman at the session. The first item of business was the inheritance of the widow of the deceased. (The widow took no part in the discussion.)

CHEMWOK: We are finished with everything important and now must determine who should be guardian of the family. In the old days we would not have spoken of this now, but later, when beer is brewed. I would point out the person to be guardian should be the brother of the deceased, the one who is next to the deceased himself.

He was interrupted by the first wife of the deceased's father, who harangued the crowd in a very cross way, saying she had "heard yesterday from brothers of the deceased that nobody was to inherit the woman, but if they say that, then who will look after the children?"

A son of the deceased, a precircumcised boy of about sixteen or eighteen years, then got up: "What you are saying about this is all a nuisance. Nobody will inherit my mother." A clan member responded: "You are too young to say this sort of thing." Next, the deceased's father's brother's wife got up and confirmed that nobody was to inherit the deceased's widow.

CHEMWOK: Do you think that this young man here [pointing to the youthful son of the deceased] is old enough to look after the cows and the other properties of this woman?

WOMAN: It doesn't matter. The government will look after these things properly.

SON: My mother is not to be married by somebody else.

CHEMWOK: You are too young to decide. It is up to us. It is not your wife, it is ours and we are responsible for her and for you, too. I suggest the name of Kamuchinok. His father and the father of the deceased are brothers and he has no wife. I am asking the old men to talk to the widow about this.

SELUK (who is the next younger full brother of the deceased) : The next to the deceased is the right person to inherit the woman and look after the children. The men have suggested my name, but I am not interested in this. But Kamuchinok is the right person. I agree I should support the children, but I don't want the woman for my wife.

YAKOBO (another brother) : Another thing is to ask the widow. You have so many brothers from the same father, you could forget about the right person being from the same mother [citing precedent to support this]. Ask the widow whom she wishes.

WOMAN: Seluk should be the right person and shouldn't refuse at all. If he doesn't like her, all he must do is wash ashes from his brother's wife and eat vegetables with the wife and children [the ceremonial act to establish her heritability; washing the ashes is a figure having reference to the ceremonial sexual intercourse]; and, if not, Aribasi should be the one if Seluk refuses.

ARIBASI: It is a bad thing and I can't do it. There was a Kisa ceremony here which I performed. [This reason is obscure to me, but it was supported by the men.]

WOMAN: Who knows this man Kamuchinok? I have never seen him until the deceased died.

OLD MAN: Listen, you sheep, Seluk is the one to wash ashes and eat the vegetables with the children. After that, Kamuchinok is the right person to stay with the woman. You are just shouting for nothing. What you should do is to ask the widow and it is up to her to choose whom she'd like to stay with.

WOMAN: We want to know who is washing ashes. Seluk should be the one. It is then up to the widow to find who will be her own husband. You should slaughter sheep for meat for this purpose.

MOTHER OF DECEASED: We don't have a sheep.

MAN: All right. Find a sheep and we will buy a sheep. Subscribe 1 shilling each and we will get sheep tomorrow at the market. Festo, you must go to the market to find a sheep, but be careful to buy one with horns.

I later discussed this dispute with two of the brothers, including Seluk, who gave me the following exegesis:

Choosing the man to inherit the wife was the first thing to be done and there was considerable difference of opinion: (1) that she should not be inherited at all; (2) that she should be inherited by the brother next to the deceased, Seluk [this seemed to be the dominant male position, but was not shared by Seluk himself; it was, I believe, the final outcome]; (3) that it should be the aret brother, Kamuchinok, who has no wife and therefore could use her (his father and the father of the deceased were full brothers) ; (4) that the wife is to decide later but that Seluk is to wash the ashes (Seluk agreed to support the children, but does not want to take her as a wife) ; (5) that it should be Festo Aribasi, the oldest son of the fourth wife, who claims that because he performed the Kisa ceremony here he can't do it, to which the men agreed.

From the deceased's senior half brother, I received the following two days later:

The brother that follows the deceased is the right one to inherit. If the widow refuses the real brother of the deceased, she may choose any from the sons of another mother. In this case Seluk should have been the one, and he is the one to "eat the meat" with the widow. We must then find another brother. Seluk knows that the widow will not agree to marry him. That man is a very cruel man and mistreats his wife, and she is afraid she may be treated the same. He beats his wife from time to time. Seluk agrees to provide for her children even though he doesn't take the wife. This is a customary procedure. He must send the children of the deceased to school and, when boys and girls are to be circumcised, is responsible to arrange for that and pay all the costs. When these boys want to be married, he is the one to bargain the bride-price and it is his responsibility to pay the cows and goats and other charges. If he can't pay these things then the other brothers of deceased must help—all brothers, irrespective of mother. Seluk has been sleeping in the house. When we find the ram, that is the day we decide. After that Seluk may go away, if he so wishes, or if the woman refuses him.

In the old days it was the same. People of the aret had to find a suitable person, but still she can refuse a person; but she must take a man of that aret, who need not be of the same kota.

I tried to find out who she wants but she refuses to say until the day they eat the meat. I feel that if Seluk refuses it should be his younger brother, Mwayet.

My father and Kamuchinok's father were brothers. Kamuchinok's father died and his wife was inherited by my father, and my father got Kamuchinok from her. Therefore, Kamuchinok cannot inherit our wives. If we allowed him to do that, all our family will die, because Kamuchinok's mother was not married by my real father but by my father's brother. [A man who is himself a son of an inherited wife cannot inherit a wife unless there are no other brothers whatsoever. This was pointed out by Kamuchinok's sister and seconded by the old men.]

The argument between the men and the women at the meeting was that somebody suggested Kamuchinok and the women said that it was impossible, that Seluk should be the correct person, and he refused. It is always the custom, so as to find the right person, to have this kind of discussion.

The Sebei claimed that nowadays a widow may be inherited by a son of the deceased (by another wife), a custom that started in the Mbai region, but that this practice was not followed in earlier years. I have no case evidence of such an occurrence.

Personal possessions in Sebei were never extensive and are not today. They are, however, taken by heirs. Of particular importance are a man's spear, shield, and stool, which become the property of the oldest son; they are symbols of his authoritative position in the family as reconstituted by the father's death. Before these or any other personal possessions may be taken they must be anointed ritually with beer and sheep fat to free them of the father's spirit. The other items, according to the instances I observed, seem to be taken by whoever makes a satisfactory personal claim.

Guardianship and Disinheritance

Most of my information on guardianship has been implicit in the foregoing discussion. The basic rules are simple: the man who inherits the wives, or the residual legatee of the cattle, assumes guardianship of the immature children of the deceased. In the former case, the man who inherits the wives takes the land and cattle as trustee for the children and cannot "use" them himself.

When a brother inherits a wife and she has children, he is given cows for feeding the children, but he cannot claim these cattle as his own. He must keep them to feed the children of the woman he inherited. He cannot slaughter, sell, or use them for bride-price for another wife. [Field notes]

Chelegut's father died and his father's property, including his wife, was inherited by Kaptyemogin. Kaptyemogin used the cows, and when Chelegut grew up he was told that his father's cows had been used up. Chelegut took a case against Kaptyemogin before the kokwet, which ordered Kaptyemogin to give Chelegut two cows. [Case 235]

When the guardian is an older brother, the same rule applies.

In the division of Kambuya's property described in *Kambuya's Cattle,* certain animals were allocated to the younger half brother of the herdsman who took over Kambuya's herd. These animals would be cared for by the herdsman, but they and their progeny would remain the property of the younger brother. Caring for animals would include necessary sales and exchanges—the guardian had the right to make contracts—but this would still be done as legal representative for the boy.

When the mother dies, a young child may be taken by another relative to be cared for. Case 234 (p. 36) illustrates a guardianship by the mother's sister.

Among the Koin tribe, a youth who had lost his father might be circumcised early and thus raised to adult status by legal-ceremonial fiction, but the Sebei do not follow this practice. Such an act enables the youth to enter into contracts and take charge of his own animals. Such a policy would have been more important during the period when circumcision was often delayed into maturity.

With adequate justification, a father may send his son out of the house, refuse to give him cattle, and refuse to pay bride-price, though normally such things cannot be done. I have no measure of the justification for such an act, except as indicated in the following.

Malinga Kamachin was very rich. He had five sons. The second son misbehaved by disobeying his father's instructions, insulting his father, and refusing when asked to graze the goats. His father sent him away. I asked him why he sent his son away and he said that was the punishment given to sons in the old days. The son never got married. He cannot bring a case against his father, because he misbehaved. [Case 236]

Such a son could not bring action against the father to pay his bride-price. Sebei informants spoke as if disinheritance of the son was possible, but I doubt that this notion is correct, strictly speaking. The son cannot be obstracized from the clan. There was dispute as to whether the son in the above case might inherit cattle when his father dies. Again, spiritual matters intervene: "Such a man might take a case; the people say that he is the father of your grandsons, and he will be given two or five cows—not many, depending upon how rich the father had been." [Law Conference]

Missing Persons

A missing person is declared dead by means of having his widow undergo a funeral ceremony. (I did not hear of this happening in the case of missing women or children; the likelihood of occurrence would be less, and, furthermore, there would be little or no legal point to such a declaration.) I attended one meeting held to determine what to do; there was some gossip that the man's body had been found, but, if this was true, it clearly was not officially admitted. The senior man of the aret presided, and a number of other clansmen were present.

This is a family kokwet to arrange the appropriate funeral ceremony for a man who is missing and presumed dead. The ceremony establishes, in effect, the death of the man and arranges for the inheritance of the widow and responsibility for the children. It is not a unique occurrence, as appeals to precedent were made.

The meeting resulted in a number of decisions, as follows: that a ram was needed for a ceremony of smearing and for treating the children; that the same ram could be used for both; that the woman should engage in only one day's mourning; that there would have to be a ceremony of friendship for cows [by means of which the two herds can live together] and to chase away the bad oyik of the deceased; that Sirar [a clan brother] would inherit the wife; that Sirar had the responsibility for getting the ram and other things necessary for the ceremonies; that the ceremony of friendship of the cows would require the presence of one of the true brothers [who were not present as there had been ill feeling among them] of the missing man.

The decisions were reached by mutual agreement; no one appeared really to dominate the decision-making. No one spoke for the interests of the widow, and there were no women present at the kokwet. The actual "funeral" took place nine days later. [Case 127]

In another case brought before the modern court (Case 4), the woman asked for a "divorce" from a man who had been missing for three years, but her petition was summarily denied.

Affiliation in Sebei Legal Action

In every society the individual articulates to his community through formally defined membership, by means of which he derives the statuses that determine his rights and obligations with respect to others in the community. This factor is so important in Sebei that we have chosen to illuminate this part of Sebei legal institutions first, despite the fact that to do so requires that we borrow information from later sections. Let us summarize this section by reexamining the basic principles.

First, in matters pertaining to rights and duties, in their formalized manifestations, women are clearly subordinate to men. A woman is, legally speaking, dependent upon her father until she is married, when the father through negotiations allocates her to another man. The community defines the privileges so transferred and may intervene when the husband oversteps them, but, as the woman's public status is essentially a dependent and a limited one, we must concentrate our attention upon male roles. We hasten to add, however, that the woman's role is not necessarily meek and submissive. Through informal actions, through the power of her individual personality, through masculine fear of the occult powers of women and the potentialities of sorcery, women may exert considerable influence upon the day-to-day affairs of Sebei life; and though they may be beaten, they are not discounted in the affairs of men.

A man's basic rights and obligations are established through the circumstances of his birth. He is thus placed in the constellation of a household, a communal and collaborative unit with its established rights to resources. In considerable measure his subsequent rights are dependent upon matters of birth order and the established rights within the household of his own mother. Most important, the circumstances of a man's birth place him in a specific agnatic social group, interdependent with his fellow clansmen. Furthermore, they place him in relation to other specified clans, with attendant, though dilute, rights and obligations—that is, those of his mother and his father's mother. Finally, his birth also places him in a pororyet, which is normally his for life, and this also gives him rights and puts him under obligation. Even his age-set affiliations derive from the circumstances of his birth, though in this instance the time, rather than the parentage or the location, is the relevant factor.

These legal statuses an individual can, in varying degree, alter during his life, or they may be altered by outside events over which he has little or no control. Normally, however, they are not altered, and the individual's legal position is basically established at birth.

It is well to anticipate here the manner in which affiliation operates with respect to the other major sectors of legal action in Sebeiland: violence and property. As we shall see, the law of violence has as its central underlying thesis the assumption of clan unity and clan responsibility, a demand ultimately enforced by the spiritual unity of the kin group. On the other hand, property is essentially a private right. Yet property is to a considerable degree acquired by virtue of the affiliations defined in this sector, and is even more clearly protected by the collaborative action of groups so formed. We will have to concern ourselves with the important interrelation between property rights and the ties of personal relationship, but the discussion of this matter has to be delayed until the other aspects of Sebei law have been set forth.

PART TWO: The Law
of Violence

In this section I examine acts in which one individual harms another, whether by physical assault or by slanderous or abusive language, whether directly or by means of witchcraft, whether it leads to death or to physical or emotional injury. I am concerned with the legal definition and status of such acts and the sanctions against their commitment. I believe there is an underlying unity to Sebei concepts regarding acts of a harmful nature, though, as we shall see, not all matters dealt with in this section fall within the unity thus formed. Let us first examine the nature of this unity.

The law of violence is essentially clan law, and acts of harm against a person are viewed as being either actually or potentially against his clan. Legal actions in redress of such wrongs are therefore actions by the clan. Similarly, the act is seen as being an act of the clan as a whole and not merely of the individual who actually performed the injury; retaliation is therefore against the clan and not the individual.

It has already been made clear not only how clans are formulated, but also that the identification with the clan is not a matter of choice. Indeed, the unity of the clan is a spiritual unity from which there is no escape; it places upon each individual the burden of mutual support to his fellow clansmen.

This law of clan retaliation in Sebeiland applies fundamentally to killing, not to lesser forms of violence. Or, put the other way about, lesser forms of violence enter into the realm of clan interaction to the extent that they represent a threat of escalation into murder. Therefore, as we shall see, the acts that we would call assault and battery either are disregarded as inconsequential and therefore remain outside the realm of law, or they are regarded as possibly leading to an interclan killing and therefore must be given serious consideration. Such consideration can best be seen as efforts to prevent the act from leading to murder or to retaliatory feud or sorcery. The same reasoning can be applied to verbal abuses—slander, false rumor, and the like.

The realm of witchcraft and sorcery is not so clear, and we shall leave the discussion of witchcraft as a delict to a subsequent chapter. One difficulty lies in the fact that acts that appear to be and terminologically are the same are not the same in Sebei legal attitudes. For acts of sorcery are at one and the same time a most serious crime for which a special ordeal and punishment is reserved, and also a major means of redressing wrongs—a veritable handmaiden to the prosecution of the law. It is to the second of these functions that we must give some attention in this chapter.

All deaths in Sebei are considered to be due to some supernatural force (unless they are murders), either witchcraft, a curse, or the action of the spirits. If a tree falls on a man or if he dies in a lorry accident, the death is not an accident but is due to supernatural forces. The only exception to this general assumption is in the case of a very old person who is assumed to have died a natural death, called a sweet death or *kelil*.[1] Any man who dies while still able to get about and do normal work, even though he is an old man, is not so regarded; kelil is limited to persons who have reached a really advanced age. Whenever a Sebei dies, there is immediate and widespread discussion as to the possible source of his death, with inevitable suspicions of direct witchcraft.

But we must not assume that the Sebei blame every death on some act of witchcraft. There are many supernatural sources of death. A "legitimate" curse against the clan for some past act may be responsible, or a person may have unwittingly done something that brought upon him the action of a curse, or a curse imposed upon another clan may have run too long and is now having a reflexive action on the clansmen of the person who imposed it. Death may also be brought on by the spirits of

[1] The root form *lil* is a verb form referring to longevity.

the dead ancestors because they have become displeased at some slight or by the failure to perform some ceremonial act. Elements of a more fatalistic kind may also bring about death: a wife of an ill-fated clan, the look of a person who has the evil eye, the working out of some ill omen—all these can bring death without the operation of a human or spiritual will. A person may suffer death as an evil consequence of the breach of a tabu. A sick Sebei will seek out the diviner (*chepsokeyontet*) to discover the source of his illness; the family of the deceased may do likewise and certainly will discuss the possibilities at considerable length.

There is a pragmatic, almost experimental, approach to the problem, for though there are many sources of illness there does not seem to be a clear means of discovering which one is involved in any particular instance. Thus the Kaptui clan, galvanized into action by the death of one of its members climaxing a long series of losses, endeavored to organize along modern formalized lines so as to raise funds in order to rid themselves of the possible cause or causes. They listed no fewer than seven possible sources of the evil influences that were invading them: (1) sorcery resulting from the fact that a man whose mother was a member of the Kaptui aret (a "nephew of the aret," in Sebei reckoning) had committed a murder; (2) *surupik* (a form of curse) had been initiated by a clan member against the man who had caused two children to be burned, and reciprocal effect was feared; (3) some clan members had eaten meat of a stolen cow (which they had purchased), and the owner did surupik against those responsible, so that the clansmen had eaten ritually tainted meat; (4) during a famine many years ago, a clansman killed his sister whom he found stealing beans that were ripening in his field, and sorcerous revenge was feared; (5) surupik was done by a man against an unknown person who had burned down his house, and there was a fear (with what foundation, I don't know) that the arsonist might have been a member of the Kaptui clan; (6) during a famine many years ago, a clan member killed a herd boy whose cattle had broken into his field and eaten some maize, and retaliation by sorcery was feared; (7) a member of Kaptui clan killed a

man's cow but denied having killed it, and they fear the owner
has done surupik on this matter. A wide range in circumstances
and time could therefore operate as a source of death. The clan
planned to meet such of these forces as it could in order to
preserve the remaining members from a similar fate.

We witnessed a ceremony in 1954 for the removal of a curse
that was causing the illness of a prominent Sebei—a curse that
was originally pronounced at the time of Baganda control over
Sebeiland in the first decade of the twentieth century.

Spiritual forces, particularly as exemplified by oaths, act as
prime sanctions against illegal or improper behavior. Curses of
one form or another may be pronounced in response to behavior ranging from outright murder to a minor infraction of propriety. They may operate against an unknown miscreant as well
as against known or suspected actors; they may be taken against
strangers or against the members of one's own family; they may
be invoked over body parts in case of a murder or over a gourd
of urine in cases of false accusation. The threat of an appropriate curse is frequently heard, as is oathing to assert innocence of
an accusation.

These two aspects of Sebei culture—clan identification and
witchcraft belief—join together, for the clan is a spiritual as
well as a social entity; it is a sodality tied by a common ancestry,
which is to say that it shares the same dead. What is still more
important is the fact that sorcery, at least in its more important
forms, operates against the clan rather than the individual. In
modern times, at least, the Sebei are more motivated toward
clan solidarity out of fear of spiritual forces than they are out of
fear of direct physical retaliation, and I believe this has always
been true.

A clan need not retaliate with blood vengeance nor await the
action of a curse; it may accept a payment in cattle as compensation for a murder. Such compensation is negotiated between the
two clans in terms of a general set of expectations and values.
The livestock is contributed by clansmen in general; this motivation is not merely the generic welfare of their own clan and
the desire for peace among their fellowmen. Rather, a failure to
settle a dispute puts each clansman in jeopardy of being killed,

either outright and immediately as an act of blood vengeance, or by means of a curse pronounced against the clan.

Neither in clan action nor in sorcerous retaliation does the community—in the sense of a geographically delimited set of coresidents—have any role to play in juridical affairs. The community, through the kirwokik and by social pressure, may bring two feuding clans into negotiation and may help them resolve their difficulties, but it cannot intervene, nor can it enforce its decision. There is reason to believe that this was once entirely the state of affairs in Sebeiland, though perhaps at that time age-sets may have played a more prominent role in matters of law.

Now, however, there is another institution that takes action in instances of legal offense, and through it the community does have a role and does have the power to act. There is considerable evidence that this innovation, though clearly antedating the first appearance of Europeans in the area, is a recent one. The community asserts the right to punish an offender under the sanction imposed by the ceremony of *ntarastit,* which was glossed by interpreters as "passing the law." (It was impossible to obtain any etymological breakdown of this word, which informants say means simply the law. Dr. Montgomery calls my attention to the word *ndara* in closely related Nandi, meaning remorse or anguish.) This ritual, initiated by the prophet, is held periodically (variously indicated as three to five years, but apparently actually when the prophet feels that the level of moral compulsion has so reduced itself as to require a reaffirmation). The last ntarastit was probably held shortly after the beginning of the twentieth century, before the Baganda conquest of the area. The ritual is a public oath held in specified places in each pororyet, starting in the eastern sector of Sebei territory and moving (in accordance with the general pattern of Sebei-wide ceremonies) westward until all the pororisyek have performed it. It consists chiefly of an oath by all adult men of the pororyet who swear a kind of fealty of acceptance on the pain of supernatural death. All circumcised men gather naked at the specified location and, before an altar of implanted selected branches of ceremonial significance, swear as follows:

"Anybody who kills anybody passing by (or who takes things belonging to others, etc.) , he will die." They thrust their spears at the altar in unison each time as they name a different kind of offense. The ritual apparently brings any delict into the jurisdiction of the pororyet, which can then punish the person or clan responsible.[2] The punishment takes the form of destruction of property—killing livestock, slashing plantains, destroying crops, taking stored grain, and even burning down houses, or any combination of these. This punishment does not legally eliminate the demand for compensation of the injured clan in cases of murder, though in none of the cases I collected was compensation ever paid.

The pattern of action is succinctly put in the following case:

Ngelach of Kapkepen aret of Kapeywa pororyet killed a man named Chepkowo of Kapunkor aret of Kapcheptemkoñ pororyet, soon after the laws had been passed and members of four different pororisyek, Kapcheptemkoñ, Chema, Tegeres, and Kapeywa, went and fought the Kapkepen aret. They slashed their bananas and took animals in punishment because the clan had broken the law. [Case 165]

One participant in the Law Conference had "brought back two goats, a he-goat and a she-goat." He went on to say: "You can punish the murderer's clan by taking property because they broke the law, still the murder is not forgotten. The clan of the deceased must take revenge by killing a member of the murderer's clan or can accept compensation paid by that clan." Finally: "The time we punish in this manner is when we insist that the laws be obeyed and the time that we don't do this is when the law is not in effect. . . . In the third year, laws become weak and are forgotten and if the pororyet tries to take this kind of action, there will be a war." Thus:

Shortly after markets had been established, a man named Mwoko said to the people as they were dispersing from the market: "Who is that man?" The reply was: "That is Kapchepet, who is a poor man

---

[2] I use the term "punish" here not only because the interpreter did so, but because I think it was viewed as that. It was not a fine, and it was not compensation; though individuals made off with goods, they thought of the act as punishing the individual for a wrong done.

with no relatives." Mwoko stood up and speared the man to death, saying: "This is a poor man. Who is going to take revenge?"

Matui [the prophet] said that such killing must be stopped; he initiated the ntarastit ceremony and the people stopped doing things like that. Matui said to the people that they had "forgotten our laws"; that "this will be the last man to be killed." [Case 206]

Ntarastit, then, gives the community the sanction to act; it places the kokwet in the position of being able not merely to right matters that have gone awry, which, as we shall see, appears to have been its chief function, but actually to take over the function of punishment. It is not without significance that a supernatural sanction is involved, nor that the sanction has the form of an oath. We return to these considerations in the last chapter. The ntarastit is invoked in cases of murder, as has already been shown. It is my impression, however, that it is more readily brought to bear in cases of theft.

With these considerations, we turn to the law with respect to delicts involving interpersonal injuries.

CHAPTER 5 *The Law Regarding Murder and*
Other Inflicted Deaths

The Sebei Definition of Murder

The Sebei recognize a category of delict which may be called murder; they distinguish such acts from killings by accident or inadvertence, and they recognize that a person may under certain circumstances kill another without its being viewed as a delict.

A Sebei definition of murder, based upon general statements and distinctions made in various contexts, may fairly be formulated. It may be defined as the act of one person killing another when

1) it is a purposeful, intentional act, and not an accident;
2) it is not adequately motivated by prior actions of the murdered man or his clan;
3) the decedent belongs to a clan other than that of the person doing the killing; and
4) the decedent is a Sebei rather than a member of an enemy tribe.

According to the Sebei, a death caused by witchcraft may be murder. Because of the special circumstances surrounding witchcraft, and particularly because it is handled differently from murder by direct physical means, I am treating the discussion of delicts involving sorcery in a separate chapter.

The Sebei do not recognize insanity, drunkenness, or minority status as a meliorating consideration in matters of killing. If it is determined (to the satisfaction of the Sebei) that a death was caused by an injury inflicted by another, no matter how much earlier the assault had been made, the act is still viewed as murder and treated as such.

Murder is called *katokyi; tokyi* means "to aim at something." The Sebei do not indicate degrees of murder, but they do recognize forms of homicide that are not murder. In such instances neither vengeance nor compensation is proper, but a ceremonial payment may be demanded and a cleansing ritual is requisite.

Killings Not Considered Murder

The Sebei distinguish between intentional and accidental killing. Just as the term for the former includes the notion of aim or intent, the term for an accidental homicide is *kalel*,[1] which is built on the verbal stem *lel* meaning "to err." The following cases were brought forward particularly to illustrate the point:

Arapelilya of Kapchepai clan killed Kamwandil [another Sebei] of Kapyis clan during a battle with the Elgeyo tribe. There was no legal action because the many witnesses who were present knew that Arapelilya had not done it intentionally. [Case 117]

Arapletu was hunting in the bush. He saw Tenwenu moving in the bush and, thinking it was a bush pig, speared him and he died. The people decided it was an accident. [Case 160]

The Sebei also recognize justifiable killing. They call it *kachiker*, which is the passive verbal construction meaning "having been repaid," from *ker*, "repay in kind."

Mutey of Kapchoken clan was insulted by a member of the Kapkepen clan and killed him. Mutey was taken before the High Court and convicted of manslaughter [by European magistrates] and sent to jail. After he served his jail sentence and returned home, people of the two clans sat and decided he must pay the ceremonial compensation [see below] rather than indemnity. [Case 159]

This case was presented as an exemplification of the recognition of just cause for the act. It was later explained that the people of the pororyet must determine whether the person killed had misbehaved, and if so, then "the matter is just forgotten," except the ceremonial payment that has the force of re-creating amity between the two parties.

The Sebei are not entirely clear as to what acts of a person

---

[1] This term is not to be confused with *kelil,* sweet death, discussed in chapter 4.

constitute justification for killing him. The only item mentioned in the context of the discussion, other than the case of insult already cited, was that one might justifiably kill a person found secretly in one's cattle kraal. The person's presence in the kraal is presumptive evidence of an attempt at either cattle theft or witchcraft. Case data indicate several circumstances that justify a killing, and in no case would a justified killing be considered a murder: killing a person of a clan in retaliation for the murder of one's clansman committed by a member of that clan (Case 96, p. 99); killing a clansman who repeatedly causes trouble, for example, a recidivist thief; or after warning, killing such a person of another clan (Case 214, p. 176). Though one informant indicated that a person might justifiably kill a man found in flagrante delicto with his wife, others denied it and no cases came to light; in view of general Sebei attitudes toward adultery, it is unlikely. Self-defense was not mentioned as a justifiable cause, nor do I have case data on it. Men have killed persons in their own clan (see pp. 107–108), often because the latter have been causing trouble for the clan, but this type of killing has already been eliminated from the definition of murder.

Both accidental homicide and justifiable killing require the ceremonial payment (*chiker*) of a cow, bull, and sheep. The payment is not viewed as compensation or restitution, but as a ceremonial cleansing. Bomet said: "They give these animals to close the matter; otherwise members of the other clan will get mad. If a man thinks about his clansman having been killed and gets mad about it, other members of his clan will say, 'No, this matter is finished,' and will stop him from doing anything." The acceptance of such payment is tantamount to acceptance by the clan of the nature of the death and would prevent it from taking either direct or magical revenge; hence, it is an important element in legal procedure.

A man may kill a person of another tribe with impunity, though it was felt that to do so when the person was on a friendly visit would be an improper act and one that might, of course, escalate into a large and dangerous conflict. It is, however, less clear who, for this purpose, is properly considered an enemy. Specifically mentioned were the Bagisu, Nandi, Masai, Pokot, Karamojong, and Kitosh. Yet even here, one man who killed his Mugisu wife paid compensation to her family (see Case 166, p. 94). The killing of persons in another Sebei tribe (that is, between Mbai, Sor, and Sapiñ) was clearly murder, and apparently the sentiment extended to the Koin, Bok, and other Sabaot units even though they did not share the same prophets or engage in common ceremonials. The matter remains ambiguous; one member of the Law Conference said, "The Koin used to fight with us and we regarded them as enemies; we have just recently made friends." Other informants said that no Sabaot persons could be killed as enemies. It appears, however, that this friendliness is a product of Europeanized pacification.

From the viewpoint of Western law, the fact that the killing of a close relative is not viewed as murder represents the most unusual and unexpected aspect of Sebei law; yet the logic of legal action in Sebeiland, which considers the clan as the legal entity with respect to killing, makes this attitude fully comprehensible. In one fratricide case the leader of the clan was quoted as saying: "One life has been destroyed. We cannot lose two men from the clan. The deceased was a bad man and deserved to be killed" (Case 163).

In none of the four cases of fratricide was any real compensation demanded.

There were two full brothers, Seluk and Twintay. Seluk killed Twintay, who had a wife and two children. No compensation was paid. This happened a few years ago. [Case 162]

Barsile was annoyed with his younger brother, Sabila, when they were quarreling around the beer pot. The younger one kept accusing Barsile of bewitching the family and thereby giving him a bad name. Therefore Barsile killed Sabila. Barsile then ran away and stayed with his uncles of the Kamari clan. No compensation was paid and the matter was forgotten. They were full brothers. Sabila's widow was not inherited by Barsile but was married by somebody of another clan. [Case 170]

In one instance, however, the land of the brother who did the killing was divided among his clansmen:

Two brothers of mine, Chemgani and Ragan, fought and Chemgani killed Ragan. It was later found that Ragan was a man who repeatedly misbehaved and fought other people. The clan discussed what to do and decided that all of Chemgani's land should be divided among other members of the clan. Only land was given, not cattle. [Case 161]

Similarly, a son may be killed by his father:

During "Baganda times," when the Baganda ruled Sebeiland and brought much trouble to the land and made people work, Arapchemasyandich of Kapchesi clan became very irritable. One day he came home and saw his son in the courtyard and suddenly speared him to death. Nothing was done because the son was of his own blood. [Case 168]

The other two instances in which a man killed his son were discussed in similarly cavalier fashion, but both killings were considered accidental.

It is interesting that there are no cases on record of patricide; I do not know if this omission reflects reality, is an expression of suppressed fear to bring forth such cases, or is merely an accident of data collection. There is sufficient evidence of father-son hostility to warrant an assumption that the temptation exists, but it is also true that a man fears his father and would fear his father's spirits. In the absence of informants' direct statements, however, these remarks must remain speculative.

In three cases dealing with killings internal to the clan, the persons stand in a more remote relationship than brother, father, or son, and none of the killings was undertaken as a consciously designed means of getting rid of a clansman who was causing difficulties. One instance was described as follows, though it might be viewed as an instance of a clan ridding itself of a troublesome member:

A man killed a member of his own clan. They were sitting around a beer pot. One man removed the chair of his clansman. He threw it away and put his own in its place. He had been doing this sort of thing daily, but when it occurred this time, the man became annoyed and said to those around the beer pot, "Why does this man do this?" The people responded, "He does this often; why don't you wait by the road and kill this man?" So he followed the advice of his friends and speared his clansman to death. [Case 163]

When separate lineages (*korik*) are involved, however, the matter becomes more serious. In one instance (Case 84) the kota members made a surupik curse (see chap. 6) against a person of a different kota who killed one of their men. After many years the avenged kota began to lose many of its members, so that in 1927 they arranged to remove the curse ceremonially. This kota "had to pay a compensation of one heifer, one bullock, two she-goats, and one ram, and also to give a beer party," but the compensation appears to have been merely the payment of the ceremonial chiker. One informant said that within the clan, land was used in compensation; but our data are not entirely consistent on this point, as we can see. What is clear, however, is that the normal sanctions of law do not apply within the clan, except at times between different korik. We must appreciate the fact that the korik may separate themselves ceremonially (Case 151), and that interkota killing therefore represents a kind of borderline situation, for the clan (though clearly a unit) is not an undifferentiated group of people, and proximity of kinship is a factor. This emerges in other contexts. In later sections we show that men kill their clansmen who have been creating difficulties for the clan.

Killing Involving Women

The case record includes no instance of murder executed by a woman, but it was agreed that in that event, vengeance or compensation would be sought from her natal clan, not from that of her husband; the vengeance would be taken on a person of equivalent stature to the person killed, and not necessarily on the woman who committed the act. It will be recalled that an act of such a kind by a woman is justification for divorce (chap. 3). If a woman is killed, the compensation is taken by the natal clan and not by the husband. Compensation for the death of a woman depends upon her reproductive potential, but is less than for a man.

Very few of my cases involve killing of women. One instance suggests that killing women is not viewed as a very grave matter. A woman who had been caught stealing from a granary (Case 204) ran away from her husband, only to be killed by a man

who came to be nicknamed "woman-slayer" (*kuparkor*)[2] because "he was always killing women." His nephew asked why
he did this, and he merely said he did so "because women are
lazy and always stealing food or begging it" (Case 205). He
was not punished and died kelil at an old age.

The following is the only case involving a man killing his
own wife:

> Matui fought with his wife, the mother of Mangusyo, a Mugisu
> woman. They quarreled and Matui threw her into a large clay pot
> (*koruset*) in which they were boiling water for beer, and she boiled
> to death. Her Bagisu relatives came, and compensation was paid
> right away: five cows, five goats, and one sheep. Mangusyo was given
> two of the five cows, and the sheep was killed for the people who
> were gathered; the Bagisu took home the remaining animals. She
> was old and had grandchildren. [Case 166]

The case is confused by many circumstances: Matui, a prophet,
was a very rich and a very special man; the wife was old and past
childbearing age; she belonged to another tribe; and the death
might have been considered accidental (though it was not so
indicated). The compensation is, in fact, close to the amount
normally paid as bride-price, but this consideration may not be
relevant.

On the other hand, a man who brings about the death of a
woman before marriage must pay the bride-price.

> Chepirot's daughter eloped with Oyorer. The two went across a
> swollen river, and the boy managed to get across but the girl was
> caught by the water and drowned. Oyorer had to pay the bride-price
> as though she had lived. [Case 152]

> Cheptonkin's daughter became pregnant before being circum-
> cised. She died during circumcision and the boy was ordered to pay
> full bride-price for her. There was no other compensation. [Case
> 154]

A woman who died bearing her sixth child, however, required
only the payment of chiker (a bull and a sheep) to her parents
(Case 153), "to comfort her parents for what they will lose in
beer." If a woman for whom bride-price has been paid dies, and

[2] *Kup* is a prefix denoting masculine gender; *par* is the root form for "to
spear"; *kor* is the stem form for "woman"; hence, "he who spears women."

she has children, then the family of the woman must provide another daughter "to look after the children." If a woman dies in her first childbirth, the dowry is returned (or another girl is given the man), but the chiker is kept.

. . . "Let us clarify. If a woman dies bearing her first child, the husband had no benefit from her, so the dowry is paid back to him; but actually the father-in-law does keep a cow and a sheep and this compensation is the same kind of consolation for deprivation as if she had died bearing a subsequent child. This payment is called *chepo-rir* ("payment for crying"; *rir,* "cry" or "weep"); it is to satisfy the spirits of the dead (oyik)." [Case 153, discussion.]

Other Considerations Regarding Killing

Neither insanity nor drunkenness is a factor in distinguishing murder from other killing, as already noted. All persons are treated as being responsible for their acts. We have no case evidence regarding accessories to murder, though in a sense all clansmen of the killer are implicitly accessories; however, if two men act together, both are held at fault, and indemnity will be shared by their clans. A boy who commits murder is as much at fault as an adult, and vengeance will be taken on the clan; an example is Case 18, in which a murder was committed by an uncircumcised man (a status socially equivalent to a boy) whose clansmen had to pay compensation to the victim's family.

Abortion is not considered a crime.

My wife, Yapchemwanya, and I quarreled. She became very annoyed and took a stone and hit her stomach until the baby came out. I did not know what to do with her, so she is still at home. [Case 172]

Infanticide apparently is not a legitimized practice, but neither is it a legal delict. The incidence of death of at least one twin is inordinately high, and one informant indicated that the middle child of triplets always is squeezed by his siblings and dies. Women often abort illegitimate children. A man may divorce a wife who repeatedly causes abortion, but the act is not itself illegal.

Suicide appears to be relatively frequent; it is often used by women primarily as a means of pressure on men, particularly when they are not allowed to marry whom they want. It apparently is fairly frequent among men, though I have no incidence rates. Incitement to suicide is not considered a crime.

Puruch Chesokey was taunted by neighbors who kept saying that he is the person who was doing the bewitching in the village. Samayiri was the one who did the teasing. Puruch became very annoyed, so he committed suicide. No compensation was paid. [Case 175]

My brother, Busyendich, found our sister sitting outside the house and said to her: "What are you doing here? Why aren't you out working?" And he beat her so that she ran away and hanged herself. The following day a man came by and said he had seen our sister hanging in a tree. They took her down and buried her. There was nothing more; there was no compensation or revenge, for the family did not want to lose two children. [Case 173]

Yet one informant at the Law Conference said, "If you beat your child and he hangs himself, members of the clan can come and ask what you have done; they can take property such as cows and divide it among themselves as punishment for causing the death of a clansman." No supporting cases were cited, and the statement is in conflict with attitudes toward killing one's own child.

Determination of Guilt

In Sebei legal theory a murderer cannot hide the act, for all persons who have killed a human being, whether friend or foe, whether in revenge or in cold blood, must undergo an appropriate cleansing ceremony. The disease *(kulelekey)*[1] from killing without taking the proper medicines causes a man to itch all over until he scratches himself to death. All informants were fully agreed upon this point, and that no man would ever hide the fact that he had killed a person; moreover, "You never find Sebei killing anybody with whom he has not been fighting." This generalization obviously does not apply to cases of witchcraft. We cannot, of course, go beyond our informants' statements here; if they firmly believe it never happens, then it follows that there are no open court procedures to establish guilt or innocence. Ultimately, the matter rests upon sorcery, to which we turn later.

Justifiability and the question of intent are, however, matters for determination. Our data do not indicate how these issues are decided, other than that, as in Case 117, "there were many people present as witnesses [to the killing] and they knew it was not intentional." Though insult was given in two instances (Cases 83 and 159) as justification for a murder, it was not so regarded in another (Case 55). I do not know what factors are responsible for this difference—whether it was the greater fault in using abusive words in front of the man's mother-in-law, as in Case 83, or because the man being abused was a poor man and

---

[1] This is the reflexive form of *lel,* meaning "to err"; both the killer and his victim are referred to as being in a state of kulelekey.

his abuser was rich. But in the final analysis, the determination
of guilt is part and parcel of the procedures for redress.

General Procedures for Redress

At the Law Conference, Richard Bomet outlined what is in
fact the general procedure for redress of wrongs when he said:
"I want to make clear to you what the major laws about killing
are. First, it was the law that you should not kill a person, because some member of your clan will be killed and, second, everybody in the clan must suffer if compensation is to be paid. If
neither revenge or compensation is had, then they will have to
do sorcery, and this is a most dangerous thing, because it is
more serious and is not forgotten. The clan who has not paid
compensation or been avenged—their children will all die, and
even nowadays you can see people doing ceremonies to get rid
of these curses so that people can live."

This clearly is the text for the remainder of our discussion on
the law of murder. In it I show that there are the following procedures with respect to a redress of wrongs in the case of murder:
(1) The clansmen of the injured party may take immediate
revenge, which should be done in hot blood. (2) The clansmen
of the murderer may seek to pay compensation for the killing.
(3) The clansmen of the murderer may themselves kill the
murderer in order to avoid further penalty. (4) The pororyet
may take action to punish the clan of the murderer. (5) In the
absence of the first three of these (and presumably irrespective
of the fourth), the clansmen of the murdered man may seek any
opportunity to avenge the death by killing individuals or taking
cattle. (6) Finally, if none of the above succeed, the family of
the murdered man may make a ceremonial curse against the
clansmen of the murderer, which continues until it is removed.

Revenge as Redress for Murder

In this section we deal with the first and fourth of the items
listed above. Strictly speaking, vengeance is the method of choice
while tempers are hot; if there is a delay, then a peaceable
settlement should be sought. If, however, the clansmen of the
murdered man do not want to initiate a settlement, then a state
of feud exists between the two clans; they do not sit down at the

same pot of beer, and the clansmen of the victim seek every opportunity to even the score.

Immediate redress is indicated in the following cases:

Before the Baganda came to rule in Sebeiland, Chilla of Kaptui clan killed a man of Kapsume clan and was, in turn, killed by one of the Kapsume men. The two clans had a ceremony of peace and there was no further fighting between the clans. [Case 96]

Members of Kapsulel and Kamelkut clans were at a beer party. After much beer had been consumed, they started fighting and two Kapsulel men were killed on the spot. One Kamelkut man, named Psakey, of the Ñongki age-set, was killed. His son is of Chepelat age-set. Both clans then left the area. The fighting had taken place at a beer party for clearing bush, and by the time they were weeding the fields after planting, the Kapsulel clan decided to avenge and even the score of dead. The Kapsulel men came to a place where a very strong man called Cheptipin, of the Kamelkut clan, was weeding his land. Two men of the Kapsulel group showed themselves at the top of a hillside and the man tried to escape but he was surrounded and was speared by the Kapsulel clanspeople. The Kapsulel people then reported their vengeance in a kind of chant. This made the score even and there was no further fighting. [Case 54]

It need not be the murderer who is slain in revenge; indeed, when there is a clear difference in status, a person equivalent to the murdered man is sought:

A member of Mangusyo's clan killed my father. The murderer was a poor man and my father was rich and had a large family. Though the murderer was close by, they did not kill him; they killed Mangusyo's father, who was rich and had a large family as my father did. [Case 156]

There may be a long period during which a feud exists, but eventually the feud is expected to result in a compensatory killing:

The quarrel between the two clans started when Kapkepen people came and took a Kapchay girl by force. The Kapchay people formed a group to take the girl back, and they started to fight and one of them was killed. Now vengeance broke out and one man of the Kapkepen was killed too. That was the end of the quarrel. The girl captured was a Ñongki age-set but the quarrel ended in Maina age-set times. There was no ceremony of peace. [Case 149]

We cannot know exactly how long a time elapsed, but presumably at least half a dozen years and probably much longer.

When a person has killed a man in vengeance he is supposed to seek out a high place and shout, "The killing is finished," thus announcing his act and initiating a settlement of peace. The end of the feud relationships must be given ritual publication, presumably to make all members aware of the close of the feud and to assure that both clans accept the reality of peace. The ceremony is known as *kiyirikowo* (*yiri*, "break"; *kowo*, "bone"). A bullock is killed, the femur is stripped of meat, and the bone is thrown against a stone until it is broken, or it is braced against a tree and struck with a stick until it breaks. Also, the tail and ears of a dog are cut, and a bowstring is severed. Both of the clans involved in the case eat the meat of the slaughtered animal, which is furnished by the clansmen of the person who committed the initial killing.

Settlement by Compensation

In the normal course of events, according to informants, it is the clan of the murderer which initiates action for a settlement; I

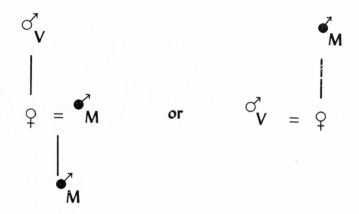

do not know if it can be the other way about. The go-between (*kiyokintet, kiyokik*)[2] is normally a person related to both clans, for he is safe from being killed while making the approach. Go-betweens are persons who are married into the clan

[2] The root form *yoch* means "send"; hence, "messenger."

of the victim: as the Sebei would say, any husband of a daughter of the clan, or any father of a wife of the clan. The relationships marked M in the accompanying diagram illustrate the proper relationship for kiyokintet, where V = clan of victim and M = clan of murderer. The kiyokintet goes to the head of the clan, saying: "We come here crying, asking for mercy." The injured clan demands compensation, but the matter is subject to bargaining, which takes place before a kokwet involving the whole pororyet, with explicit appeals to precedent. The following case gives the general flavor of the approach to settlement.

Chonkeywa of Kaptyepot clan and Chilla of Kapit clan, both of the pororyet of Tegeres, had a quarrel while the people were gathered together having a beer party for harvesting the land. Chonkeywa apparently teased Chilla, who was a young, uncircumcised man, because he could not play with him, and as a result of this taunting each took a shield and spear and began jousting. Unfortunately, the young man wounded the older in the stomach, so that the intestines came out and he subsequently died.

The Kapit people who were gathered there took the goats and sheep belonging to both clans [apparently being herded together] and ran away. But later they separated the goats and sheep that belonged to the other clan and returned them to the son of the deceased. The two clans refused to meet each other at beer parties and they stayed apart.

After some time had elapsed, the Kapit people asked for a settlement so that they could be friendly again and have peace. When it came time to arrange for the peace (two years after the murder), the *aryemput* horn was blown and the people from both clans assembled, along with many people from the pororyet. When the people gathered, they invited kirwokik from other villages [apparently also other pororisyek] as well as kirwokik from the villages of the two principals. These kirwokik did not belong to either of the clans of the disputing parties. They met at a place called Chepañ, near the Cheseper River. There were four kirwokik in this case, but it was said that had they not arrived at an agreement, they would have asked more kirwokik to help arrange the settlement. But it should be clear that the kirwokik have no power to punish the offender, for this rests on revenge.

Thirty goats and sheep and thirty head of cattle were requested by the clan of the deceased, and these were paid. Each Kapit man had to pay something, a goat or a sheep from an ordinary person and from a rich man, a cow.

When the compensation was paid, a ceremony of friendship was held. Mei, a half brother of the murderer, and a person apparently similarly related to the murdered man were the principals in this ceremony. These were young men, not clan heads. The two men each took hold of a ram and started stabbing it with a knife. After they had stabbed it, they left it dying and ran to the river, where they bathed together as an expression of their peaceful relationship. After they bathed, the two men who killed the ram skinned it, and taking the right thigh cut it with a knife to show that their enmity was over.

After the ceremony, whenever there was a celebration with beer, no one could break the law or have a feeling of enmity between these two clans. [Case 18]

It is obviously of the greatest importance to know how the amount of compensation is arrived at, but unfortunately only rather general statements can be made. Though informants repeatedly quoted a standard amount, this "standard" varied from one informant to the next, and in no actual case did the amount correspond to any of these standards. The amount agreed upon at the Law Conference was thirty cattle and thirty small stock, but one participant later said he felt it should have been forty each, while elsewhere fifty was suggested. It seems clear that the figure would be only a base against which to bargain, and quite likely that it varied with time (as some data suggest) and with area, in conformity with the relative availability of livestock. The participant in the Law Conference who felt the figure was inadequate came from the area of highest concentration of cattle.

Among the factors that specifically entered into the determination of amount of compensation were the following: sex of victim, age and particularly the likelihood of more offspring of the victim, faults previously recorded against the victim's clan, economic circumstances at the time.

Compensation for a woman is less than for a man, and depends upon her age. The following generalization was made at the Law Conference: "There are three different compensations made when a woman is killed: (1) when a woman has just married and not yet produced children, ten cows and one sheep are paid because of her possibility for bearing many children; (2) if a woman is of middle age and has some children but is still able to produce more, payment of eight cows and one sheep would be expected; (3) if she is an old woman, five cows and one sheep would be paid." The only reported case in which a woman's death was compensated is given on page 94 (Case 166) ; five cows, five goats, and a sheep were paid, an amount somewhat larger than indicated in the generalizations above, but the circumstances were very special.

Other cases likewise reflect a good deal of variation in amounts paid. In one case the offer of fifty head of cattle and ten sheep was not considered enough by the injured clan, so the other agreed to pay more. When it failed to do so, a member of the injured clan took a heifer by force (Case 57) . In a case reported as occurring around 1911, involving the son of the prophet Matui, twenty cattle and twenty goats and sheep were paid (Case 115) . Another case involving the sons of Matui indicates a compensation of eighty cattle and twenty goats (Case 148) . In the case of a man who killed two people (a man and a woman) and then hanged himself, it was decided that thirty head of cattle belonging to his estate should be divided between the clansmen of the man and the clansmen of the woman (Case 158) . In a case where ten cattle and ten small stock were paid, it was specifically indicated that the amount was small because the man who had been killed was very old (Case 240) . The small compensation of five cattle and an unspecified number of goats and spears (Case 39) was explicitly seen as influenced by the diminution of livestock in Sebei country as a result of rinderpest and other diseases that had decimated the herds. A case that was settled after a curse had been imposed required payment of six cattle and one sheep (Case 7) : "The amount was small because they had lost many people and the others took pity on them." Relevant circumstances are indicated in the following case.

When Porowey killed a man of his nephew's aret for suspected sorcery, the injured parties wanted to refuse the cattle offered, saying that they were not enough, but it was pointed out that the man was old and had a family and also that he was a wizard. They asked the people if they would be willing to pay compensation for the people the wizard had killed. Finally the clan accepted the pororyet's judgment. [Case 38]

Compensation is closed by the payment of an additional sheep (called *cheptismet*) [3] as a ceremonial payment, for "if you don't, the relatives of the deceased's clan can take cows from the murderer's clan and say that the compensation has not been paid." The clan of the deceased must offer a ram to be killed (for a ceremony called *korosek*) [4] and the meat is shared between the two clans. Members of the two clans can then "sit around the same beer pot, for the matter is forgotten." A clan may ask for an extension of time; presumably the ceremony of peace awaits the full payment, but this fact was not definitely ascertained.

Reported cases do not include any instance of an effort to arrive at a peaceful settlement which failed and led to subsequent avengement of the murder. There are cases, however, in which the vengeance took place much later than the murder. For instance, in the quarrel between Kapkeben and Kapchay (Case 149, p. 99), the former had taken a girl by force in Nongki times, and in the ensuing fight a Kapchay man was killed; it was Maina times, that is, the next circumcision set (we cannot tell whether this was a matter of six years or twenty or more), before the vengeance was satisfied. Of course, many cases that remain unresolved come to light only when the guilty clan suspects that sorcery is operating upon it.

Though compensation is regularly seen as being paid in livestock, and never in land, in a few cases land was in fact uesd as the compensation. According to one of the women in the Law Conference, land is regularly accepted when the killing is an intraclan affair. We have already noted a case where land was thus used (Case 161, p. 92).

But the transfer of land also occurs in interclan disputes. Thus, after the murder of a Kapit aret man,

The Kapit people demanded compensation for their deceased; the Kapchemwor refused and the Kapit people claimed a field of land near their area as compensation. The Kapit people used that

---

[3] From *tis*, a stem form of verb meaning to pour cold water into very hot water to cool it down, and *met*, "head"; hence, "payment to cool down hot heads."

[4] From *korosyontet*, one of the plants used in the ceremony.

land until 1949 when a Kapchemwor man opened a case against them and took it as far as the District Court. The courts upheld the Kapit and the District Commissioner is quoted as saying: "If you want a son murdered by the Kapit people you can have your land back." [Case 17]

Yet the matter was not adequately and legally resolved by the transfer of land, and the two clans are still enemies and "cannot meet at a beer party, lest there will be revenge."

A fight that escalated from a woman's quarrel resulted in the killing, by a man named Arapsumoni, of a man of Kapsumpata clan.

Right then Arapsumoni and his wife and clan members immediately left the area, going to Kapkop to seek refuge, and left all their granaries and things, taking only their cattle, goats, and sheep. The pororyet divided the food they left. So Tiyoy and his family occupied the land as compensation. The land still belongs to the Kapsumpata people. [Case 83]

Again, this instance does not represent a true legal settlement; rather it is an extralegal "compensation" resulting from the flight of a weaker clan fearing retaliation by a stronger one. It appears to have taken place when the Kapsumpata were pushing eastward along the Mount Elgon escarpment, being forced out of their western area by the more numerous Bagisu. All these cases of land settlement appear to have taken place in the more agricultural sectors of Sebeiland.

We have little specific data on how the clan assesses its members for the payment fee, and none on how the stock is distributed. The former is indicated by such statements as "all the Kapit had to contribute animals" or "the rich men had to contribute a cow, the poor ones had to contribute goats." There is some indication that most of the stock went to the kota of the deceased with the remainder distributed among the other korik. "Mangusyo paid most of the cattle because he did the killing, and the cows were divided among the kota of Mwantil; none went outside" (Case 148). My general impression from watching Sebei in action is that each instance was separately negotiated with considerable haggling, but that an underlying sense of responsibility did operate to make possible the collection of animals. Who paid what would depend upon such factors as relative wealth and social standing, closeness of kin tie to the person responsible, preexisting obligations, performance on prior demands, and the personality of the individual.

Pororyet Action under Ntarastit

The community has an interest in the resolution of conflicts and presumably puts pressure on both parties to accept the negotiated agreement, but quite clearly it has only powers of persuasion. It is only after the ntarastit ceremony has been held, after the law has been passed, that the pororyet may take action against the person who does wrong. There are several cases involving theft, but only two involving murder, in which pororyet action was taken.

A Kapyis man murdered a man of clan not known, above Atar. All the people went from here to restore law and order. The Kapyis people ran to the forest with their cattle, so that all the people of the pororyet could take was the millet that was in the granaries. Some came from as far as Mbai. It is partly a fight, so women do not join in this. The men carried home the millet and each person keeps what he has taken. The matter was not finally settled because the Baganda arrived, and no compensation was paid by the Kapyis people. [Case 87]

We noted earlier another instance of pororyet punishment under ntarastit (Case 165, p. 86). The description of this same case as it was also told me by an old informant makes clear that the punishment was against the clan, not the individual, but apparently against only that sector of the clan which lived within the pororyet of the murdered man. The case reads:

Ngelech left Kapkapen and murdered a man of Kapunkor clan in Kaptapkoy near Kapchorwa. He "broke the law." All Kapkapen living in this area had their crops slashed and their cattle slaughtered, but not members of the clan who live in other areas. They destroyed the crops from Kapkirwok to Munarya and Kamatui [three contiguous villages]. Mwoko called in the prophet, Matui, who came and stopped the destruction, saying that it had been enough. The Kapungor people nevertheless intended to avenge the case, but before they could, the British government came in, so there is still a debt owing Kapungor clan. [Case 86]

A punishment for theft, on the other hand, is against the individual rather than the clan (Cases 56, 68, and 204—separate recordings of the same case; Case 203), except that in one instance of recidivist thievery (Case 216) the whole clan became involved. These matters are dealt with in detail in chapter 10.

The small number of cases of pororyet action suggests that it was not a very frequent occurrence, while the recounting to me of several instances more than once indicates that the action had a dramatic impact on the Sebei.

Clan Punishment of Its Own Members

Inasmuch as the clan is responsible for all murders committed by any of its members, it is reasonable that the clan should have the power to punish troublemakers. One clan simply aided the process of revenge:

A man called Kamai of Kapchemo clan, who was either Ñyongki or first Maina age-set [1870–1890], killed a man of the Kaparo clan, who had two wives. Kamai escaped to Koin tribal area after the murder. His clansmen sent a report to the Kaparo people that "the murderer is leaving and we don't want him to leave a debt behind." The Kaparo came to Kapchorwa and killed Kamai. There is no bad feeling between these clans as a result of this case. [Case 53]

Or they may simply not protect a troublesome member:

In Kapchorwa, a man named Kapenkich of Kaptare clan used to fight all the time and had no friends at all. People of Kaptui clan killed him. When people heard this they said they didn't believe he was dead, but that he deserved the death; everybody, including those of his own clan, were happy; they were glad to get rid of him. [Case 157]

If a kota is seen as the source of difficulty, a ceremony of separation may be performed, whereupon each kota becomes a distinct clan.

In asking whether the kota can chastise a member of the clan for causing trouble, my informant, Boror, indicated the case of the Kapsumpata expelling the Kapsachor with a ceremony of separation. The case was told to him by old people and had happened before his birth. They are now completely separate clans and cannot share beer when it is "brought for girls." The Kapsumpata people brought the matter before Matui, saying that they wanted to separate because this group are killing other clans and our people are being killed for nothing and have been paying compensation from time to time. Kapsachor people agreed to the separation. [Case 151]

The clan may also take matters fully into its own hands:

Maykut Kapyenkin of Kapsumpata clan was mad and people made songs about what he did. He used to collect any herd of cattle he could find and bring them home. Each time he collected cows the clan would discuss the matter and find what he did wrong and return the cows to their owner. At last he killed two young Bagisu tribesmen. On this occasion the whole pororyet came to fight the Kapsumpata clan, because he was killing people who were just walking about on the road. The whole clan was annoyed and decided to get rid of him. His own brother and other members of the clan agreed that they should send a young child to invite him to the brother's house for beer. There was, of course, no beer; he came and he was beaten to death by his own brother. [Case 164]

Other such instances reported concern the elimination of recidivist thieves (chap. 10).

Sanctions of a Supernatural Kind

Sorcery is the silent partner in the business of law among the Sebei; the ultimate sanction a man may apply in the redress of a wrong is to ensorcel the person who wronged him. Thus in order to understand Sebei law it is necessary to appreciate the nature of the supernatural as the Sebei conceive it. Chapter 7 deals with witchcraft in both its legal and illegal aspects, and offers a general classification of occult powers as they are involved in the machinery for the redress of wrongs; the few general remarks made here may be placed in broader context by consulting pages 113–117.

The major occult power serving as sanction against delicts is the oath and the curse. Though I see no clear distinction between these two in Sebei thought, I regard the former as a swearing upon the truth or falsity of a statement, in which unseen powers act to punish the person who forswears, while the latter is the hurling of an imprecation, either with or without magical paraphernalia, against a person for some grievance.

I use witchcraft in the more special sense of manipulating occult powers in such a way as to harm another without justi-fiable reason. Sorcery here is used as the overarching term embracing all these concepts.

Thus as I am using the terms (and insofar as I understand Sebei attitudes, it is their conception as well), there is sorcery that is used as a legal means of redressing wrongs and there is sorcery that is black magic. Both are viewed with some fear and distaste by the general public of Sebei, but only the latter is itself a legal delict. The Sebei also believe in certain fatalistic (or at least unwilled) evil forces such as the evil eye, but these play no role in the business of law.

In this section we are concerned with the sorcerous means of redressing the wrong of murder. For this purpose, the Sebei resort to *mumek*, a public oath taken in respect to a known suspect; to *sekutet*, a private curse against a known suspect; or to *surupik*, a public curse against whoever may have been responsible for the act.

The essence of all these forms of behavior is (1) that they operate against the clan of the person who has committed the act; (2) that they can potentially harm the clan of the person who initiates it, especially if it is not removed when the target clan has admitted responsibility and requests release, or when the harm to the opposition has run its full course; and (3) that hence they are a dangerous, serious matter. They are generally resorted to last, that is, after all other means have for some reason failed. My first contact with the curse concerned the ritual removal of one laid down by a clan during the time the Baganda were administering Sebeiland. It was against a man (and his clan) who had been awarded an indemnity by the Baganda court, whose decision was unjust and whose jurisdiction was suspect in the eyes of the loser.

While sorcery, especially the oath or the curse, must be viewed as a prime sanction of the law, it is not in the usual sense a legal institution. It is normally evinced only when the clansmen against which it is directed have refused to admit guilt, and it remains operative until they sue for peace and ask to make restitution, or when it appears to be having a reflexive action on the clan that initiated it, and the clansmen wish to remove the curse. A number of such instances have already been brought forward, and here we need only recapitulate some of the elements in the operation of the curse.

We will recall that the Kaptui aret was concerned over its loss of personnel, and listed seven possible causes, most of which were the operation of curses known or presumed to have been made (p. 83). Some of these were for murders committed, others for thefts, and at least one was presumably for being an innocent victim involved in a theft. Another case cited was a murder that took place about 1912 which caused numerous deaths in the Kapchoyik clan, so that they settled the matter in 1928 (Case 7). One case indicates the use of sorcery as a retaliatory measure between two korik of a single clan. The curse was never removed because the clan as a whole had been scattered by a more powerful one in the nineteenth century; much later (1927) the clan gathered and removed the curse, which was beginning to have its reflexive effect. I cite this case in full because it indicates the surrounding attitudes and procedures.

Among the Kapchemwoñ clan, a man of one subdivision killed a member of another. So the members of the group who lost a man took the jawbone and femur of the murdered man and mixed them with medicine and with a piece of the flesh cut from around the spear wound, and buried these together in a hole in a fig tree (*mowet*) and closed up the hole. They also buried some of the things in the ground where the body had fallen. The members of the Kapchemwoñ clan were subsequently forced to run away from the area by a more powerful clan [Kapsumpata] and did not settle this murder. The people of the clan subdivision nearly all died out.

Recently, as they knew about the quarrel from this early time, they came to me [the informant] to inquire about the matter and I showed them where these things had been buried. As it happens, my father was related to the Kapchemwoñ clan [his father's mother's clan]. The man who had done the bewitching, fearing that he would die and that bad things might happen, subsequently told me where he had buried these things in the ground and in the fig tree, so that someone would know and the people could save themselves.

Thus it was that in 1927 the Kapchemwoñ people gathered together and asked me, who was their neighbor, to show them the two places. They brought a ram which was slaughtered at the place and they sprinkled blood where the bones had been buried. I was the one to perform the ceremony and to bless the place and make the bewitchment end. They took away the things that had been buried in the fig tree. They used a kind of plant (*moykutwet*), which is chewed together with the fat from the tail of the slaughtered ram and "dried beer," and sprinkled this mixture, using a vine called *sinantet*. They also spewed some on the place, and asked that the matter be forgiven. This was done both on the tree and at the place where the bones had been buried. Then all the things that had been buried were put on the leaf of a *kokorwet* tree and were burned. The murderer's group had to pay one heifer, one bullock, two she-goats, and one ram as compensation to their kinsmen of the other group, and to have a beer party.

The bewitchment that was done is called *sekutet;* the removal of this curse is called *pitet,*[5] and the compensation is called *kwayet.* If a person does *sekutet,* it will harm the people of the group against which it is done, but when they all die out, then it will come back on the group that does the bewitching. Therefore it is important to make the *pitet* ceremony before all persons of the cursed group die out. [Case 84]

It should be noted that the informant was a very old man (second Maina age-set) ; as the murder had been committed before the clan was driven out of the area, well before the advent of the first European, the resolution of this conflict was delayed about fifty years.

Although the incidence of the use of these forms of sorcery and curse does not appear to be very high, the sociological force and the psychological threat seem to me to be of first-order importance. Perhaps several personal experiences involving mumek will illustrate the problem.

In 1962, after his kraal had twice been successfully raided by Pokot tribesmen, Kelele suspected that one of his neighbors who was married to a Pokot woman had assisted and guided the raiders. He asked for and obtained a kokwet of the local community and threatened to do mumek against the neighbor who, he asserted, had behaved in an inappropriate manner the night of the second raid. The kokwet, deeply concerned, dissuaded Kelele from the act of mumek; yet the threat remained, for there was the strong possibility that Kelele would resort to surupik. The anxiety of the local leaders was great.

[5] From *pit,* "to bless by spitting."

Shortly thereafter I was at a family kokwet concerning the accusation by the mother of a young wife that her daughter's senior wife was doing witchcraft against the daughter out of jealousy. When I was asked to recommend appropriate action, I cautiously suggested the possibility of mumek. The kokwet, deeply exercised by my proposal, quickly denied that such a thing should be done. Later, when the accused wife herself suggested mumek to assure her innocence, the family demanded a full hearing before neighbors of the village, with beer; in short, the threat escalated the controversy from a family affair to a community one.

There is no doubt in my mind that today, and presumably to a greater extent in the past, the threat of sorcery underlies every dispute between individuals, whether it is explicitly made or not, and that acts of sorcery, though feared, are not outlawed but are viewed as an appropriate means of rectifying wrongs done. Very ordinary disputes may lead to one or another disputant's suggesting an oath to support his accusation or to reinforce his innocence. At the same time, even the supreme crime of witchcraft may, as we shall see, be countered with witchcraft. Sorcery therefore is an important part of the legal machinery of the Sebei.

The Manifestation of Supernatural Forces

The supernatural world of the Sebei plays an important role in their legal activities. We have already seen that sorcery is the ultimate court of appeal, that the oath has been transformed into a ceremony giving sanction to community law, and that the commonality of the oyik gives the clans the spiritual unity that is necessary to their corporate action in matters of law. Thus, the manipulation of the unseen world through oaths, curses, and witchcraft plays a positive and essential role in the apparatus with which the Sebei maintain order.

At the same time, witchcraft has a potential for evil, and the practice of killing or harming others through the use of occult powers is an act against which the Sebei feel that they must take redress. This aspect of witchcraft is discussed in the present chapter. First, however, we should examine the diverse acts by which Sebei endeavor to harm others through the manipulation of supernatural forces. In an earlier chapter it was made clear that while the possibility of sorcery is always recognized, and while accusations and suspicions abound, the Sebei do not assume that each death necessarily derives from an unwonted act of sorcery. It was exceedingly difficult to obtain data on witchcraft practices, either past or current, and I offer these data with the recognition that they are far from perfect. One hears accusations, gossip, and discussions of measures of retaliation and protection, but one does not knowingly talk to practitioners or hold sustained discussions of standard practices. Perhaps as nice an expression of the problem as can be found is that of the saza chief at the Law Conference who said, "Let me make this clear: I have tried to find a *ponintet* and have failed. These old men here might be, but if you asked them, they wouldn't tell."

⌣ Witchcraft is called *panet* when it is a fait accompli, *ponisyet* when it is still in progress. The words derive from the verb stem *pan,* "to bewitch," in its transitive and intransitive aspects. The person who engages in witchcraft is called a *ponintet.* There are several varieties of witchcraft; some have separate terms and some do not. The general term is applied to the use of sorcery to cause illness or death without special provocation. It is also applied to the form of sorcery that makes a boy or girl cry during circumcision, without, so far as I could discover, any terminological distinction.

The countermagic against sorcery is called *tortayet,* a form of magic causing the person to do something he would not ordinarily do. It derives from the verb stem *torte,* meaning "to push," and presumably has reference to pushing a person into action he would not otherwise take. It can push him out of a tree or into the path of a snake or lion, or it can induce him to have intercourse with his own sister, or, as in one case recorded, bewitch his own relative.

A form of sorcery known only to two clans—Kamichaki and Kapunyey—is known as *kankanet.* I was told that it is not true witchcraft. It is not viewed as evil, for it works only against persons who have committed a specific act, and is used only in retaliation. A practice known only to the Koin tribe is *wiratet* (from verb stem *wir,* "to throw") .

The witchcraft that women perform on men is called *ntoy-enik,* probably derived from the verb *ntoy,* "to lead," since it makes the man subject to the woman's will. The woman who engages in such act is called *chepkerkayantet,* a word compounded from the feminine prefix, *chep;* the verb stem *ker,* meaning "to close"; and *ka,* "house," having reference to the woman's closing the house to other wives. The chief purpose of such magic is either to prevent subsequent marriages or to keep a husband from loving his other wives.

The person who acquires the stuff of witchcraft—the hair, fingernail parings, excrement, or other body effluvia necessary to the performance of ponisyet—is called *kopuket,* a term derived from the verb stem *puch,* "to sweep" or "to clean." The person who collects these things is not necessarily the ponintet himself, nor need he be the person who has requested that the witchcraft be done.

There is also a good deal of evidence that modern Sebei are borrowing or importing witchcraft medicines from other tribes in Uganda and Kenya, and that many of the Sebei believe the imports are more potent than their native powers. As I have no data regarding these forms of sorcery that impinge on matters of law, they need not be discussed here.

The use of oaths and curses is even more important than sorcery. If I understand Sebei sentiments and attitudes correctly, oaths and curses are awe-inspiring and terrifying, and are not to be entered into lightly. They are not viewed or treated as being illegal, however, because they are invoked against persons who have already initiated a harmful act, and thus are instruments of redress; furthermore, they do not work unless the person is in fact guilty of the suspected act. They are terrifying because they can also bring harm on the party initiating an oath or a curse, either after it has played its retaliatory part or if the accused is in fact innocent of the act he is suspected of. Inasmuch as oaths and curses are not legal delicts in Sebei belief, they need not be discussed further here; we have already seen them in operation. It must be stated, however, that the Sebei consider the oath an important element in legal procedure, for testimony on oath was an invocation of the spirits against an individual who forswore himself. It was not unreasonable of modern Sebei to feel that the evidence of testimony under native oath was far more convincing than that of witnesses in a modern court who could, in native sentiment, lie with impunity and whose testimony was therefore always considered suspect.

The Sebei also recognize that certain persons are possessed of the evil eye (*lakanek*), and that others are possessed of bad birds (*taritek che miyotech*); literally, "birds that are bad"). Such persons cause harm through no will of their own. Although they are unfortunate and their existence may be damaging, they are not committing a willful evil act and they are not accused thereof. It has already been noted that a woman may be divorced because she is possessed of bad birds; but she is not thereby being punished for an evil act, in the Sebei view of matters.

One other aspect of the supernatural elements in legal affairs must be examined: the ordeal. Trial by ordeal seems to have occurred only in cases of suspected witchcraft. This ordeal consisted of drinking a concoction made of crushed seeds, though no living Sebei admits to knowing the plant. The knowledge was limited to the Kapchay clan, whose members administered it. The medicine is known as *kiroroyek,* and the ordeal takes place in an open area in the western part of Sebei territory, where the Kapchay clan is located. The accused and a representative of the accusing clan (the clan of the presumed victim of the witchcraft) drink some of the medicine while sitting in the hot sun. The medicine has the effect of causing a person "to become like a drunkard." After the medicine has had time to affect the accused he is asked a series of simple questions, such as "How many fingers am I holding up?" or "What am I holding in my hand?" If he cannot answer these correctly, it demonstrates that the medicine has "caught" him. The clansmen of the victim may then club him to death on the spot with impunity. If he is not affected, then he is presumed to be innocent. I do not know what happens if the man of the accusing clan is affected.

Apparently, an act of witchcraft potentially involves three persons: (1) the man who knows how to bewitch and sells either his services or his knowledge to another person; (2) the man who wishes to bewitch another and purchases this service or knowledge; (3) the person (*kopuket*) who collects the necessary hair or other body parts, natural effluvia, and the like. It seems logically possible that all three might be the same person, but they need not be. It is not clear whether the kopuket, or the man who sells the witchcraft stuff, is held to be legally responsible, but certainly the person who actually uses it—who performs the witchcraft act or hires it performed—is held responsible. The kopuket would certainly be considered guilty if he is a neighbor of the victim. In modern law, all three are guilty, but I do not believe that this was the case aboriginally. It is not viewed as a wrong to be in possession of the witchcraft medicine, and it is considered impossible either to discover if a man has such a thing or to prove that any substance serves such a function. I do not know enough about the process to be certain of the character of these diverse roles, but it is clear that the purchase of witchcraft knowledge involves training ("the men go into a house together naked") and that "one does not buy medicine as one would a piece of cloth." As kankanet can be practiced only by two clans, it follows that it cannot be sold, but only passed on from generation to generation. A clansman may, however, sell his service.

Apprehension, Judgment, and Punishment of Witches

When a person is ill or a relative has died, he, his neighbor, or his close relations seek out a diviner (*chepsokeyontet*) to determine the cause. If the matter is serious, and particularly if the divination suggests witchcraft, a second, third, and fourth diviner will be sought for confirmation. The first effort (in case of illness) is to make the man "release" his victim: "If somebody gets sick and goes to the diviner, and the diviner names the person who did the magic, then the sick man's relatives catch that man and punish him by bringing bowstrings and tying one finger or thumb and sticking thorns of the *tunkururwet* or *chuynet* trees into the finger or arm and break the thorns off, and tell him that he is known as the one who did the magic and that he must undo the magic of the sick man" [Law Conference]. Thus:

Kaptyemelil of Kaptyepasa clan bewitched Malinga. Malinga went to a diviner, who named Kapchemelil. The relatives caught Kapchemelil and tied his arm and put thorns in it, and the man asked to be released, saying that Malinga would get better. They took Kapchemelil to Malinga; a porridge[1] was prepared from the bathing of Malinga and was shared by the man and his accuser. Kapchemelil spit some on Malinga, saying: "Mama [mother's brother], you had better get well." He recovered on the following day. [Case 186]

---

[1] This form of oath is known as *kuyechin musarek;* the body of the sick person is washed and the water is used to make a porridge, which both must drink.

There was no further punishment of Kapchemelil for this act.

An example of the handling of witchcraft cases is the following:

At the time the Baganda were here, before the Chumo circumcision [*ca.* 1910], a man named Sawani of Kapsulel clan was suspected of witchcraft and of killing two brothers, Sukuta Kapsikwa and Punuka Kapsikwa of Kabay clan. The Kabay people consulted three diviners and then they went to Sabilla, the son of Sawani, and took him to the fourth diviner, who said to Sabilla: "Why did you come here? It is your father who bewitched these two people." Sabilla told his relatives that it was his father who was doing the bewitching and that there was no way to defend him "and so we had better get rid of him." Sawani was taken to Kapkiroro and given the ordeal medicine. He "got drunk" and was beaten to death and was left there by his relatives. There was no further payment because Sawani's death finished everything. [Cases 34, 187]

Again, and more simply:

My father's brother, Sindet, bewitched Ali's father; they took the matter to Kapkiroro at Kapchay and drank the *kiroroyek*. He was "caught" by this medicine and was beaten to death. [Case 155]

The ordeal may be used in cases of illness and may result in punishment, as indicated in the following:

Ptoyem of Kapcheperen clan accused his half brother (by the same father), Lelbel, of being a *ponintet*. He accused Lelbel of causing his wife to become seriously ill. When the medicine "caught" Lelbel, he was given a warning. The people of the pororyet went to Lelbel's fields and took all his ripe bananas and his yams, which they shared. Then the woman recovered from the illness and this served as a warning to Lelbel. [Case 32]

If a man is innocent, presumably the ordeal will have no effect, and he is freed of guilt and punishment:

Kamwentuy Arapchemakor of Kapchepasa clan was suspected by the Kamelkut clan of having done witchcraft against Kitoy Arapteng. Kitoy's brother acted as accuser and drank the medicine along with the man accused, but neither of them was caught and thus there was no punishment. Kitoy subsequently got well. [Case 33]

In another instance (Case 113) the man was found guilty, and was beaten and left for dead; he recovered and lived on— without further punishment.

The Sebei seem not entirely to trust the medicine, to judge from one case. The instance regarding Kapchemelil, discussed above (Case 186, p. 117), had a sequel. Though the people thanked him for making Malinga well, "Kapchemelil did not stop doing magic. He went on and bewitched a girl of Kapchemungen aret. Relatives of the girl consulted a diviner who mentioned him as the one who did the magic. The girl's relatives came and beat him to death. The girl recovered and is still alive." It was explained that the people were impatient because Kapchemelil had performed magic often and was well known for it, and that "he had escaped the ordeal twice. He had a root which he chewed to cool his eyes" [Law Conference].

"If a person suspected of witchcraft has escaped the ordeal many times, but still the relatives of the deceased are not convinced, they can go to a third person [another specialist in witchcraft] and ask him to do *tortayet* on the suspect, so he will kill himself or be killed by an animal or something like that" [Law Conference]. This witchcraft makes the *ponintet* turn his magic on himself or his own relatives.

My grandfather, Mwoko, bewitched Kapyakan of Kapyamet clan, whose relatives went to a Mugisu diviner. When they came back they did tortayet on my grandfather and he bewitched his own son to death. [Case 188]

Thus the ultimate sanction against magic is magic itself.

Lesser Witchcraft

Two forms of witchcraft are widely known: (1) the knowledge of magic that will make the initiate cry or bleed excessively during circumcision, and (2) witchery used by women against men. The former is learned by all members of both sexes at the time of initiation; the latter is learned by all women at the time of their initiation; both represent the most important secret lore that is passed on during these ceremonies. I understand that there are other kinds of sorcery which are widely known—

chiefly for causing illness. By and large, the details were kept private from me.

The witchcraft knowledge against initiates is a strong element in the social control of youth. In Sebei there is a firm distinction between initiated persons, who are men and women, and the uninitiated, who are mere boys and girls. Among the Sebei, any man or woman may scold or chastise any boy or girl, and for the latter to refuse a request or to be rude to his elders is a breach of conduct. The sanction against such behavior is the use of sorcery (or the potential of such use). Furthermore, though sexual activity among youths is not a major delict, it is considered quite improper for a woman to have intercourse with an uncircumcised boy. This act, too, is sanctioned by the possibility that it will cause excessive bleeding or crying during circumcision. A youth is asked on the eve of his circumcision whether he has insulted an adult or slept with a married woman, and he must tell his parents. The bleeding caused by the latter act is stopped by the use of a piece of the undergarment of the woman. One informant said:

I mentioned about a man I had insulted, and my parents were informed of this and went that very night and looked for him and kept him through the night so he had no chance to do such magic. All the men of my father's age-set watched him very carefully and told him, "If my boy cries you will be stabbed to death." But he swore that he hadn't arranged anything like that. If my father had not been strong, the man could have said, "Yes, I've done that and the boy did wrong to insult me, and I demand payment so I can undo such a thing." In such a case he would undo the magic in front of the family then and there.

Salimu Laleyo lives beyond the Sipi market. He is of Kapsamsama and he insulted a woman of Kapkeben clan. He insulted her and beat her, but I do not know the kind of insult. So during circumcision he cried and kicked the person who was performing the operation. She admitted having done it. No case can be brought; she can be beaten, however. [Case 90]

Strictly speaking, it would seem that such a use of magic is justified in Sebei eyes and therefore not a delict. Whether it happens without justification and is then considered a delict, I cannot say. The one girl who "cried the knife" during an initiation that I witnessed told me subsequently that she knew who had caused her failure, but I do not know what action was taken.

Men all assume that women have a corpus of magical knowledge which they learn during their initiation and can use against men; the women do nothing to disabuse the men of this belief. The magic, called *ntoyenik,* may be directed either to enfeebling the man, to causing him to be gentle and therefore not a warrior, to preventing him from wanting a second wife, or to causing him not to love his other wives.

"The husband ceases caring for the other wife; he neglects her, doesn't sleep with her, and the like—one can tell. Also he becomes very 'polite'; he doesn't fight and if he goes on a hunt, he trails behind and doesn't even spear the animal, but throws his spear on the ground." [Law Conference]

A man may divorce his wife for such magic.

Chepsonkol had a wife, Cherimur, who had love magic. He loved her so much that he divorced the other five wives, even though Cherimur was barren. She was the first wife. So the members of the clan collected everything that belonged to her—clothes, baskets, goods, and all the things that belong to a woman—and put them outside the house and dug a hole in the roof of the flat house in which they were living. She was sent away for good. The man remarried two of those he had formerly divorced and two others, and four children were subsequently produced. [Case 19]

Aside from divorcing a wife, there is no punishment for this kind of witchcraft. There is a ceremony, carried out within the village, which discovers women who are doing such magic (and persons who have the evil eye), and it is believed that a woman who does such magic will die in childbirth, or at the time the next crop is harvested.

Women also do sorcery to prevent others from having children by "tying their blood." Several current cases, more in the nature of gossip, came to my attention. Perhaps the following case (though in the end it came to nothing) will indicate as well as any the character of this behavior.

Yapyeko, wife of Yeremia Chemaiko, the sister of my mother, had three children and then stopped for a long time without having any

more children, so she decided to go to a diviner. She went to a Mugisu named Alima who lives at Kapteret, accompanied by two other
persons. The diviner finally indicated that when she had had her
last child a number of people were present and her neighbors on the
upper side of the house—one of the wives—had bewitched her. He
said that unless she did something about this she would have no
more children, and asked for 30 shillings. However, Yapyego could
not get 30 shillings, but in another month found herself pregnant.
Before that there had been a growing hatred between herself and
the neighbors, but when she found herself pregnant she forgot that.
She decided that the diviner was not right. [Case 93]

Accusation of Witchcraft in Conflict Situations

While it is difficult to learn much that is specific about the
performance of witchcraft and the persons who control such
knowledge, another aspect of supernatural beliefs plays an important role in the disputes and interpersonal conflicts that take
place in modern everyday life in Sebeiland. This is the accusation of witchcraft. Such accusations are a frequent form of
threat and from time to time raise major issues that lead to open
hearings. The accusation often seems to be more a means of
coercion than an expression of personal conviction. In one such
case a woman made an accusation against the senior co-wife of
her newly married daughter. It is my belief that the woman did
this for personal satisfaction, though it might have been to
improve her daughter's position in the household. None of the
people at the hearing seemed seriously to entertain the notion
that the senior wife had actually engaged in the witchcraft.

Another instance sheds considerable light on the use of such
accusations and the procedures for their resolution. The dispute itself included many elements, and the witchcraft aspect
receded into the background during the hearings, possibly because of our presence. I am inclined to think, however, that the
relatives wanted to avoid the issue of witchcraft, which they
hoped would be taken care of by a ceremony of cleansing, even
though the cleansing had to do with "bad oyik," not the witchcraft itself.

The case is also of value as a means of understanding both the
background sentiments that enter into a specific dispute, and
the informal manner in which decisions are reached, at least in

domestic matters. The background material was gathered by my wife through discussions held with the two co-wives and their husband; she and I were both present during the hearings that culminated the discussion. (The matter was heard at the time of the Law Conference, which prevented our checking out details and being present both before the hearing and subsequently. These circumstances are responsible for certain limitations in the quality of the data.)

The case revolves around a junior wife whom we shall call Maria, her co-wife, whom we shall call Yapcherkut, and their husband, whom we shall call William, one of the more widely used Christian names in Sebei today. The matter took place near Sipi, where William has a small shop and beer parlor. The matter at hand began in April when one of Maria's two houses burned down. Each wife accused the other of arson. Some weeks later Maria was made to suffer by the oyik, the spirits of the dead. She said, "At night I have bells ringing in my ears; people tell me it is the oyik. The oyik don't allow me to eat—I can take only three bites of plantain porridge. When I get the lamp ready at night, I can see shapes coming toward me and going around and around on the wall and on the roof and they tell me this is the oyik, too. I never have seen these things before. The people tell me they are Bagisu spirits [Maria's mother was a Mugisu]. At night I hear the oyik running outside and I know I am going to die. One day I bought beer and sprinkled it around the house for the oyik, but that night they came and beat me all night and in the morning I vomited blood. Also, some oyik had intercourse with me. I can't sleep; the oyik came and say, 'Wake up! Wake up!' When I sleep in the house my feet become swollen and my head very hot. If I sleep elsewhere, I am also very afraid, but the oyik come only once to where I sleep and it feels a little better. When I sleep in my own house, it feels very cold at dawn, and I cannot pull my bedclothes over me because my hands are shaking with fear." These manifestations appeared to Maria after she had gone to the Muslim diviner who had "read his book."

According to the senior wife, Yapcherkut, "The Muslims sent oyik to look for the one who burned the house and they found Maria. Now she is very sick. The oyik come with knives and say they must kill her. My husband knows that Maria wants to kill me. This is a very serious matter and people will make many words on it. Maria is going to make beer for certain persons to drink [to send away the oyik]. This may cure her, but if it does not, our husband will send her away. Maria tells people she is trying to kill me, but I do not die because I have very strong oyik."

Maria herself said that the Muslim gave her medicine to bury in the place where the house burned down, having told her that it was done by a man, who had done so at the request of a black woman. (The Sebei regularly identify one another by complexion; presumably Maria was referring to the co-wife.) He have her the medicine to cause the man to die, but "I waited and waited and no one has died since." Maria agrees that the medicine brought the oyik. She called another Muslim to remove the medicine but he could not find it. This man then tied medicine on her head and put some in the fire, which caused her body to shake so that she ran away. When she returned, she could not find any trace of the fire or of the medicine. When she put the medicine on the fire she began to feel "strange, different," and knew the medicine had turned back on her and would kill her—"because the man and woman have stronger medicine than mine."

Maria subsequently made beer in order to hold a ceremony for chasing away the oyik, but nobody came to perform the ceremony, as it was the date for collecting payments for coffee sales. She therefore sold that beer in order to have money to buy maize to make beer later. A week or so later Maria was in further difficulty. According to some reports she had got drunk and gone to bed with a schoolteacher. Maria herself denies having slept with the teacher, though he had come to the house where she was and had gotten drunk and had slept in William's bed. William was very annoyed and planned to take a case in court because the teacher had been abusive to him, and because he was selling European medicine without a license. William will no longer go to Maria's house and will not let her come to where he lives in the back of his shop. "He loves only Yapcherkut, who uses medicine to make him love only her." Maria is prepared to get a divorce and leave the children with William.

Maria again brewed beer; it was ready one day in early August, and a group of about fifty relatives and neighbors gathered for the dual purpose of resolving the conflict in the family and performing a ceremony for driving away the oyik. It is, of course, only the former purpose that engages our attention. By the time we arrived at the scene of this combination kokwet and ceremony the people had all gathered, and very soon after we arrived the hearings began. The group was scattered—both men and women—over the slope extending above Maria's house, without any discernible order or any clear focus or leadership. What leadership there was, was taken by Maria's maternal uncle, who both led the questioning and set the conclusions.

Maria began by listing her complaints against her co-wife. She did not include the charge of arson, but accused Yapcherkut of collaborative work in the harvesting of beans (which I did not record), of witchcraft against her (Maria's) children, and of quarreling over the use of land.

Concerning the second complaint, Maria began: "I had gone to dry maize, and Yapcherkut came in my absence and jumped over my children and the older child started crying, and Yapcherkut came out and laughed. . . . She didn't laugh once, but in three places: inside the house, outside the house, and in the granary." The mother's brother asked her if she had told this story to her husband, and Maria answered: "Yes, and William asked the other wife to come. Before any of this happened, I had been given a cow to milk in order to feed my child and that other woman was jealous. When he asked her whether she had done this, she jumped over her clothes and swore that she had never done this to the child. William asked if I had seen her jump over the children and I said that my child had told me so. I told him I saw her after she had left and she had laughed out loud. This proves she had done this thing. Then William went to Yapcherkut's house and I prepared food, but this other wife took the food from my fireplace and gave it to William." Someone asked if it was Sebei custom to jump over a child (presumably a rhetorical question in support of Maria, but conceivably asked by a Mugisu who was present), to which William responded: "Only after spearing a man can you jump over him; but not when he is still alive."

Maria went on to say that before all this had happened her co-wife had hidden the feeding bottle for her baby. "When we quarreled, she brought the bottle back after she had made a hole in the bottle and cut the nipple."

MOTHER'S BROTHER: What did the woman take the bottle for?

Someone responded by saying that it means that she is going to bewitch it, and the uncle agreed; however, the local appointive chief (who was present but not administering this kokwet) said that if a person takes and returns it, it means that she has failed to bewitch it.

At this point Yapcherkut, who had up to then been quiet, said: "These are mere lies. I never saw the bottle nor did I ever bewitch anything." She also denied having jumped over the child, saying: "I went to the house to get fire. The child was in the far side of the house. I went only to the fireplace."

Someone then asked if the child became sick subsequently, and Maria said that the child was sick at the time, but "she recovered after being jumped over." To this Maria's uncle responded, without apparent irony: "She did well, because after she jumped the child it recovered. Is there anything else you want to bring out?"

MARIA: I went to the field and found a bunch of plantains that had been taken, and I asked another woman what had happened to it. Yapcherkut heard me ask this and again asked me what I had said and then told me that I should have my own plantain field by my own house.

There was further discussion of this accusation, but it was not recorded. Then the older wife spoke.

YAPCHERKUT: I am a friend of hers, for all the things that were paid in the dowry for Maria came from my house; therefore, why should I make this trouble? Our husband had three wives, and the first wife died. She had two plantain fields. After she died, I enjoyed those fields, but when her sons grew up, they took back the fields that had belonged to their mother. Our own plantain field was given to Maria, so now I have nothing and I had to go back to my original field. After awhile, William had to divide this field between us. Soon after he divided the field, I refused to give some to Maria and asked William to plant a field for her, but he has refused. So I took a case against him, which I lost. The court told me, "You are a mere woman and the land does not belong to you." I don't want Maria to use this plantain field. As soon as Maria ceases to use this field, we will return to friendship. Another thing, Maria brewed beer and I went to work in the moyket, but Maria sent me away from the work. The women working on the field stopped Maria from doing this, for you can't refuse somebody the privilege of working in a field. When we finished the moyket, I went to get water for Maria and she threw that water down.

MARIA: I admit to throwing down the water.

At this point one of the neighbors expressed his surprise at the accusations and the fact that each of these women was going to a diviner. At this point the mother's brother interceded: "Let me shorten the matter. My judgment on this is that Maria should brew beer and start a new plantain field, and that you, Yapcherkut, if you are doing witchcraft, you should throw that away. You must sit together and enjoy food and beer together and be friends."

WILLIAM: I know the behavior of both my wives. My first wife, when we have a quarrel and fight, soon after the quarrel we can cook food and enjoy it, and anyone who comes in would not be able to tell that we had been fighting. But if I quarrel with Maria, she never leaves that fight. Even after six months she still discusses it. If later I again quarrel with Maria, she goes on reminding me what happened before. It happened that I was coming to Kamukei's house during the night and I passed here and saw something white in the bush and found the man still there. The man was lying in the bush with Maria. I forgot that man

and we all came into my house. Still I forgave her for this, because I am a Christian. So I don't like a person to go on being
annoyed for a long period of time. My third wife, Maria, is the
only one who is misbehaving herself. [We must recall that William had a wife who died.]

MARIA: You have blamed me, but you neglect me. You don't eat my
food or sleep in my house. You have told me you do not love me.
Yes, I did that, because you neglected me and told me I should
look for another husband.

A neighbor spoke up: "We, the people of this sangta, see that this
quarrel is of long standing and it is because of the plantains. We
therefore say that William has much land. You plant a new plantain
field for Maria and she is to stop using the plantains from the old
field from today."

To this, William agreed. But after some further, unrecorded discussion, he said: "I think that woman [Maria] has bewitched me."

MARIA'S BROTHER: You say that you aren't strong enough to serve the
first wife?

WILLIAM: No, that is not the question.

MARIA'S BROTHER: This argument has happened before, but the
sangta has sat together and made these people friends.

MARIA: You say that you are going to stop me from taking plantains
from the old field. Do you mean to say that the field that is to be
planted this year is to feed my children?

MARIA'S BROTHER: You take your children to your husband and say
to him: "Here are your children. You take them and feed them."
We came here to learn the quarrel and have learned that it was
the plantains. Should we come now to the disease that is trou-
bling Maria from time to time?

MARIA [to William]: You are neglecting me and staying away from
my house.

WILLIAM: I have to do my work. I can't neglect it and stay here all
day.

At this point William went off to show some of Maria's relatives
that she was not keeping her plantain field in good order, and one
of the members of the group explained the essence of the kokwet to
me by saying that Maria had made three accusations: a claim that
Yapcherkut took more than her share in the collaborative harvesting of beans; Yapcherkut's jumping over Maria's child and laughing
(which Yapcherkut "proved" she had not done by jumping over her
clothes as a form of oath) ; and the quarrel over the use of the plantain field. William had in turn accused Maria before her brothers of
being lazy, of holding a grudge after quarrels, and of sleeping with
someone.

With that the formal kokwet ended and the ceremony of remov-

ing the oyik began. Involving mutual blessings by the relatives of
the principals, it was presumed to have restored peace and harmony
among them. After this ceremony the whole group gathered around
the pots and drank beer together.

My wife called on Maria several weeks later. She was living in the
back of William's shop. She said that he did not want her there, but
as she could not live alone in her house she was keeping quiet and
he had not sent her away. She seemed lethargic.

This detailing of a single instance of conflict affords us more
insight into the legal processes of Sebeiland than may appear at
first blush. First, it reminds us that in domestic quarrels of this
kind—and doubtless in more far-reaching ones—the issues are
not single and monolithic, but are involved and intertwined. It
is in this context that witchcraft accusation becomes a part of a
more extensive set of issues, and incidentally is eliminated by
the process of oathing. We see also the role of Maria's relatives
as protectors (in theory) , but actually under the strong motivation of restoring peace and maintaining the status quo. Finally,
we see the role of the ceremony as an endeavor to reinforce harmony.

CHAPTER 8

*Other Acts of Violence
and Personal Injury*

Assault

According to Sebei legal practices and attitudes, physical damage done by one person to another in a fight or an act of aggression is not in itself a matter of grave consequence. If the injury is slight, the person may hope to fight back or may simply disregard the matter; if it is grave, the action taken is based upon the fear that the injured person will die as a result of the wound inflicted.

Injuries caused by fists or sticks, where no blood is drawn and no bones are broken, are entirely personal matters and remain outside all mechanisms for settlement. A man so injured would not be justified in avenging the injury by harming a clansman of his assailant, nor would his own clansmen take any action in the matter.

If spears or other weapons are used, or if bones have been broken or major injuries sustained, the assailant is expected to pay a goat to the victim. This goat is called *cheptikiryontet* (from the verb *tikir,* to stop something from running down a hill) .

Festo of Kapkepen clan stabbed Marich and cut the tendon in the back of his leg. Marich was sick for a long time. A goat was paid in compensation. [Case 179]

Though informants spoke of the giving of the animal as a compensation, it is better seen as a ceremonial peacemaking. The goat must be brought by the assailant to the injured man and slaughtered for him by the assailant himself, "to help make him well" or "to bring back his blood." If the injury is severe enough to require a payment, the amount is always one goat; it is the same regardless of the severity of the injury or its permanent and incapacitating character, regardless of the status of the two parties or their relationship to each other, and regardless of the justification or provocation for the act.

The matter remains personal between the two individuals, but if the assailant refuses to slaughter a goat, "the members of the man's own clan would force him, because they would fear that the injured man might die and therefore a member of the clan would have to be killed."

Chemnoñ came to my father's home and insulted him, and my father lost his temper and stabbed him so that he became seriously ill. Chemnoñ's father came to my father's house and told him to offer a goat and threatened to spear him if he failed to give him one, so my father did. Chemnoñ's father took the goat and slaughtered it. My father didn't have to do the slaughtering, as is normally the case, because they are both of the same clan. [Case 180]

In this instance the fact that both men were of the same clan is, in view of attitudes toward intraclan killing, somewhat enigmatic; I do not know if they were of the same kota. If a feud is not likely to ensue, there is less pressure upon payment.

An old man of my clan named Purkeywa fought another man and wounded him on the hip with a spear. The man who was speared lived in Chema, far away, and he didn't die. And because he was living far away and didn't die, no compensation was paid and no revenge was taken. [Case 178]

The law on assault thus distinguishes between minor injuries, which it regards as inconsequential personal matters (and hence outside the institutions of law), and grave injuries. The latter, which may result in death and hence invoke the machinery of clan feud, are seen as important. The law provides a penalty that is not so much an effort at either punishment or restitution as it is an effort to establish the basis for ensuring that if death should ensue the matter would be settled amicably. Assault law is thus an adjunct to the law of murder.

There is always the possibility that a grave assault may end in death and lead to a feud; the payment of the cheptikiryontet is a means of preventing a feud from happening. Should the person subsequently die, "the goat is regarded as a witness; that is, it is proof that the injury had caused the death." The assailant does not remove his responsibility by making the payment; indeed, he has given overt recognition of his liability for the compensation. I believe this would prevent retaliation by revenge or sorcery, unless of course the assailant later refuses to pay the indemnity.

Abuse and Slander

The Sebei are much given to bickering; they have a rich repertoire of curses of a purely verbal kind, and they are gossips. Like physical assaults, however, verbal encounters do not enter into the realm of legal action until they threaten to arouse conflicts that might lead to murder or witchcraft. The following colloquy at the Law Conference communicates the basic attitudes:

A. MUZUNGYO: If a person, sitting around a beer pot, says to another person, "You are stupid," that is simple and doesn't matter, but if a man goes about spreading bad things about another man, then he deserves killing.

J. FLEMING: You make a distinction between verbal insult and spreading bad news about a person?

KAPTYEMOIKIN: A verbal insult is a minor thing, but spreading bad words is more serious. If I am married and a neighbor goes to my parents-in-law and says that I am doing wrong things and then comes to me and says they are saying bad things about me, this may create a fight between me and my parents-in-law, and somebody might die. In such a case, a man might take the matter to people gathered at a *moyket* [work party] or he could take it to the pororyet council. The first time a man is brought before the council and it is confirmed that he was spreading such rumors, he is warned that he must stop this. If he continues, he will be punished and he may be killed, and if he is, there is no compensation to be paid.

J. FLEMING: Any form of punishment other than killing?

A. MUZUNGYO: At the council, the insulted person is not given permission to do anything to the insulter, but if the insulter continues, they may fight. One may kill the other, or there may just be a fight. If there is a fight, that finishes the matter.

E. CHELAKAM: If the insulter kills the insulted, he must pay compensation, but if the insulter is killed, then no compensation need be paid, as he had been warned.

A. MUZUNGYO: If the insulter is strong and beats the insulted, then the pororyet must find a strong man to fight the insulter and

cool him off. If they fight where there are people around, and
people see that the insulted man isn't strong, they will go to the
assistance of the weak man, so he has a chance to beat or spear
the insulter.

w. GOLDSCHMIDT: Can you provide a case?

KAPSILUT: I have no example, but I know that a person who does
that is beaten on the head so that bad words are beaten out of
his head.

ALI MUSANI: He must be beaten when other people are around.

J. FLEMING: What if many people are repeating and spreading rumors?

ALI MUSANI: If many people said I heard something from so-and-so,
it is obviously just rumors and would be forgotten.

This discussion suggests that insult is distinguished from slander, that the latter may lead to a major offense and thus is
punishable, and that the settlement is made directly between
the parties by means of a fight, but that the clans of each (and the
community) have a vested interest in seeing that the slanderer
is punished. The case material on these matters is slight and
unclear. One case that is celebrated in song was summarized as
follows, suggesting that slander involving accusation of witchcraft makes murder justifiable:

Aramwoko spread news against a man named Arakita, saying he
was a bewitcher. When Arakita heard this, he was annoyed. One day
he went to collect a bundle of grass, carrying with him a kind of
spear called *morontoyit,* which was poisoned and used for killing elephants. He waited by the side of the road and speared the other
man. After that he was protected by members of his clan. I do not
know whether compensation was paid. There is a song about this
story. [Case 185]

In modern court action one man was jailed for two months
because he used vulgar abuse against the chief (Case 46),
though his words may have been no more than an expression of
pique and a display of power. In another case the court admon-
ished a man for abusing the mother of the woman he was
endeavoring to marry, and told him to give up the woman
(Case 139).

False accusation in a dispute may be settled by swearing an
oath, as when a man who was accused of sleeping with his
father's young wife urinated into a gourd and asked his father

to join an oath on this (Case 249), or in the case regarding witchcraft brought forward by Maria (chap. 7). Another instance of false accusation was resolved by the clansmen of the accuser, who paid a voluntary fine to the man accused (Case 89).

Like assault, slander and abuse do not seem to be, in themselves, primarily matters for legal action. When minor, they are disregarded, even though it is feared they may escalate into more serious crimes, particularly witchcraft and the accusation of witchcraft. Because verbal offenses themselves border on witchcraft in Sebei eyes, such escalation appears to be an everpresent threat. The law seems designed to prevent it from happening.

Sexual Offenses

In Sebei, certain sexual acts are viewed as wrong—as "very impossible," in the words of my interpreter. The basic concept is *sokoran.* We might gloss this as "sinful," but "sokoran" does not invoke supernatural sanction or postmortem punishment. It is sokoran to engage in incest, which among the Sebei means to have intercourse with one's sister, mother, father's sister, or father's sisters' daughters; with one's own daughter or one's brothers' daughters; with the wife of one's neighbor; with the daughter of any member of one's age-set; with any other member of the clan of one's wife or any member of the clan of one's mother; or with the wives of one's brothers. The woman's role in these acts is also sokoran, but "the man carries the heaviest sokoran; he is the most responsible."

Acts that are classed as sokoran do not necessarily invoke the formal action of clan or community, but the informal sanction of ridicule or abuse:

Cheromboch slept with his sister and impregnated her. When it was discovered, both were despised and shouted at by people for doing this. Neither ever married. The child died. [Case 181]

Such a person would be known for this behavior, and as in the case cited, would not get married. Some informants said that a man who had engaged in an incestuous act would be beaten on the head, but only if he answered the taunting rudely. Apparently neither the retaliatory machinery of clan action, the formalized intervention of the community, nor the recourse to witchcraft or other supernatural actions is brought into such a case. For those who would make the distinction between law and other realms of social behavior, incest is a matter of morality rather than of law. The rules are, nevertheless, quite explicit and the "punishment" is quite real.

Some of the above-cited acts carry an implication beyond the realm of sexuality. To have intercourse with a brother's wife or a wife's sister is viewed as expressing a wish that the brother or the wife, respectively, should die (for if they did die, the man would then inherit the brother's wife, or be given the wife's sister), and he becomes suspect of engaging in witchcraft against the brother or wife. The suggestion of witchcraft brings the matter more firmly into the realm of legal institutions, and more formal action may ensue:

> If the members of the wife's clan find out that her husband is having intercourse with one of her sisters, they become annoyed and ask the wife to come to their home and to remain there. They later invite the husband to beer and accuse him. The penalty is to pay a sheep to the wife's parents and brew beer for them. They would say: "you are bewitching your wife. Perhaps you wish her to die so you can take her sister." After paying the sheep and the beer, the man takes back his wife and the sister marries somebody else. The sister is not punished, but she is blamed. [Law Conference]

In other forms of sokoran intercourse, as with an aret member of the man's mother, no punishment or compensation is involved, but only loss of respect and taunting. These can, of course, become severe sanctions, and such a person may find it uncomfortable to enjoy beer in the community.

One of the strongest tabus of Sebeiland is against intercourse with the daughter of a member of one's age-set. The man would be beaten by his age-set mates' wives and might be cursed so that he cannot have children. He must brew beer and slaughter a cow for his age-set, presumably as a ceremonial release.

It is recognized that a man may have intercourse with a woman without knowing that they stand in a tabued kin relationship. The following discussion at the Law Conference reveals the attitudes toward such an act:

SAMARI: It might have happened because the age-set members were scattered about and you may have got hold of a girl on the road and you didn't know she belonged to an age-set mate. If you have intercourse not knowing, then you are sorry only and there is no compensation, but if you do it intentionally, knowing the girl belongs to an age-set mate, you must pay compensation of *tinkyontet* [iron bracelet] given to the girl.

BOMET: You must feel very much ashamed and everyone will tell you you did wrong and sometimes you must give a sheep (alive, not slaughtered) to the girl.

P. SALIMU: You may have a sister who is married to a man who lives far away from you, and you don't know her, and you meet her daughter and have intercourse with her. When you find out, you feel badly, but if you didn't know each other, you are not blamed.

W. GOLDSCHMIDT: Are some sokoran more serious than others?

A. MUSANI: If intentional it is very bad; if it is accidental, it is called *sokoran kelel* (accident).

W. GOLDSCHMIDT: Is it more serious to have intercourse with a true daughter than with a daughter of the same clan but of different kota, but still you know she is of your clan?

SAMARI: It is the same, if you know.

Extramarital intercourse is not viewed as sokoran, nor is male adultery. Nor, I think, is female adultery considered sokoran. Though it was said in one place that a man might kill another found having intercourse with his wife, no cases were adduced, and in discussing sexual matters in the Law Conference, Richard Bomet said: "In the olden days there was a law that if you found somebody having intercourse with your wife, you took the matter before your elders; if you lost your temper and killed the man, you would have to pay compensation." To this was added: "They blame him [the wife's sexual partner] and tell him if he continues he will be killed. To the woman they say, 'If you continue, you will be divorced.' Neighbors belonging to the same clan blame and ridicule her and she feels ashamed and stops." No compensation may be demanded, but on repetition, a woman may be divorced (see Family Law) or a man killed (see below).

The Sebei recognize extramarital sexual intercourse as a wrong only when it is either repetitious or habitual behavior, or when several (two or more) men have intercourse with a woman by forcing her. The word for rape is *kotiñet,* from the verb *tiñ,* which means to hold something down. It is not viewed as possible for a lone man to rape a woman, that is, actually to force her into sexual intercourse. An example of a habitual offender is indicated in the following:

> It happened once in Kapchorwa that a man forced many girls sexually. One old man got annoyed because this man had taken his daughter, and he speared that man to death. No compensation was paid; all agreed that he was a bad person. [Case 184]

It is sokoran for a man to rape an uncircumcised girl, and shameful for a circumcised woman to have intercourse with an uncircumcised boy. An uncircumcised boy is viewed as dirty. It was said that in the old days uncircumcised boys and girls did not have intercourse, but today it is recognized as usual, and is not condemned.

A case of rape brought against two men (one of whom held the woman) was heard in a modern court, and though the actual rapist was scolded ("You are always taking women by force; you should not do that—only by talking"), no action appears to have been taken (Case 25).

It is considered sokoran for a man to have intercourse with a woman while she is asleep, or to engage in sodomy with her. No data on fellatio were obtained.

The Sebei would clearly regard homosexual behavior as sokoran, if they practiced it. Sebei informants know about homosexuality from other people, but they absolutely deny that it occurs among the Sebei, either now or in the past,[1] and I am convinced that they are correct in this assertion. They made no effort to deny transvestitism or other acts they know are repugnant to Western society, or to hide the following case, which was reported as a unique (and amusing) item:

---

[1] Bomet, who would have learned of homosexual practices at his European-operated schools, said that the Sebei would regard homosexuality as very bad.

I heard that two men of Kapsumpata aret were sleeping in the same house and while one was asleep the other had intercourse on him. That man, when he woke up, knocked down the other fellow and had intercourse on him. Old Marakan told me about this. [Case 183]

Male transvestites (*chepwoynto*) exist,[2] and their behavior is accepted. Some do not put on female attire but behave like women. The existence of female transvestites was denied. The following statements were made about transvestites at the Law Conference:

w. GOLDSCHMIDT: Are chepwoynto circumcised with men or women?
GENERAL RESPONSE: With boys. They never cry when circumcised.
w. GOLDSCHMIDT: Could a chepwoynto go to war?
GENERAL RESPONSE: No.
J. MALINGA: Sometimes the chepwoynto build their own houses, that is, put up poles and build walls [men's work], but they can't put up roof or thatch; that has to be done by moyket [work party].[3]
w. GOLDSCHMIDT: Do you say *"takwenyo"* [women's greeting] or *"supay"* [men's greeting] to them?
GENERAL RESPONSE: "Takwenyo," and it will answer *"yeko"* [woman's response].
R. BOMET: If you tease a chepwoynto by saying "supay," he will respond with "yeko." I know an example of a boy who when he was eight years old wore boy's clothes and appeared to be normal, but who recently became a chepwoynto; he wears women's clothes. In olden days, chepwoynto dressed as men but acted as women.
E. CHELAKAM: There is another example; a person named Sumotwa dresses like a man but acts like a woman, carrying wood on his back.
A. MUZUNGYO: Another example is Muchali, who dressed as a woman. He was circumcised at the same time I was. When dancing before circumcision he joined the girls but when morning came, he stood to be circumcised with the boys. However, when they were taken to the house for healing, he was taken to a separate house and stayed by himself. After the final circumcision ceremony, he turned up dressed as a woman, with beads, etc.,

[2] *Chepwoynto* may be derived from *way*, "to wander"; a hermaphrodite, being a physical infirmity, is viewed as *solwet*.
[3] Women never put on thatch, as modesty deters them from climbing up on the framework.

and he still dresses that way. He has never paid taxes, either. He has big packets of razor blades and shaves every day so his beard won't show. When there is beer he goes with the women to collect wood and bring water, and serves others as women do. He is my pinta mate and I greet him "supay," but he answers "yeko."

Animal contacts are sokoran.

Somebody had intercourse with Tentera's cow and it was killed right away. The man who had intercourse had to pay another cow to Tentera. He was told, "Take your wife and give us another cow." Nothing else was done. [Case 182]

A man who has intercourse with an animal is neither sent away nor formally punished, beyond having to replace the animal. The animal is not eaten, but burned. It is said that women will despise such a man and will not marry him. It is not viewed as serious if done by a boy, though he will be whipped and the animal must be replaced by his father. The act is treated as sokoran, but in addition, since property is spoiled, it requires restitution. It was not considered possible for a woman to have animal contacts.

The regulation of sexual conduct is largely reinforced through endemic moral attitudes, and misconduct is subjected to the sanction of informal social pressure—light or severe, depending on the nature of the act and the degree of moral wrongness it has in the eyes of the community. Sexual acts, however, may enter into the more formal aspects of legal action. If the sexual misconduct of a wife is strongly felt by her husband, he has the right to punish her personally. He can also, if he feels she is disloyal to him, bring community pressure on her to change her ways, and should she persist he can divorce her and demand return of his bride payment. If sexual misconduct destroys property, restitution may be demanded. If the act implies the death wish against another person, this itself is a serious breach that requires at least a ceremonial indemnity of atonement. But only when the actions threaten seriously to disrupt the community, as in the case of habitual behavior, does the community feel compelled to act. We see, therefore, that though sexual behavior is basically sanctioned by social pressures based upon deep-seated moral sentiments, a sexual breach can enter the realm of litigation.

General Remarks Regarding Minor Acts of Violence

Throughout this book I have avoided making a firm distinction between what is and what is not law. Rather, I have started with the assumption that there are certain regulations regarding proper conduct and certain acts that are regarded as breaches of propriety against which the community applies sanctions or lets the harmed party supply sanctions with impunity. Yet, among the Sebei, as among most peoples, there are breaches of propriety which for one reason or another do not merit sanctions. When this is the case we feel intuitively that we are leaving the realm of law. We enter the realm of morality or etiquette or the inconsequential. Precisely where the boundaries are differs from one culture to another.

The discussion in this chapter leads us across such boundaries. The Sebei do not consider fighting or slander a matter for any kind of sanctioned retaliation or community action unless it reaches certain specified degrees of violence. They do not regard malicious speech as actionable until it takes the form of a threat against the peace. They do not regard adultery or extramarital intercourse as actionable unless it carries an implicit threat of sorcery, or is done under particular circumstances.

The Sebei do recognize, however, that if a quarrel gets too bloody it may lead to a murder and the eruption of feud, that if the malicious talk is so directed as to create distrust between individuals it too may lead to bloodshed, and that repeated adultery may lead to the disruption of the marital bond. They therefore apply sanctions to minimize the disruption in the event of escalation. In a sense, there is no Sebei law in the field of minor violence; rather, there is only the preapplication of law relating to murder, witchcraft, and the family in those instances where there is a substantial threat that present behavior will lead to breaches in these major legal areas.

There is a second boundary between what we intuitively feel is law and what is not: the realm of morality. Sexual desire is taken for granted by the Sebei, and there are no strong sanctions

against normal extramarital sexual intercourse among adults;
even occasional adultery by women is not a legal offense, though
the woman may be beaten by her cuckolded husband. Except
for rape (as defined by the Sebei) and repeated adultery, sexual
offenses as such appear never to enter the realm of law. They do
enter the realm of law when the behavior carries the threat of
witchcraft, or when it "spoils" property, as in animal contacts,
but only for these considerations rather than for the sexual act
itself. There are many other rules, however, where the infraction evokes moral revulsion, contempt, or derision.

PART THREE: The Law
of Property

CHAPTER 9

The Law of Property and
the Rights of Ownership

General Characteristics of Property Law

The resources and material goods of Sebeiland are divided according to Sebei law into two categories: those that are the product of nature, the provision of God, to which man has added nothing, and these are all in the public domain; and those in which some investment of labor or human skill has been made, and these are held as the private rights of individual adults. There are no major and significant variations of this basic dichotomy, though we will find some embellishments and minor discrepancies. Bushland is freely available for all to use, but cultivated land is owned by individual men; natural water holes are a public resource, but a dug step well is the private right of the man who dug it; salt caves are freely available to any stockowner, but if a man has broken off and stacked some of the mineral rock, it is his personal property. There is a consistency in the applications of this basic rule of property which the Sebei themselves fully recognize, though so far as I could discover, it was not given any specific terminological form. It derives ultimately from the basic assumption of a pastoral people that the grass, water, and salt are available to the people, or put another way, that livestock have free access to the resources necessary for their existence. From the pastoralists' point of view, then, stockownership is not dependent upon the ownership of other resources. I think this an important basic element in pastoral law.

The public sector of the natural resources includes the following:

1. All bushland or open land on which animals can graze.
2. All free-flowing or standing water.

3. All mineral deposits, including salt, pottery clay, iron ore, cosmetic clay.

4. All natural growing plants, including those used for medicine, grass for thatching, trees for housing, wild fruits or vegetables, and the like.

5. Wild animals.

So far as I can tell, these resources belong generically to the Sebei; that is, they are not limited to either the sangta or the pororyet, but may be enjoyed by any Sebei person with whom there is a peaceable or friendly relationship. Thus I was told that one could not prevent a man from another pororyet from using salt or graze, that a fight could occur only over the cattle themselves—that is, if someone stole, damaged, or killed an animal. I do not believe the distinction between tribes within the Sebei or Sabaot group would matter either, though obviously hostility that had developed from some other cause would effectively hamper the sharing of resources.

There has been some recent erosion of public rights, though the essential distinction between public and private ownership has not been destroyed. Nowadays, trees on land that is cultivated are generally regarded as the private right of the owner, and a person would not be free to cut a tree on another man's land. Trees are frequently planted to serve as future house posts. In the Bukwa area of Sebei it is increasingly common to fence land, and nobody may cut grass for thatching on another person's fenced land. On the other hand, Sebei who have settled on the plains in recent years and who try to claim a larger area of land than they have actually cultivated have not had their claims sustained in the courts. The criterion here is whether the land has ever been cultivated or not. As one man, speaking of his own land case on the plains, said: "If land is plowed, then it is considered the property of the man who plows it; but if you haven't plowed it, then anybody can take it" (Case 118).

The private sector of the economy includes the following:

1. Livestock, chiefly cattle, goats, and sheep; also a few donkeys.

2. Cultivated land.

3. Bee trees.

Above. Litigants before Sebei County Court on circuit, waiting while a witness affixes his thumbprint to the transcript of his statement. Near Binyinyi, 1954. *Below*. Group of old men discussing a legal case at the Law Conference, Kapchorwa, 1962.

"Breaking the sticks." Negotiations in arranging brideprice. Tegeres area, 1962.

Above. A compound household in the rich plantain-growing area of Sipi. *Below*. Men enjoying the ceremonial meat and discussing the claims against the estate of the deceased. Benet area (highland zone), 1962.

Above. Pokot denying cattle theft to a government askari while Sebei soldiers watch. Pokot territory near Kapsirika, October, 1962. *Below*. Diviner shaking wooden bowl to seek the cause of an illness. Kaptyai area, 1962.

Above. Group of men in formal kokwet, Kaptyai area, August, 1962. *Below*. Men engaged in cattle trading, official Ngenge market, August, 1962.

The "kotyak" pacing off the space a woman is supposed to cultivate at a work party. Binyinyi, 1954.

Above. The elder Kapsilut addressing the assemblage at the ceremony for the release of Matui's spirit. Kaptyai area, November, 1962. (The poles are hollow bamboo tubes which serve as cases for beer straws.) *Below.* Men clearing bush at a work party. Binyinyi, 1954.

Women cultivating at a work party. Binyinyi, 1954. The Sebei plains are in the
background.

4. Houses and manufactured goods such as clothing, weapons, tools, utensils.

5. Medicines and magic.

The Sebei spoke of having slaves, but this appears to be a misconstruction, for it cannot be said that persons may be owned in any real meaning of the word. There is no sale of persons, nor would a poor dependent be estopped from leaving. During famines children have been exchanged for food with people from other tribes, in a form of sale, but this appears to be an extralegal deficiency adjustment. In some sense it might be possible to treat wives as legal property, but on the whole I do not think this practice would accord either with our use of the concept or with Sebei attitudes.

For the most part, private ownership of property is the simple and unassailable right of the individual. And with some minor exceptions, the individual of legal competence is the adult (circumcised) male. These exceptions may be briefly noted here, though a more extended discussion of some of them appears later.

1. *Clan rights to land.*—Some informants said the clan owned the land, and in a few cases the clan had prevented the sale of land by an individual member to a member of another clan. In some parts of Sebei, clans (or clan sectors) settled and occupied contiguous areas and the clan elders endeavored to hold the unity of these lands; they certainly could prevent the sale of land to an undesirable person. But they do not themselves sell the land, hold land, or allocate its use. It is not proper to speak of clan (or kota) holdings or even to assert that clans have a residual or partial right to property, but rather to recognize the corporate rights of the group over its members (as persons) which could prevent individuals from taking action inimical to the welfare of the clan. Furthermore, clan elders might have to decide matters of inheritance which were not obvious, and thus appear to be allocating land, while in fact they are concerned with matters of family law (see also the section on land, and the discussion of family law).

2. *Subsidiary rights.*—Both wives and sons have certain allocated rights to land and cattle. This allocation, made by the

husband-father, gives certain privileges of use to the wives and the right of inheritance to her sons (as against those of her co-wives).

3. *Property of minors.*—A minor (uncircumcised) son inherits rights to both land and stock upon the death of the father. They are held in trust for him, normally by the man who inherited his mother, but, if she is dead, by his older brother or his father's brother. The minor may not make contracts with this property, which his guardian may do, but there is strong moral pressure on the latter to husband his ward's resources.

4. *Personal possessions of women.*—Women have the recognized ownership of certain personal goods (clothing, utensils) to which the husband holds no rights. She also has a right to dispose of some of the product of her labor as farmer; she may own goats in her own name, and now apparently even cows obtained through sale of her farm products.

5. *Public property.*—Public property, as distinct from public domain, are goods held by the community as a corporate group. The only Sebei public property is the place of meeting for the kokwet of the sangta or pororyet. Use of such lands for private purposes is forbidden.

An old man named Sayekwo Arapseluk of Kapchoken clan tried to cultivate the kok [place for holding kokwet] and was stopped. He was afraid of disobeying because he might be cursed. [Case 200]

Keeping in mind these exceptions and limitations, it may be said that the adult male has a kind of fee-simple right to property that is in the private sector of the economy. The rights normally are acquired by the individual either by attachment (as of cattle through raid or by settling on unoccupied land), inheritance, or exchange. He is free to enter into contracts regarding these goods, including their rental or exchange, with full rights of alienation (except as noted above). When subsidiary rights are vested in a wife, he is expected to consult her in making such contracts, but is not bound by her will in the matter. These rights emerge more clearly in the following sections of this chapter, in the chapter on contracts, as well as in the discussion of family law.

What we particularly want to emphasize, however, is this: while the law of violence is fundamentally legal action between clans as corporate groups, the law of property is fundamentally law between individuals. Private property is not clan property; thefts are acts by individuals against individuals, contracts are negotiations between individuals. This may seem surprising, inasmuch as acts of violence must, if a peaceable solution is to be found, be translated into cattle, but it is nevertheless true.

Land Law

To appreciate the character of Sebei law with respect to land, it is necessary to review land-use patterns as they have varied in recent Sebei history and as they vary spatially today. The Sebei were primarily pastoral until about 1800, being chiefly concerned with their cattle, secondarily with their goats and sheep, but also cultivating millet and sorghum. Though they lived on the mountains, they cultivated some land on the plains, where they went only in large groups for mutual protection against predatory animals and neighboring tribes. They used forest lands similarly. These areas were not occupied, but were used only as cropland and hunting area. Presumably these outlying lands were supplemental to the lands on the escarpment, though Sebei informants emphasized the outlying lands. Well before the first European contacts in 1890 the Sebei had acquired plantains, either from the Bagisu who had pushed the Sebei out of the southwestern section of the Elgon massif, or from other Bantu-speaking people. Plantains were moving from the western sector eastward along the north escarpment in mid-nineteenth century, and became the major crop in the relatively humid northwestern part of Sebeiland. The north escarpment was only lightly populated. The Sebei claim that at an earlier era they lived on the plains. Military pressure had forced them onto the mountain, and constant raids (perhaps aided by diseases of man and beast) were also responsible for the low density on the north escarpment. Though the Sebei do not live in the forest, they occupy the open lands above the forest line. (A few Sebei formerly lived in the forest, but never in large numbers.)

The Sebei have adopted two European-introduced crops that affect land use: maize and coffee. Early maize was less successful than a later variety introduced directly by European settlers (it was more productive and less hard) which is now the second food crop in Sebeiland, being far more important than either millet, sorghum, or root crops. Land found in relatively large flat plots is cultivated by ox-drawn plows, also a late introduction. Coffee was introduced just after World War I and is an important source of cash. It is generally interplanted with plantains, and like plantains is a permanent crop with intensive usage of land. The flatter lands of the Bukwa area, and the influence of the white settlers in neighboring Kenya, have encouraged the fencing of land, the use of the plow, and the marketing of surplus maize. The plow is rapidly transforming the plains from a grazing to a farming area.

Today in Sebeiland we find a variety of circumstances, varying regionally in response to diverse environmental factors and historical forces: intensively used plantain and coffee fields (predominantly on the western escarpment), fenced and plowed fields (predominantly in the eastern, Bukwa area), mixed fields and pastureland in varying proportions (on the central escarpment), downs and forests with small garden plots (in the highland area), and open, unfenced pasture range (on the plains). Everywhere, except in the mountain region, there has been an increased intensification of land usage, a process that started long before the territory had contact with Europeans and is particularly characteristic of the fertile but dry plains today. A recognition of these regional and temporal diversities is essential to an understanding of Sebei laws regulating control of the land.

Unless we distinguish between ownership and territoriality, Sebei statements regarding landownership will appear contradictory. Some informants stated that the clans owned the land, while others insisted that land was individually held, though all recognized that within the clans each individual has his own rights to the land. "In Mbai," one informant said, "we find about twenty members of one aret living together, so that the land there is called by the name of that aret. But inside that they divide it privately. Each person has individual land divided by planting a long-living bush called *senchontet*. That bush cannot die; even some planted by our fathers or grandfathers are still growing."

The ancient Sebei settlement pattern appears to have been in age-graded encampments or manyattas; but some areas were settled by clans, or clan offshoots, which occupied them as a unit, so that there are still villages named after the clans that occupied them and villages where one clan forms an overwhelming majority of the population. These are found chiefly in that part of the western sector of Sebeiland (the Mbai tribal territory) where farming was the predominant economic activity and into which Sebei, who had taken to plantain cultivation, and who were displaced by Bagisu pressures in the southwest, had pressed. A good deal of evidence suggests what propably happened is that when Sebei took to farming they tended to hold together as clan units: they fought as clan units, they fled as clan units, they resettled as clan units. They sometimes paid for the right to take over an area; they sometimes simply pushed out the weaker clans. It is in this western area that reference is made to the difficulty in being "a clanless man"—that is, settled among persons of an alien clan. It is in this area, too, and in this limited sense, that the clan became briefly a territorial unit. there must have been some allocation at the time of initial resettlement, but once the Sebei were settled in, and once land was allotted to clan brothers, and when all the arable land had been divided, this land then became the private holdings of the individuals and their progeny. The clan retained, through the political-kinship powers of its elders, the right to screen sales; whenever a sale (which required witnesses and could not be done privately) was proposed by an individual, objection could be raised in terms of group welfare.

My father went to buy land from Psiwa's father but Psiwa's clan members refused to allow him to buy it. They simply said: "We do not want you to bring a man of another clan to live in the middle of us," and also asked the seller where he would grow his own crops. Psiwa, who was present, said that his father had to accept the ruling of the elders. [Case 198]

Indeed, it was not always the clan; the village might be exercised over a sale that endangered its members:

Bumet Barteka of Kaminwa clan came from Kaserem Pororyet and tried to live in Kapsilut. Somebody told them that he had been sent away from Kaserem because he was a witch doctor. The Kapsilut people took the land back and sent him away. Barteka had to wander about; he tried to make friends but failed and finally he died. It was explained that it was the people of the sangta rather than of the clan who held the meeting to decide whether to allow him to take the land. [Case 195]

Thus there came to be a kind of clan quasi-territoriality in parts of Sebei, where the clan as corporate group having a concern with its own integrity exerted an influence over the sale of land. This system never overrode the freedom of access to open land which characterized Sebei pastoralism, though manifestly as open land tends to disappear the rule is of diminishing consequence. But the quasi-territoriality of the clan did not last, and furthermore it never had the character of rights—either subsidiary or overriding—to the land, for clan leaders neither disposed of nor allocated lands once the territory was settled. Clan powers are best understood as the obligations associated with group affiliation, not as rights to property.

The picture I reconstruct of Sebeiland of a century ago, before plantains (as well as maize and coffee) became important, is one of a sparsely populated landscape where the primary occupation was livestock husbandry, and farming was secondary if not ancillary. Under those conditions the Sebei could hardly place a great deal of emphasis upon landholdings. I suspect that at that time landownership was not an important element in law, and that only the actual cropland, or worked land that would sustain a subsequent year's crop, was considered a private right; that is, it was really the labor investment that rendered land into personal property. But, as the Sebei had a strong sense of private property with regard to livestock, they had, so to speak, a built-in set of legal customs favoring private rights which could be adapted to real estate. Much of land law, especially patterns of inheritance, is closely parallel to the law of cattle ownership. I believe the Sebei now tend to project back into the past their present attitudes.[1]

While it is entirely clear that uncultivated land is freely available to existing livestock regardless of ownership, and while it is also true that any cattle may run over a harvested field in which nothing can be destroyed, the stockowner nevertheless must keep his animals out of the fields and gardens of his neighbor.

An old man named Arakita Sabila claims that the goats of Wilson Cheminingwa are getting into his banana field each day. He claims Wilson should pay 11 shillings damage and 5 shillings fine. [Case 21]

If animals damage crops, the owner is liable for compensation. The only exception is that when a field borders on an established trail leading to water or salt, the person cultivating the land must fence it off from the trail.

Sebei inherit land patrilineally (though it is worked chiefly by women). A number of instances were called to my attention, however, in which a man moved into an area, married a local woman, and was given land by his father-in-law. He was expected to give a feast, which formed a ceremonial expression of his membership in the pororyet, and if he did so he had a permanent claim to the land. When there was still a good deal of vacant land, as was particularly true of the dry central sector of the escarpment from which the Sebei were driven in mid-nineteenth century by Masai raiders, land was simply taken up by individuals, though they made (or at least now make) some effort to justify their claim on the basis of clan ties with former occupants. This pattern continues to operate on the plains today. An early settler on the plains justified his claim to take up the land on the ground that his stock had been urinating in

[1] We must recognize that the Sebei are nowadays wary in discussing the subject of landownership, for fear that their rights (both individual and tribal) may be jeopardized by too close a look at the old procedures. I believe I have elicited enough case material and details of history (including clan histories) to support the views here expressed, though at one time I thought individual Sebei were suppressing information on clan rights to protect their private rights.

the streams above the area, and the urine had washed down with the water, and thus his stock had, in effect, used the area. But his argument was no more than rationalization; not all claimants had lived just above the land to which they went. The plains settlers tend to claim a large area of land, but as they cultivate only a few acres, and have done so for but a few years, much of the land has never been under the plow, and others (even from other tribes) may take up and plow virgin land. Such preemptive claims have been supported in the courts.

There is a tendency today for some men to build up their landholdings. One man I knew well in the western plantain area was regularly lending money, taking land as security, and buying up property, thus translating his free capital into land in a manner comparable to similar behavior with respect to cattle. Land disputes are now a frequent occurrence in the more densely settled sectors of Sebeiland.

Each man allocates land to his wives for cultivation, and a woman's permanent right to such land is subject to abrogation only by her husband. A husband will take some land away from his first wife when he marries a subsequent one, and he may take land that his wife has been cultivating and give it (in earlier times) or sell it (nowadays) to another person. Members of the Law Conference, including the women present, asserted that formerly a woman had no say over such a matter, but nowadays they can enforce their objections—presumably through modern courts.

Each wife normally cultivates her own land, fills her own granaries, and feeds her own children with the product of the land. Sebei sell or exchange both preharvested crops in the field and granaries of maize or millet; such sale cannot be made by the wife without permission from her husband, nor by the husband without the wife's agreement. Thus, while the land is recognized as belonging to the man and allocated to the women, the product of her labor must be recognized as jointly owned. A woman might take some of her grain and exchange it for small household or personal items. Nowadays they take stems of plantains and similar products to the market, and considerable income (by Sebei standards) is obtained by some women through the sale of *waragi* (distilled native beer). So far as I can tell, most of such money remains in the hands of the women.

Sebei wives are frequently jealous of their land rights, and our case record includes several quarrels between wives over land use (notably Cases 122 and 238). Sons also are jealous for their mother's right, for they themselves will inherit the land allocated to their mother (Case 138). But ultimately the right of reallocation rests with the husband, though evidence suggests he prefers to avoid involvement in such disputation.

Livestock Ownership

Cattle were the most important resource of old Sebei, and remain important economically and socially. Cattle transactions formed a basis for social solidarity, they were (as we have seen) the base for settling disputes, and they were used for bride-price. Cattle are an important mark of status in all parts of Sebei, and overwhelmingly so on the plains, where their numbers are large.

Each clan has its own earmark for cattle, and these brands are used as an aid to identification in case of theft, but there is no evidence whatsoever to suggest that the clans have ever been the unit holding rights to livestock. Clearly the clan holds no rights—even so limited as we found with respect to land—with respect to livestock. The clan does have a concern with regard to its constituent members, and can press a clansman to sacrifice an animal, or to contribute a payment, for the welfare of the clan. But this responsibility cannot be regarded as a corporate right in the herd. In fact the community, as distinct from the kindred, can also exert pressure on the individual to make such sacrifices, as I witnessed when the plains people created a warrior bivouac as a protective measure and wanted animals to slaughter for their feast. Similar occurrences are reported in connection with pororyet ceremonies in the past.

Livestock transactions are regularly engaged in. As they are discussed in detail in the chapter on contracts, here we need only point out that they are freely entered into by the owner and that his right to do so cannot be hampered by any other individual, except for the persuasion of his wife under certain circumstances, and for general community pressure to husband his resources and preserve the integrity of his herd.

Though the men own the cattle, certain rights may be vested in wives and minor sons. They are usually allocated by the husband-father. A cattleman is expected to give some of his animals to his wives in a ceremonial anointing. His herds are thus divided between those formally allocated to each wife and those he holds in reserve (*tokapsoy*). The wife might have animals from other sources, given to her by her brother-in-law or by her father, but this is unusual. (Sons are also given cattle from time to time, particularly at circumcision, and these form the nucleus of their herd or their bride-price. I do not think they can use them in contracts prior to their initiation.) Whatever the source, the wife's rights in the cattle permit her to milk the cows and utilize the milk for her household and to feed her children; the husband is not to sell or exchange these cows, or to use them for bride-price without her permission (though there are constraints on her against refusal) ; the cattle are to be used as bride-price only for her sons and not for other sons of the father; her sons inherit the cows upon the father's death. In the event of divorce the woman cannot take the cows with her, even if they have been given by her own father (but if she has sons, their rights are unimpaired by divorce) ; she can neither initiate nor conclude a contractual obligation with respect to them, nor slaughter them. Her rights are thus clearly circumscribed, and beyond daily use are unenforceable in law, albeit generally honored. It must be remembered that men fear the magical powers of women, and I suspect few men would freely disregard the wishes of a wife with respect to the disposition of cattle that were given to her. Furthermore, if she has sons, they will insist upon the recognition of their mother's rights. These rights extend to the progeny of cattle indefinitely (calculated only through the cows, the bull that sires an animal being disregarded), including those obtained under contractual exchanges for her animals. She has no rights whatsoever to the tokapsoy, which the husband generally uses to obtain subsequent wives, though these cows are assigned to wives for milking, and though a woman's sons might expect to get a share of the tokapsoy either upon departure from the ménage or by inheritance. Nor are her rights, if she is survived by sons, abrogated upon her death; the cattle are held in trust until the sons are initiated into manhood.

The rights of a son to his father's cattle are ancillary to those of his mother. He has no rights in his father's tokapsoy, only an expectation of receiving his portion either when he marries and establishes an independent household, or when his father dies.

Houses and Chattels

Each wife expects to have a house of her own built for her. This was true in the early days when Sebei lived in rectangular houses and is true now when they live in thatched rondevals. The house, however, legally belongs to the man; he can marry a second wife and force his first wife to share the use of her house until a new one is built.

Minor chattels owned by men are spear, shield, bow and arrows, quiver, herding stick, beer straw, stool, sleeping skins (and nowadays slat bed), clothes and personal ornamentation, beer pots, gourds for storing milk, knife, ax, pick for cattle salt, baskets for carrying the salt, and eating basket.

Minor chattels owned by women are personal clothes and ornaments (particularly her cowry-shell girdle), sleeping skins, drinking calabash, hoe, beer straw, walking stick, water pot, milking gourds, saltmaking apparatus, winnowing and food baskets, mortar and grinding stone, knife, and smoking pipe. Most of these items a woman takes with her in case of divorce, particularly if she brought them with her. There was some discussion as to whether she took her hoe with her—one of the major items in the domestic ménage of the pre-European Sebei.

Some of these possessions are more closely associated with the person than are others, are more vulnerable to use in magic, have to be specially anointed when inherited, and the like.

Wild Game and Bees

Hunting is a secondary activity, but not inconsequential. Elephant hunting was particularly important from about the 1880's

(when Swahili traders entered the area) until after World War
I. Wild animals are public property, and may be hunted without regard to property rights or territory.[2] A person hunting
alone simply keeps the animal. Most hunting appears to be done
in groups; any person may organize a hunting party, but he receives no special rights by having initiated the activity, nor is he
in a position of leadership. The man who first strikes the animal
(whether or not he draws blood) gets it, but if another finally
kills it, he is entitled to a foreleg. In a large party, the kill is
divided: the ribs of one side of the animal, and the chest, liver,
and spleen are roasted and eaten by the hunting party while
they are at the place of the kill. The man who first struck the
animal gets the head, the back or thighs, and the skin. The
second person who spears gets a foreleg, and if a third person
has speared the animal he would get the biggest part of the
intestine and a piece of meat from the neck. The person who
started the animal gets a piece from the back called *paswet*.

But this orderly arrangement was not followed on the large
animal hunts occasionally undertaken on the plains and initiated by the prophet. The following is from the Law Conference:

W. GOLDSCHMIDT: Did Sebei ever organize hunting parties?
SEVERAL: Yes.
W. GOLDSCHMIDT: How was a hunting party formed? Does it have a
    leader or is it just formed and people go off together?
KAPTYEMOIKIN: The prophet Matui used to pass out orders telling
    the people where to hunt. The people would hear the *kontit*
    being blown and then news would go round that at such and
    such a place you should hunt. The kontit was blown in the af-
    ternoon and the people knew that tomorrow would be the
    hunting day.
R. BOMET: When it was blown, each pororyet in turn blew so that all
    could hear. They also called out that there would be hunting
    a certain animal "kota" [figure of speech for variety of game].
W. GOLDSCHMIDT: What kind of animals?
SEVERAL: Any kind.
W. GOLDSCHMIDT: Do you have a captain of hunt; how is hunt organ-
    ized?

    [2] Nowadays, of course, there are strict game laws; this statement has
reference entirely to aboriginal custom.

KAPTYEMOIKIN: A man named ———— was sent by Matui and organized us here. [The name was not recorded.]

W. GOLDSCHMIDT: How were the food and skins divided among the people?

MANGUSYO: We didn't skin the animals, and we fought over the carcasses; the strongest man got the most meat.

R. BOMET: The one who did the spearing gets the head of the animal; the one who does the killing never gets good meat.

MANGUSYO: Because they are fighting and are trying to cut the carcass with knives, sometimes they cut one another. An animal can be divided properly if it is killed in the forest; fighting over the carcass occurs only on the plains. Hunting in the forest was not organized and Matui didn't blow his horn. Just a small party would go to *masop* [up the mountain].

W. GOLDSCHMIDT: How was a small party organized?

MUZUNGYO: Anyone who wanted meat would go to the forest and call Ho Ho Ho. Everyone knows he is going to organize a hunting party and anyone could go with him.

Pit traps can be dug without restriction and are the property of the man who digs them. He is not considered liable for damage to person or livestock, and it is claimed that such would not occur, as the traps are not put near houses or kraals. A man might give a beer moyket, getting others to do the work; but it would still be his trap, and he has sole right to the game caught. A man finding an animal in a trap belonging to another man gets the right foreleg.

Elephant hunting used to be a fairly important source of wealth because of the ivory trade, and in the past some Sebei were particularly interested in hunting these animals. The tusks were traded for cattle. Values reported were from one to four cows for each tusk. If a man kills an elephant, the tusks belong to him. Cases 58 and 207 concern property matters that resulted from hunting elephant (see pp. 178–179).

If a poisoned arrow is used, the poison is purchased from a specialist, and he is to be given the left tusk.

My father borrowed a poisoned arrow from Kaptomom Psenger and shot an elephant with it, but it didn't die from his arrow wound. Somebody else shot it and it died. So my father took the right tusk and the other man took the left one. My father exchanged the right tusk for a heifer and when it produced a calf, my father gave that bullock to Kaptomom Psenger. [Case 241]

This case makes clear that the first person to shoot gets one tusk; the person who kills gets the other.

Beehives (*mwengket, mwengkonik*) are privately owned, and a person who has established a right to use a tree has it in perpetuity. The tree right is separate from the land. Apparently only one hive is placed in a tree.

Psekuton made a beehive and was the first person to put it in a certain tree. It got old and broke down, and later Kamakanka of the same clan hung his beehive in that tree. When Psekuton found this out he quarreled with Kamakanka, after which the latter had to take the hive down. [Case 196]

In the highland area, bees are an important economic asset; individuals have sections of the forest in which they keep their hives, and such areas are recognized as a private right. The following case, though regrettably sparse in detail, exemplifies this right.

I took a case against Aramatui in 1943. I claimed that Aramatui came and put his beehives on trees in my area, and the case was decided in my favor. I had twenty hives. He was ordered to remove his beehives. [Case 141]

I was also told that Sebei in the highlands hold private grazing rights, and while a member of the Law Conference said "I think it may be true today," there was denial that it had been so in the old days or that one could prevent others from grazing the land. Unfortunately, there are no relevant cases.

Medicines and Magic

Medicines and magical knowledge may also be seen as private property. It is not the substance that is owned, for that is insignificant; rather it is the knowledge of how to use it and the right to do so. A person who knows either curative medicine or harmful magic may charge for his cure or for the use; he may also sell the knowledge or give it to his sons.

Normally a person acquires knowledge of a medicine only after it has cured him of a disease. He may then request that the doctor instruct him, and he acquires not merely the knowledge of what the relevant medicinal plant or plants are and how they are handled, but also a right to use this knowledge. If the medicine is to be efficacious, the buyer of the knowledge must brew beer, take a calabash of it to where each plant grows, and spit beer as a libation upon it, while his instructor says, "This plant should be sweet to you and you should use it in the way I do to make people well." The price for such knowledge varies with the gravity of the disease that the medicine cures: "If it is a light one, a sheep or goat is enough; if it is heavy, a cow must be paid." The purchase of knowledge is a separate transaction from the cure previously received. Some medicines are quite widely known. Medicines may also be taught to one's sons or daughters who have not undergone the cure, and apparently certain specialists come to know a wide variety of treatments through their relatives. The knowledge may be transmitted to more than one person, and the seller is not impaired in his continued use of it. As I noted in the preceding section, poison for arrows can also be purchased, as can the right to make it.

Sekutet is a form of sorcery (curse) known to only a few people, who are hired to perform it; they are paid only when the target's clan, because it is losing personnel or cattle, requests its removal and makes payment to the person who requested the sekutet. The payment to the specialist was said to be one heifer. Black magic can also be hired and can be transferred by sale, as with medicine, but I have no specific cases involving purchase.

The Individual Character of Property Rights

The data set forth in this chapter support the position that essentially property is privately and individually held and is not in any true sense owned by the corporate group or by the community. I had anticipated that clans and clan segments would hold some property rights, that the privileges of owner-ship of livestock, land, and chattels would in some measure be shared by the corporate group. On the basis of this assumption, I pressed questions quite closely. We have already seen that the ambiguity expressed by some Sebei regarding land can best be resolved by assuming that clans have rights over the persons of their constituent membership where the welfare of the clan is at stake, but not rights over their property. On matters other than land, there is no ambiguity whatever; all rights are private rights.

The test of this generalization lies in the fact that if a person takes something from his father or his brother, the deed is regarded as a theft and is clearly actionable. The Sebei were quite definite (in response to direct questioning) on this point, and supplied specific case material. Thus while a man cannot (in the legal sense) murder his brother, he can steal from him.

There was a time when Musani, father of Mangusyo, went to his father's brother, Psomo Ngerenet, during a famine and stole a gourd of millet which had been kept for seed. When asked if he had done it he denied it, and the people performed the mumek oath. They stayed until Musani married and lost three children, and then they performed the korosek ceremony of peace. [Case 208]

One of Konyi's cows was stolen by his elder son, Chuma Bartega. The father tracked the cow until he found it. He invited the sangta people to a council. Konyi lived below Kaproron at Lelketi and his son lived in Kwanyi below Kapkata; and the council was held at Kwanyi sangta, where the father accused the son and the case was adjudged against the son. Konyi gave his son a strong warning not to do that again, but left the cow with him, so nothing more happened. [Case 209]

One time my father made beer and asked the people gathered at the beer party to slash the banana plants in the field that had not been given to him by his father. My grandfather fought with my father over this. The people judged the case against my father, but his father was kind enough to give the son some of the land, but also he warned him. This happened when the Baganda had just arrived, while we were paying one rupee tax, at Kapsumpata in Chebonet area. [Case 210]

General Discussion on the Law Relating to Property

In this chapter, the general legal attitudes with regard to the things of the Sebei world have been set forth. These rules and assumptions underlie the laws relating to theft, which is the subject of chapter 10, and contractual arrangements, which is the subject of chapter 11. Much of what has been set forth here is substantiated in the case material presented in these chapters, though some comes directly from informants' statements. Some of the matters with respect to property are also involved in the law of affiliation, particularly the chapter on the family.

The things of the Sebei world are divided between those that are public and those that are owned. The realm of private ownership comprises those things to which human labor has contributed value. The basic feature of this ownership pattern lies in the essentially private, individual nature of property rights. The freedom of the individual to use, sell, or make contractual arrangements regarding his possessions is relatively unimpaired. With respect to land, pressure against a particular sale may be applied by clan or community, but on the grounds of undesirability of the buyer, not on grounds that he is not competent or free to make the contract. With respect to cattle, there may be moral suasion to maintain a herd intact, but no pressures enforceable in law. The individual may also have established obligations to his wives or sons, but these are obligations he has himself entered into. The same applies to property of less economic importance. All in all, the degree of individual right with respect to control of material things—those that enter the realm of property at all in Sebeiland—is fully equivalent to that generally found in American law, where such rights are, of course, also subject to limitation.

CHAPTER 10 *Theft*

General Concepts and Orientation

The taking of things belonging to others is recognized as a delict by the Sebei. This is implicit in the legal recognition of property rights. From the fact that theft, unlike murder, is regarded as a personal delict rather than a clan action, it follows that punishment is essentially against the individual, not the clan. Furthermore, and most importantly for the formulation of a Sebei legal theory, action against theft is community (sangta, pororyet) action rather than clan action. Thus, while the kokwet and actions taken under the ntarastit ceremony only occasionally come to bear on matters relating to violence, they play a major part in matters relating to property; conversely, the clan has only a minor or ancillary function in serving the law of property. The clan role can best be understood as a standby role, for delicts with respect to property may incite either curses or violence, which in turn may require preventive action by the clan. The normal course of events is to bring delicts involving property before the community. They may also, however, be handled by means of sorcery. They are never handled directly by clan feud, though clans may act either (1) to remove a curse initiated because of a property conflict, or (2) to chastise or kill a recidivist thief who is endangering the welfare of the clan by his actions.

The Sebei distinguished [1] three basic kinds of property delict:

1) *Chorset.* This may be glossed as theft, for it is the taking of something by stealth, without the knowledge or awareness of the owner. It may apply to any form of property, but it is generally the taking of food, personal goods, or (nowadays)

[1] The terms and concepts were supplied by informants during the Law Conference. Efforts were made to determine their more explicit meanings.

money. It does not apply to cattle (so far as our case record indicates) , and informants said that cattle could not be taken by stealth. It does, however, apply to sheep and goats, which are frequently stolen.

2) *Kimngonget* or *kipnganget*. This is taking by force, and may be applied to cattle-raiding internal to the Sebei community. There is no etymological evidence for its meaning. Raiding of enemy kraals is *setet* (from the verb *set,* "to raid cattle") , and such a raiding party is *luket*. We have no clear cases of kimngonget.

3) *Ngokisto*. This may best be glossed as false claim, though one informant expressed the idea that it was an unmotivated crime. There is no Sebei etymological evidence, but the Nandi *ngac* means to accuse falsely, while *ngokisto* has been defined as guilt in Nandi.

The Sebei do not appear to have any clear ideas with respect to accessories to delicts involving property. We have one modern case (Case 44) in which a man was fined for having in his kraal one of a group of stolen cattle, but the higher court overruled the lower court's decision, so it gives us no information. There is no explicit concept of recidivism, but a person who regularly or habitually steals is known as a *chorintet,* "thief."

Procedural Matters: The Nature of the Kokwet and the Kirwokik

Though reference is made to the kokwet in earlier sections, I have withheld full discussion up to this point, where its relevance is clear. First, we must appreciate that it is a very general term. It may be applied to a family council, a clan council, a village or a pororyet council; it is used when an issue is brought for discussion and determination before a group of men around a beer pot; and it is used for the modern governmental district council. The model for the kokwet, however, is surely the council of the pororyet, and it is this council that I describe.

When a man has lost property through theft he calls an alarm, and people of his sangta (note, not his clan) endeavor to find and follow the tracks of the thief. If the thief is found, punishment may be directly meted out; but if it is not, the person whose property was stolen may ask the kokwet to hear his matter. He will go to kirwokik in diverse villages of his pororyet and ask them to come at a certain time. They may collect at any suitable place, though there is a recognized meeting place (*kok*) in each pororyet and sangta. The kokwet includes all men who are interested, and persons are expected to appear. Men are not forced to come, but a man who stays away from the kokwet is despised and people would call him *puswok*. The term has reference to someone or something that is left behind; it is used for a cow that continues to graze when the cattle have returned to the kraal. By extension it means a lazy or good-for-nothing person. Women and uncircumcised boys may attend—and it is considered good for the latter to attend—though they may not be heard. Women are invited to participate in matters involving women, and under these circumstances are presumably privileged to be heard.[2] The men of each sangta sit together, the kirwokintet of that sangta in front of them. There should be several kirwokik present, but there is no one who presides over the group.

When the men have gathered, the man making the accusation addresses the group, setting forth the purpose of the meeting and his side of the case; then the accused person (who has presumably also been asked to be present) stands and explains matters in his terms. The kirwokik stand and express their views as they are motivated, and the public murmurs approval or disapproval of these views. Eyewitnesses are called *piko che kikese* (people who were looking), while people who were present but not necessarily observing are known as *piko che kimi cheto* (people who were present). Witnesses are not distinguished terminologically between those for one party and those for the other party to a dispute, or in any other way. For contractual matters, a man's neighbor (*latyet*, which is a formalized quasi-kin relationship) is expected to be one witness. Both

---

[2] Certainly this procedure was followed in matters handled in councils in my presence. Moreover, it was the Sebei men who suggested that women should participate in the Law Conference, and it was when matters involving women were discussed that women volunteered their opinions. They also made their feelings known at the family councils I witnessed.

sides may bring forth witnesses, and sometimes evidence (e.g., the cow presumed to have been stolen or involved in the transaction) may also be brought before the kokwet. There is no oath for witnesses, but a person who lies will not be credited in future instances. It is important that persons be present who are not members of either clan, because a person may not (or will not?) testify against his own clansmen. The witnesses are present during the entire hearing, and they dispute one another's testimony. The court reaches a decision through consensus. Any person, whether a kirwokintet or not, may speak his mind. If an agreement is reached, all present stand up "and that means the matter is closed." There appear to be no specific rules as to how consensus is arrived at; Case 18 (p. 101) suggests that additional kirwokik may be called in when no solution can be reached.

As always in Sebei law, however, the force of the supernatural stands behind its actions. Should matters come to an impasse, or should one or another of the principals specifically deny the verdict of the court, he may ask that they both swear an oath— the accused one swearing that if in fact he has done the matter he should die (e.g., "If in truth this cow is not mine, may it harm me"), the accuser similarly swearing that if he be making false accusation, he should die.

The normal procedure is to take a matter before the kokwet of the sangta in which the defendant lives, though members of the sangta of the complainant are also present. If the defendant refuses to accept the decision of that court, he may appeal to the pororyet of the complainant. In a case involving a contractual arrangement regarding a cow (Case 199, p. 150), the village council of the defendant ordered restitution, but he refused to comply and appealed to the pororyet council, which upheld the village court.

It was said that should the pororyet not reach a decision, a case may be appealed to a kokwet to which outside major kirwokik are invited.

KAPSILUT: It may be the case that a member of Kapcheptemkoñ pororyet had a case against a Murkutwa pororyet man; he would take the matter to the man's village in Murkutwa; if the man refused to pay the demand of the village council, they would in-

vite members of the pororyet of Murkutwa, and if he still refuses they would have to invite people from another
pororyet.

KAPTYEMOIKIN: If the third council makes the same decision and he
still refuses to pay, there will be a fight.

CHELAKAM: If he still refuses, people of the council will tell him,
"You are living by yourself, you are a *putkey*." [3] [Law Confer-
ence]

A person may obtain a higher court decision through taking
matters into his own hands.

Soyto married a daughter of our clan and paid a heifer as part of
the bride-price, which multiplied until there was a big herd and the
kraal was full of cows. Soyto's son came to our clan [his mother's
clan] and asked for one cow that had been paid as bride-price for his
mother, but we said: "We can't give you a cow. Your mother has
one son and three daughters; you will receive your bride-price from
your sister." The young man brought the matter before the council
and the case went against the son. Then the son organized a group
of people and when our cows were going to water, the son and his
group took ten head and drove them to a cave. When we heard the
alarm we started fighting and many heads were beaten in. The kirwokik Muse and Laypuch came and stopped the fighting and said:
"Let us go home and we shall sit in kokwet tomorrow and decide
this matter." The cows were kept in the cave and the next morning
members of the Kapcheptemkoñ pororyet invited Kono and Murkutwa pororisyek people and we met at Siron.

At the hearing the elders from these other pororisyek said that we
had been wrong to refuse. They told us it was the custom that when
a heifer was paid as bride-price and it multiplies, one should give a
calf to the son. So the kokwet ordered us to pay three head, two to
be a part of the original cow and one from our own herd—this last
to keep him from demanding more. This custom is called *put*
("pinch off"). [Case 201]

Though in the above instance the kirwokik took the initiative
in order to stop the fight, neither the kirwokik nor the kokwet
has any powers to arrest. The kokwet is a court to which a
person may appeal. It has no powers to imprison, flog, or exe-
cute offenders, but it may assess fines or (under the ntarastit
rule) plunder the possessions of the offender. We see, however,

[3] Dr. Christine Montgomery suggests that this word is based on the
reflexive form *put* of the verb "to pinch off" (in harvesting), and therefore
means "to cut oneself off."

that it does have an ultimate sanction of persuasion to compliance, at least in contractual matters, through the use of public opinion and community pressure—a power that should not be underestimated as a force to obtain compliance.

In the above discussion I have referred to the kirwokik as if they held a special office, but they should not be so viewed. A person becomes known as a kirwokintet informally; there are no fixed numbers of persons so recognized, and they have neither special powers nor special insignia of office. They are merely elders who have, through their public performance, shown themselves to be particularly astute and perceptive, to have rendered judgments or made pleas meeting with general approval. "If a man gives his views over and over again and they are wise and correct views, then he would be appointed kirwokintet" [Law Conference]. But we must not take the word "appointed" too literally; there is nobody who has the power to appoint, and what is meant is that the kirwokik will be recognized as such by the people. The Sebei speak of some who were specifically kirwokik for the sangta only (*kirwokintet ñe mining*, lesser kirwokintet) and others for the pororyet as a whole (*kirwokintet ñe wo*, major kirwokintet). I suspect this distinction holds a false specificity; nevertheless there is no doubt that certain men had a Sebei-wide reputation as important kirwokik and were often called upon to serve whenever a difficult dispute arose. They are the names old men now remember from their youth as being important kirwokik.

No explicit requirement other than personal ability was mentioned. Wealth may lend weight to a man's words, but does not in itself make him kirwokintet. The Sebei say: "One does not buy a councilorship with a cow; one buys it with the ear." One becomes kirwokintet by listening to the wisdom of one's elders. A man might be poor and have but one wife and be a kirwokintet, though a bachelor would not become one. There is no inheritance of the position, but there is a tendency toward continuity from father to son. The kirwokik are not members of a single age-set as they are among some of the culturally related tribes; any person of middle years may become a kirwokintet, and he remains such until death.

One other procedural matter deserves our attention: the use of theft to force an issue, to bring a matter before the court. I develop this point in some detail in the chapter on contracts (chap. 11, pp. 199 ff.) where it is particularly brought forward as a device in law, a delicate means of bringing into court a matter that in itself is unseemly to raise as an issue. We find, however, that a similar procedure appears to be used in other contexts. Thus, two cases cited earlier (Cases 209 and 210, p. 160) had the effect of forcing a father to comply with a request, while a similar pattern was invoked by the young man who was demanding a cow (Case 201, p. 166). This also seems to be the underlying pattern of Case 136 (pp. 169–170), a modern instance of land theft. All these instances are intrafamilial.

The Sebei gave no indication as to how a man would decide which kokwet was relevant in cases of theft. There is some indication in the analysis of approximately thirty cases involving property delicts as to what the procedures are.[4] In order to understand Sebei procedures in the treatment of theft cases, and thereby the laws pertaining to theft, it is useful first to extract the cases that were intrafamilial and intraclan from those that involved two clans, and then to treat each of the major property delicts (*chorset, ngokisto,* and *kimngonget*) separately.

Property Delicts within the Clan

Intraclan matters normally are, in essence, family matters. They are therefore usually decided at a local level, either in the sangta kokwet or even more informally at a kokwet held ad hoc at a beer-drink. In no case was an intraclan theft brought before the

[4] I do not cite numbers to indicate prevalence rates; neither the number of cases nor the mode of obtaining them makes such a use feasible. Intrafamilial cases were brought forward in the Law Conference at our specific request, but once obtained they satisfied our immediate purpose of demonstrating aspects of property rights. The general acceptance by Sebei informants of the implications of a clear case is taken as evidence that the relevant rulings constituted a principle in Sebei law as it existed in operation. Multiple cases do add to our sense of security in the reality and generality of the relevant principles. There are surprisingly few indications of conflict, either between cases or between stated rules as obtained in various contexts and the case record.

pororyet. In one instance, when two separate korik of a clan were involved, the matter was taken to the clan kokwet.

> Kwerit of the Kapchemantan clan accused the people of another kota of the same clan of having borrowed [5] his cow. They met at Kwesus in the sangta of poy, and because it was a matter internal to the clan, only the clan met. The head of the clan was Psiwa Arambuya, who acted as judge. There were witnesses. . . . [Case 37]

Unfortunately in this case the informant moved from the specific to a generalized form. He concluded as follows:

> The person whose cow was taken will bring witnesses who indicate the cows that have been slaughtered. The man who took the cows will bring witnesses, saying that when my cow was slaughtered so-and-so was present. If it happens that the neighbor is dead, his wife is appointed instead. She will tell about the sprinkling of the milk (i.e., specifically who borrowed the cow in the ceremony of borrowing) . [Case 37]

Sorcery is not frequently resorted to in intraclan delicts. Of the dozen cases I have, only two instances of sorcery were reported (Case 208, p. 160; Case 248) , and in each the thief had originally denied his guilt, so that the guilty person was not known when sorcery was invoked. The two cases were resolved within the family. Because sorcery works on the whole clan, it is too dangerous for intraclan sanction. Three modern instances of intraclan dispute were taken before the governmental court, while six were determined by the sangta or an informal kokwet, and one, just cited, by the clan.

Land disputes involving either forced taking or encroachment are more frequent among the cases I recorded than any other form of property delict internal to the clan. An instance of the former is as follows:

> My father Psiwa inherited this land from his father. It was given to me in 1950. I took the land by force, it was not just given. I claimed my father was against me in not giving me enough land. I planted coffee on it and he said nothing, but he was annoyed. Later I tried to plant coffee to straighten the eastern line and also the upper line, but he stopped me from doing that.
>   I first built a house and had the use of the plantains and planted

[5] "Borrowed" here has reference to the standard namanya exchange (see chap. 11, pp. 192–206) .

the coffee. But Psiwa didn't say to me that this land was for me. He now accepts that it is mine. There has been no court case. I believe perhaps it is because my mother came to him already pregnant and therefore he does not consider me to be his son, and that is why he has given me so little land. [Case 136]

On this subject, the father subsequently said:

I have five sons who should have been given land. He [the above informant] planted coffee and therefore he picks it, but I did not give him the land. I gave him two fields and he has bought two others, and that is quite enough. There is a case in the Gombolola court which has not been settled. I took the case last year and it is still pending and has not been heard. He failed to appear. Another son tried to take the field next to the one he took, but I stopped him. [Addendum to Case 136]

A case of encroachment is handled as follows:

Araplet accused his brother [by Sebei reckoning; they were actually sons of two full brothers] Sayekwo of crossing the boundary. The people of the village were there and walked the boundary. They examined the contours of the line on which rubbish from the garden had been heaped, to determine the boundary, and found Sayekwo guilty. There was no fine or punishment. The man who won the case made beer for the kirwokintet Barsiagi, as an expression of appreciation. [Case 72]

We also observed the local chief settle a claim between two co-wives (one of whom had been inherited), one having encroached upon the holding of the other (Case 122). The matter was settled by an informal kokwet presided over by the local governmental chief, with elders and neighbors as witnesses. Two other cases involving land encroachment (Cases 16, 64) similarly were handled by local people, without punishment but with a determination of rights.

Most significant with respect to intraclan property delicts is the fact that in no case handled by the local court was there any punishment meted out to the defendant; the court served merely to determine what it deemed to be the correct ownership right and demanded restitution. Ntarastit is never applied to intraclan matters according to my case record, and I believe that this is a correct reflection of Sebei legal action.

We may summarize the problems of intraclan theft as follows.

First, there are no reported cases that can properly be called kimngonget (forced taking) except two recent efforts at forcing a relative to give land, and these must be considered very special instances of property conflict. Outright thefts and efforts at land encroachment make up the bulk of intraclan property cases. Of outright thefts, there are two involving money, two about cattle, and one about food. In no instance of native court procedure did the matter go beyond the local community (except the case that was handled by the clan). Mumek was resorted to in two cases, both after denial of guilt by the family member.

The fact that property can be stolen from fellow clansmen and close relatives supports the conclusion that property is viewed entirely as a private matter. Still, conflicts internal to the corporate group cannot be handled in the same manner as conflicts between separate clans, for the threat of violence runs counter to the demands of clan solidarity, and sorcery is a two-edged sword when used against fellow clansmen. We are not surprised, therefore, to find that thefts internal to the clan are resolved locally and with no sanctions other than a demand for restitution.

Thefts (Chorset) Involving More Than One Clan

The Sebei did not classify the cases that were given to me, but of the instances of property delicts in my files involving two different clans, nine I have called chorset, one kimngonget, and six ngokisto.

Of the nine cases of chorset, only one was handled by the sangta, six were at the pororyet level, and two were resolved by sorcery.

Two cases, the first one heard by the sangta and the second by the pororyet, resulted in straightforward fines.

Psekuton had a wife who stole plantain stems belonging to Sikoria. She was caught by following her footprints. It was a small stem. The matter was taken before the council and she was fined two goats. They were given alive. This happened during famine time. [Case 202]

A woman belonging to Kapcharicha clan stole Aliwa's millet from the granary. She was followed to a house, where they did not find the millet, and she had not cooked any. They tracked her footprints and found the millet nearby. The husband denied that it was stolen and the wife hid herself. He tried to defend himself with a spear and an alarm was raised and the people came from Kapchilil, Kamwerimwo, Kirwogo, and Kaptanya, and reported that this man wanted to kill people though his wife had stolen some millet. After proving this, the group of people caught two of their goats; they slaughtered one and ate it together and gave the owner of the millet another one, alive, and also a hoe. They held the council right at the spot. This happened in Maina age-set times. [Case 203]

It may be that the latter case had greater importance because of the threat of physical violence, but this was not made explicit; other instances (to be cited below, Cases 215 and 216) show the pororyet demanding fines (in the form of goats to be slaughtered and shared by the people) for ordinary thefts.

In two cases involving theft the punishment was according to ntarastit. In one instance, both parties were found to be guilty.

Arapsamput stole one banana stem from a field belonging to Arapsampukot, who took the matter to the kokwet. Arapsamput said to the people, "Really I have stolen this bunch of bananas but Arapsampukot is also guilty because when I was passing by, Arapsampukot took my bracelets and necklaces." The pororyet decided both were guilty according to ntarastit. So all the bunches of plantains were cut and some goats were slaughtered. Their houses were not burned but the grass thatch was taken off and millet, utensils, and everything were taken. The people felled the granaries at the posts. We all took things. The food was just taken by whoever was there; it was not divided evenly. [Case 73] [6]

The second case involves an effort to resist punishment.

During a famine, Masopo had no food (i.e., plantains or grain) so he slaughtered a goat and divided it in two, one part for each wife. They went to a man named Sali to exchange the meat for sorghum. Sali and his brother each took some of the meat, and Masopo and his two wives returned with the sorghum, which they consumed. They went back to Sali's house at night; the senior wife got in the granary and threw out sorghum to her husband and the second wife put it in the basket. Then they went to another granary and did the

[6] I have classified this act as chorset, which the woman had done, though the man's act was kimngonget. Informants subsequently agreed that these acts should be so classified.

same thing, with the second wife inside the granary. Sali woke up; he made an alarm and roused his brother. Masopo and the senior wife ran away, leaving the second wife inside the granary. The owner caught that woman. They were surprised to find that it was the woman they had sold food to a day or so earlier. They tied her until the next morning, when they took her to Sali's house. They gathered the people of the pororyet together and told them that Masopo had stolen sorghum from Sali's house. Masopo tried to get inside his house to get his arrows. The people went into the second wife's house and found thirty goats and killed them. They knocked down the walls of the first house and took twenty-five goats from there and killed them. The people shared the meat and released the wives. Both wives ran away, because Masopo had nothing to feed them. . . . [Case 204] [7]

It should perhaps be pointed out that one informant indicated the ntarastit punishment is not used (at least in property cases) when the man adjudged thief by the pororyet accepts the judgment and pays a fine. He said:

If a person ignores ntarastit after it has been performed and does something wrong, the person harmed will go to the pororyet. The people of the pororyet will all come to where the harm had taken place, and will say, "Should we burn [the house] or should we not burn?" If the person then wants to pay compensation for the harm and maintain the peace, he will say, "You should not burn," and that means he wants to preserve the peace. If he has said that, then the old men will stand with sticks and prevent the young men from destroying his property. The guilty man will then pay a "fine" according to what he did. Then the pororyet will ask for what amounts to a "court fee"; they will slaughter an animal to be eaten by the group. [8]

[7] This case was given in three essentially identical versions; this one, taken at the Law Conference, offers the greatest detail. Sebei granaries are freestanding structures, 3 or 4 feet in diameter and 5 or 6 feet high, with conical thatched roof or lid.

[8] The particular discussion, cast in general terms, assumes that the hypothetical case involves two pororisyek, rather than the pororyet against an individual. In no instance when an actual case was discussed was there any mention of such an option for the accused; indeed, the implications are that the people of the pororyet rather wildly plundered the accused man's property and that "it was something like a fight." Only one case (Case 165, p. 186) mentions more than one pororyet involved in a ntarastit punishment. I was told, however, that within the sangta, ntarastit might be invoked for minor offenses, while in intrasangta actions, it would be invoked only for major offenses.

Though the cases thus far discussed are reasonably classified as chorset, they are singular acts of thieving; that is, there is no evidence that the persons were guilty of repeated or habitual acts of theft. They were not, in the usual sense of the word, thieves, and none of the accused were called such (*chorik*) in the case record. I have three cases, however, where persons were recidivist thieves; all seem to have been young persons unwilling to accept the codes of Sebei society. In such instances, the problem takes on a different character, for the action endangers the peace and welfare of the clan. The victims of the thief ask his clansmen to take action against him, with the result that the clansmen either restrain him or kill him. If they refuse to do so, these outsiders may avenge themselves against any member of his clan, or may kill him with impunity.

Murkenu, my aret brother, and Chelelput, of the Kapkapya clan, both stole a goat from Purkeywa of Kapchoken aret. They were arrested and accused before the kokwet. The clans of these two men each furnished a goat; one was slaughtered for the kokwet to eat and the other was taken by Purkeywa. The two clans were warned to take control over these boys. Later, however, they stole a goat from Michangana of Kapsomin clan. They were again accused and brought before the kokwet. The two clans again furnished goats; this time two each. Two of them were slaughtered by Michangana to feed the pororyet. Later the boys stole a goat from Mangusyo Kapchepkan of the Kapchoken aret. An alarm was raised and the whole pororyet came. They said: "Where are the people who are causing all this trouble? We want to see them." Sabila, a clan brother of one of them, said that he would try to "arrest" his brother. Also, the brother of the other boy said that he would try to "arrest" his brother. Sabila found his brother, and though he tried to run, Sabila caught him and killed him with his spear. When the other man found his brother, he said, "I think that other boy has been killed and that he was the thief." He thus talked his brother into coming back to the house, and then proceeded to beat him to death in front of the whole clan. The matter was reported to the pororyet, that the thieves had been killed. This took place at Kaserem during the Maina age-set famine. [Case 216]

Malyan, my father's brother's son, and Chepkesetot, my father's sister's son, kept stealing things. They stole sheep and goats all over the country. People kept reporting lost animals, and they suspected these boys. The clan was warned that it had better catch these boys and tie them in the house. The boys were hiding in the cave called Kapcheporkon. Their clansmen found them roasting meat in the cave, where they had a lot of dried meat. They took them home and tied them to the center post of the house, where they fed them for a month. They escaped and went on stealing until one day some goats belonging to Malinga Chesekoñ were stolen. When that happened Malinga did not bring a complaint to the clan but he blew a horn and the people came in answer from all over the pororisyek of Kapcheptemkoñ and Tegeres. They wanted to raid the clan because they had been too careless in holding these two boys.

When the Kapchemandan people, to whose clan one of them belonged, saw the others coming to attack, they ran to the caves with their cattle, leaving their maize and millet. The people seized the things left behind and then tracked the Kapchemandan to their cave hideout. When the Kapchemandan saw so many people coming after them, they asked to hold a meeting rather than to fight. When the two pororisyek agreed to settle, my father's brother gave two goats to each of three men, and these were slaughtered for the people who came. As Malinga was the one who blew the horn and had so much help, his goats were the ones to be slaughtered and shared by the people. The people again warned the Kapchemandan to tie and to watch these two boys, or they would seize the property of the clan.

One night, when my father and two of his wives went to Chebonet, where they had the right to collect bananas, a young boy came to the house. He had been sent by Konyi to warn the clan that a man named Kwerit had gathered people together to look for and capture those two young men. He came to our house and my brothers and I told him that our father had gone to Chebonet. When it became dark, the group gathered by Kwerit went to a lookout called Kaboto's Stone and saw that the boys had lit a fire in the cave called Koyo. They crept up slowly and caught them sitting around a fire roasting sweet potatoes which they had stolen. They grabbed the boys and ordered ropes tied around them, but Konyi said: "I am tired of these boys. I have tied them twice. The best thing to do is to kill them." So other clan members from the sangta said that so long as their own clan members agreed that the boys should be killed, they should be killed on the spot. Konyi asked some people to hold their arms and legs and then he took two sticks and choked the Kapchemandan boy, and Kiteywa choked his own brother the same way. Then their bodies were thrown in the bush. Kiteywa's clan was Kamaranga. My father was angry because Konyi had done this without his being there; he was going to tie the boys up again. It was necessary for Konyi and the other man to have the funeral ceremony and have their heads shaved. [Case 215]

The relationship of the two boys to the men who killed them is shown in the accompanying diagram (arrows point to the youths killed). The informant was a son of Kulanyi. It would appear from this incident that the persons who do the killing are supposed to be close kin, though when a man becomes known as a *chorintet* he may be killed with impunity by others if his clansmen fail to restrain him.

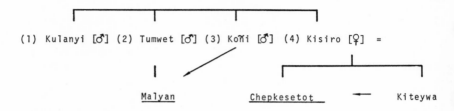

Chemonges Arapcheronko, my father's brother, was beaten to death for stealing. He mostly stole goats and sheep. My father warned him that "there is nothing except death if you behave like this," saying that "the pororyet will come and take our things and attack our kota," and "please flee from here and go to Koin." Chemonges accepted his brother's suggestion, and one of their sisters gave him a gourd of millet. This he refused, saying it was too little to support him. He was offered a second one, but he still refused it. Finally my father gave him a ewe, and so he left and went to a cave near Binyinyi. He stayed there and ate the sheep and the millet. He stole a sheep from a grazing place and ate it. Then he decided to go to Bumet, as he had a wife from that area, and from there he decided to go on to Bugisu. On the way, while crossing the Simu River, he was met by Masabo Kasire, to whom he said he was going to Kamarimba near Budadiri (in Bugisu). But the people with Masabo knew he was a chorintet and they killed him, sending a message back saying: "We have killed your chorintet." His sister cried, but they could not do anything. She asked his father to let her inherit one of his cows, and I have one of the descendants of that cow now. There had been a prior case against Chemonges for stealing goats. When they accused him and held a council, Chemonges just sat at one side and sharpened his knife. He had also stolen a goat, which they traced to where it had been slaughtered. They saw that the spleen, liver, and part of the stomach had been eaten without roasting, and thought it had been a leopard before they found the knife that he had left behind. This goat was a namanya (i.e., borrowed) goat in Chemonges own kraal. They took the remains to the owner, saying that they did not know who had done it but that they thought it was Chemonges. [Case 214]

Finally, cases of theft may be handled by the use of sorcery. For matters dealing with property, kankanet, if available (for it is known only by two Sebei clans), is the magic of choice. The following is a case in which kankanet was used.

Salimu Kapungkech of Kapkech clan spent the night at my house and left 21 shillings there by mistake. He discovered this after he got to Kaproron, and as I was not present when he returned, he asked my wife for the money. She denied she had it. Salimu left, and returned when I was present, but my wife still denied and said, "If you want, you can do mumek in my home." About two months later, my wife's mother paid a visit to Chesoweri, where she was served cooked maize. Salimu (who was Mutongole chief at Chesoweri) learned that the mother of the woman who had taken his money was visiting, and picked up the cobs from which she had been eating.

As she returned home the next day, she fell ill at Kaproron and was unable to cross the Atari River. I was sent for, and brought her home. She began to cry that she was dying and sent for a diviner, who said she had rainbow disease and ordered that a white he-goat be slaughtered to drive it away. Though this was done, the sickness did not go away, but became more serious. Later I received a message that my mother-in-law was dying: "Unless my daughter pays Salimu his money, I shall die." So I went to my wife and said: "You denied that you took the money and now your mother says you did." My wife then admitted she had taken the money but had spent all but 10 shillings. As I learned that Salimu was at Kapchorwa turning in his tax money, I visited him and asked him to take the 10 shillings, saying that I would pay the rest later. One of Salimu's brothers said: "We cannot just release your mother-in-law and accept 21 shillings. You must give a bull before we will release her." I defended myself by saying I would not pay the bull as the theft had happened when I was not present. The people at the kokwet were in my favor, because I feed so many people who come here for meetings, and they asked the brother to accept the shillings and he finally did. My mother-in-law got better in the afternoon and asked for porridge. Salimu brought the medicine he had used and "untied" her. The only expense I had was the he-goat killed to chase away the rainbow disease. Nobody blamed Salimu; he was right to use that magic. [Case 192]

The blacksmiths (who are of special clans) have their own sorcery, using some of the tools of their trade.

This old man here is of my clan and his father was a blacksmith. He had four sons. One had some bananas stolen so the father cut a stem from near the ground. He made new things and did the ceremony of cursing on blacksmith's apparatus. It did not take very long before the children of the person who stole the bananas died. When the children died their skin got as if it has been burnt in the fire. The man came forward and admitted that he was the one who did the stealing. He was ordered to find a sheep. Someone who was not a member of the clan had to dig a hole in the place where the banana stem was. The sheep was suffocated; its stomach was cut and the contents smeared on all members of the thief's clan. They had the ceremony of peace. [Case 98]

Interclan Property Disputes Involving False Claims (Ngokisto)

Six cases fall into the category of ŋokisto. Three concern false claims to elephant tusks, two involve land, and one is a modern case that reached no decision and gives no information. The use of the Sebei term was exemplified by the men at the Law Conference with the following case:

Kapkurot and a group went elephant hunting and he speared an elephant which was not killed. He chased it but could not find it. On their way back they met Kampiya with a hunting party, and Kapkurot described the elephant which had a broken left tusk. Kampiya's party sighted vultures and found the elephant at Kirwot, and knew it was Kapkurot's elephant. They found the arrow and threw it away and claimed that the elephant had been killed by the Karamojong. Kampiya took one tusk and another man took the other, and they denied that they had seen Kapkurot's elephant. Kampiya got four cows for his tusk; the other man obtained three cows. Later one of Kampiya's companions told Kapkurot that one of his friends had been exchanging tusks for cows—one was broken and the other straight, and he thought it was the elephant that Kapkurot had mentioned.

Kapkurot brought the matter before the kokwet of the sangta and accused the two men. The man who took the broken tusk readily admitted that he got three cows, and gave them to Kapkurot, who was pleased by this and gave the man a she-goat, and that ended that matter. But Kampiya denied that he had done so, saying that the animal was his. The case was discussed before the kokwet, which finally decided in favor of Kapkurot, but though Kampiya was ordered to pay four cows, he gave Kapkurot only three. Meanwhile, Kampiya migrated to the other side of the Suam River. Kapkurot went there to visit his father and met Kampiya, who by that time was a chief under the Baganda government. Kampiya accused Kapkurot of stealing the three cows from him, and the Baganda sent askaris to examine Kapkurot's cattle and decided in Kampiya's favor. So Kampiya got back the cows that had been taken by Kapkurot in payment.

When Kapkurot returned, he took a spear for killing elephants, some of the mud from where the elephant had died, and some of the elephant's bones and did magic with them, saying: "If it is I who killed you, go and eat Kampiya and keep eating his children and grandchildren. If not, let Kampiya stay free with his cows."

Meanwhile Kampiya had married and paid the cows in brideprice, and when this wife arrived at Kampiya's home, she died. When the cows went to his father-in-law they started eating feces like dogs. This man, named Maragon, sold the cows to a Karamojong. Kampiya was a man of my clan, and later two children of Kapchemandan that belonged to Malinga died, and also another wife of Kampiya. Other people of the same clan, including a man named Juma, went to Kampiya and organized a kokwet to decide, because they believed Kampiya had done something wrong. Kapkurot was invited to the council. By this time Kampiya had gone to live in Kenya. Kapkurot snatched a single cow from Kampiya. After the kokwet Kampiya paid three cows and allowed Kapkurot to keep the one he had taken. A korosek ceremony was performed to end the matter. [Case 207]

This case illustrates how a matter may be appealed to the court of sorcery. It illustrates (as do several instances) that the Baganda courts disrupted the old legal machinery and caused inequities (according to Sebei legal attitudes) which could be corrected only by sorcery.

A second case suggests that the clan played an important part in assuring compliance.

Kamwendui of the Kapkech clan was a great elephant hunter. He speared an elephant and it disappeared on the plains. Psiwa Arambuya, who was also an elephant hunter, found a dead elephant and took the tusks and sold them both for two heifers. Kamwendui followed his elephant and found it dead, with the tusks removed. He heard that Psiwa had taken them, so he took the matter up in court Psiwa didn't turn up at the meeting of the council and the Kapkech people went away. Psiwa later visited Sipi, where the Kapkech people lived, and was taken into custody by them because he failed to appear at the council. He was kept in their homes as a prisoner for a month because he was unwilling to give up the cows. Finally, he agreed to send a message to his clan to bring those two heifers. They gave the heifers to Kapkech people and so there was no fighting. [Case 58]

A case of land encroachment was brought before the sangta, but ultimately was decided by the use of mumek.

I was about ten years old when two Maina age-set men got into a dispute. One was Chelebey Mosoro of Kaptui and the other was Mwanga Kapchapkoli of Kapchepkot aret. Chelebey accused Mwanga of uprooting the senchontet, but this Mwanga denied. Chelebey called the people of the sangta, who gathered around the hole [where the plant had been uprooted] and performed the oath ceremony. Shortly afterward Mwanga died. The sons of Mwanga and his clan came and wanted to have a friendship. They held the ceremony of peace between the two clans. [Case 27]

In all the incidents involving ngokisto, the court insisted only upon restitution; there was no fine or punishment for the offense. This applies also to matters of contract, as we shall see in chapter 11.

Theft by Use of Force (Kimngonget)

The group at the Law Conference introduced the concept of kimngonget with the case cited below. The essential feature of this form of delict is that it is the taking of property by force, as distinguished from chorset, which is taking by stealth, and ngokisto, which is taking through false representation. No other case was so labeled by informants, though we have already seen an instance of a theft's being made in retaliation against a case of kimngonget (Case 73, p. 172). The subject was introduced in terms of breach of trust, and while Sali's case certainly may be so viewed, breach of trust is not the essential criterion for kimngonget. Indeed, one informant subsequently questioned whether this case is properly labeled kimngonget, as the original act was stealth. The Law Conference participants apparently held the subsequent use of open force the overriding consideration.

Once there was a man named Sali who had but one cow and a few sheep and goats. He felt that he was not getting anything more, and wanted to be a rich man, so he decided he would go and live with Mwotil and herd his cattle and eventually steal them from him. So he went to live with Mwotil and they herded the cattle on alternate days. One day he decided to steal this man's cattle, and fifty goats and sheep that belonged to Mwotil and his neighbors. They were living in Tukumo at Binyinyi, and he left that place and went as far as Kaptapkoy with the animals. When he got there he raised an alarm, as it was becoming dark and he wanted help. The people of the area answered the alarm and found him with eleven cows (including the one of his own) and the small stock, and helped him bring the animals home. He divided some of the sheep and goats among the people, giving each two or three or four, and told them to slaughter them and eat well so they would be strong enough to fight the next day.

The next morning Mwotil and his people raised an alarm, and a large group gathered. Sali had already told his people to collect themselves, but when they saw so many people coming they decided not to fight but to hold a kokwet. They asked Sali why he took the animals and if these people had owed him anything, trying to find out why he took those cows. Sali explained that he had been trying to get rich for a long time but had not succeeded and he had decided to make kimngonget [the act of taking something by force] in order that he might become rich, and that was why he had robbed Mwotil. He asked the pororyet people to support him, so he could have these cattle, and promised that if they would fight and chase away the others he would kill a bullock for them. That is why the people of the pororyet stayed. The Kapcheptemkoñ people had information that the Kono people were coming and they fought them and chased them away, but did not kill anybody. After that, Sali took a bullock from Arambuya to slaughter for the people who had helped him, giving a namanya cow in exchange. They ate the bull, and Sali kept the cattle. Later, when he was an old man, he said that he robbed Mwotil because he wanted to make kimngonget and the people wanted to help him. Sali was a *mwongintet* [a person who takes by force].

This happened when I was very young. After the Baganda arrived, Taskin Kapkamba was the first person to make an accusation. The case was decided against Sali, and he was given five head of cattle. Later Mwotil accused Sali. The case was again decided against Sali and he had to pay the five head of cows to Mwotil. One of the five head of cattle, it happened, was kamanakan from a Bumet man, and it was given to the man who owned the kamanakan cow.

[Afer some discussion, the informant said, "Oh yes, I forgot," and then completed the material on this case as follows.] Sali's son had lost many children, and also the others of the descendants of those cows became white and the cows' teats became brown. When Sali's son saw that his children were dying, he sent a message to Mwotil saying that though his father took the cattle, "Please, I would like to pay them back." Sali's son took the descendants of the cattle that had been stolen—four of them—and one of his own, and paid these to Mwotil. From that time on Sali's son produced children. There was no korosek ceremony. Sali's son changed his name from Chemonges to Labu. Labu died but has left many sons. [Case 211]

This case has a number of facets that deserve illumination. First, though the instance was cited by a nephew of Sali, there was no expression that he had done wrong, but rather that Sali had been clever. It was suggested that Sali's feeding the members of his pororyet with some of the stolen animals was "like a bribe to the judge." It is not clear just how the affair went the next morning. As I read it, Sali had convinced enough people that he should be supported so that Mwotil and those who stood with him were driven off. Ultimately, the animals were returned, but only in terms of other legal machinery—Baganda law and the use of sorcery—and long after Sali and his family had prospered economically.

A case in which it was said that the theft involved violence (and thus might be classed as kimngonget) is of interest because in this use of kankanet the person was allowed to die, despite the intercession of the prophet. The informants felt that the man was justified in not letting his victim live.

A man named Kapchokey came one day while the Baganda were here and stole Areya's 30 shillings. Areya was an appointed chief [in the Buganda authority established under the Muganda general, Kakunguru] at that time. He did kankanet on Kapchokey, who was sick then for a long time and was unable to go to the latrine and finally died. Before his death Matui asked Areya to release him, but Areya had lost his temper and would not agree to do so. There was no action to be taken against Areya.

It was explained that Areya's lack of compassion was because Kapchokey had stolen the money with violence. Furthermore, he had spoiled Areya's position as chief by taking government money. [Case 189]

The next case stands somewhere between a law case and warfare. It illustrates both the lack of unity among the Sebei tribes and the importance of ntarastit in reestablishing a measure of harmony among them.

The Mbai people were very proud that they are more numerous than the Sapiñ people. Women from Sapiñ went to buy bananas when there was a shortage of food, for the Mbai were the only people who had bananas. The Mbai people planned to come to Moyok (in Sapiñ) and take things by force. They wanted to take pots, sheep, goats, yams, and other food in the fields and in the granaries. The men came to take all these things by force and brought their women for they felt that the Sapiñ people were so few that they needn't fear them. The people at Moyok called an alarm. The people from Kapcheptemkoñ pororyet (to which Moyok belongs) and of Murkutwa pororyet got together and attacked the Mbai people and drove them back, so that the pots they collected fell and were broken and the grass was mowed down by the speed of their flight. It was raining and the rocks were slippery and many of the Mbai men were killed. The Sapiñ men told the people not to kill them at all, but to threaten them only. If it had been the Karamojong, they would have killed them.

When the prophet Matui heard about this, he ordered the ntarastit ceremony. He blamed the Mbai people. He called for the ntarastit ceremony before there could be any revenge. I attended this ceremony as a boy and stood on the rocks where I could watch the battle. These Mbai raiders were prevented from slaughtering cattle but they did get the sheep and goats.

There was no compensation case. The people here did *yotunet* [cleansing ceremony for persons who have killed somebody] but those who killed the Mbai people couldn't cut the shoulders [as a mark of honor for slaying enemies] because they were Sebei people. [Case 67]

Theft as a Legal Device

Two cases (Cases 212, 213, pp. 200–201) of theft were specifically initiated to force the owner before a kokwet. In both instances the theft was from a man who would not meet his contractual obligations. The cases are discussed in the chapter on contracts. I think, however, that such thefts are a semiformalized procedure; that by stealing a man can force a public hearing of an earlier (but not actionable) grievance. Several occasions where sons successfully forced their fathers into giving them property by first taking it have been cited, though if this occurs under modern court procedures, it does not have the desired effect. Again, one informant said that the clan of a murdered man would constantly steal from the clan of the murderer to force them into paying the compensation.

General Remarks Regarding the Law on Theft

Conflicts over property are frequent in Sebeiland; when they occur they are between individuals, and are generally resolved by the action of the community. In most instances, the community acts only to bring restitution of the property or its equivalent to the rightful owner, though it does have the right to fine a miscreant, and under ntarastit, has the further right to punish by plundering his property. A habitual thief must, however, be restrained from such action by his own clansmen. If they fail to do so, he may be killed with impunity by others. He is, in fact, usually dispatched by his relatives. It is noteworthy for our general thesis about the difference between the law of property and the law of violence that in those cases when ntarastit was invoked against property delicts, it was applied only to the individual, whereas when it was invoked against a murderer, it was applied to his clan.

Actually, the low incidence of cattle theft is surprising. Cattle are important in parts of Sebeiland, and we shall find several cases of conflict over cattle in the context of contractual law (as we did in family matters), but the number of instances of outright theft was quite small in contrast with the number of cases of land encroachment. The rarity of outright theft of cattle is the more surprising in that the Sebei belong to a cultural group that regard cattle raiding against enemies as an honorable activity, and one might have considered cattle theft acceptable among the Sebei tribes (after the fashion of the action by Sali in Case 211). I believe the low incidence reported and the specific denials of the informants reflect the reality of the situation among the Sebei, at least during the past century. Perhaps the rarity of cattle theft simply stems from the circumstance that it would be exceedingly difficult to hide the fact of such a theft, inasmuch as Sebei men generally recognize individual cattle over a wide area.

We also find remarkably few cases involving the theft of minor chattels, either in the modern courts or in olden times. To be sure, the Sebei had few personal possessions, but they did have them. It is my feeling that the theft of personal property—spear, shield, stool, native clothing, or ornaments—would constitute such presumptive evidence that the thief was motivated by a desire to engage in witchcraft that he would not readily steal personal items, which tend to have a mystic or magical connection with their owners. (This does not apply to food, livestock, elephant tusks, money, or modern clothes.[9]) Furthermore, the Sebei have magical means of harming persons who steal small movable property. We were advised, for instance, to pluck some feathers from each of our chickens so that we could use them for magic if a chicken was stolen.

The law of theft would seem basically to have been designed in terms of foodstuffs—granaries, food in the field, goats. Its application to land is probably of relatively recent origin, and the law does not seem to have developed a very high level of sophistication. Regulations with respect to jurisdiction, level of court action, and formulation of rules of punishment in accordance with the severity of the crime are generally wanting. In an earlier period of Sebei history, property was largely of three kinds: cattle, foodstuffs, and personal possessions. Of these, only foodstuffs were regularly subject to theft in the sense of chorset, for cattle could be taken only by force, while personal possessions were limited and too dangerous to steal (as their theft might be defined as an offense of witchcraft). With the shift from cattle to farming and the elimination of patterns of aggressive cattle-raiding, the nature of property delicts changed; theft of food and of chattels has become more important and land encroachment tends to dominate the court cases involving property. The legal machinery of community action, particularly the law operative under ntarastit, is a crude means of meeting

[9] Modern clothing is occasionally used in witchcraft, but the close identity with the individual is lacking, so that present-day thefts of clothing would be treated just as thefts of money or food.

the need for adequate legal institutions. Clearly the machinery did not develop the refinements necessary for meeting even the pre-European, let alone the current, needs of Sebei society. I return to these considerations in the concluding chapter.

The General Character of Sebei Contracts

By "contract" I mean the orderly arrangements, explicit or implicit, of details regarding a transaction freely entered into by two or more parties, in which there is an exchange of property or services. Contracts are important in Sebei society, and have been so from time immemorial. They play an important role in the economy of both cattle-keeping and farming, and a good deal of litigation results from breaches in contractual arrangements.

The Sebei enter into contracts for the exchange of cattle and other livestock, agricultural commodities, and land, and for the exchange of services. They also enter into marriage contracts, which have much the same character as those for goods, services, and land. (Because marriage contracts relate intimately to family aspects of Sebei law, I have discussed them in the chapter on the family.) The Sebei regularly exchange animals one for another; they exchange animals for food (in Sebei semantics the word "food" is reserved for the starchy staples, as distinct from meat, vegetables, and other comestibles) ; they enter into contracts for work in caring for both animals and land; and they sell, rent, and exchange land. Such arrangements are so closely parallel to contracts in Western law that I consider it proper to call them such. As I see it, the older contractual arrangements were quite explicit in their implications of rights and obligations of the two parties, but in the evolution of economic activities new situations have arisen, so that old contractual forms have had to meet new circumstances. The fact that they lack explicitness in these newer situations has not only led to litigation, but has created many social difficulties. In these areas there is a tendency today to reduce the basic considerations to writing.

I believe that certain general propositions hold for all contractual arrangements.

1. Contracts are between individuals, not between groups. This principle applies even to the marriage contract, though in this instance there are ancillary parties to the contract.

2. There is no law of limitation on contractual obligations. "A debt," the Sebei say, "never rots." An obligation once contracted for continues beyond the life of the individual; it may become part of the inheritance of both the creditor and the debtor.

3. A contract may be revoked by either party in a position to do so, or to put it more exactly, a man cannot take action against another for withdrawal from a promise to perform provided that restitution of the original consideration is made. Thus a man who has taken a bullock for a future heifer may withdraw from the contract by returning the bullock or its equivalent. With certain limitations upon the freedom of women, this proposition applies even to the marriage contract.[1]

4. All adult men are competent to engage in contractual negotiations; women and young men (uncircumcised) are not competent to so engage. Even when women's goods are involved, the negotiation is legally between the men,[2] though the women clearly have a voice in the matter.

5. No contract implies a time clause. There is no means other than moral suasion to force a person to perform within a limited time. A man may have to go to considerable lengths to enforce performance on a contract; however, in a community of men known personally to one another, moral forces serve to press conformity to expectations, and failure to perform may be brought before a kokwet.

6. Though in case of a dispute the testimony of witnesses is given due consideration, contractual arrangements may be made without either public ceremony or formal witnesses. This

[1] The marriage contract is not, however, between husband and wife, but between the husband (or his father) and the father of the bride.

[2] Some exception to this practice appears to be developing.

is particularly true of cattle contracts, where neighbors would know as a matter of course that an arrangement was made; in land exchanges formal witnessing has emerged.

7. In modern Sebeiland, contracts are frequently reduced to writing. Nowadays written contracts are usually employed for land exchanges, occasionally for bride-price, but never (to my knowledge) for cattle exchanges.

Ownership and Dispersal of Cattle through Contractual Arrangements

Before discussing the nature of cattle contracts, it is necessary to appreciate a few points regarding the characteristics of Sebei cattle-keeping. The Sebei, like the people of other tribes, do not each keep all their cattle in their own kraal. Hence the animals in a herd do not belong to only one man. The animals in a man's kraal fall into three categories: *sikonik* are the cattle he owns, including the tokapsoy and those smeared for his wives; *namanisyek,* are the cattle belonging to a man under the *namanyantet* contract in an exchange arrangement; and *kamanakanik* belong to another person, but are kept by him to herd. In addition to the cattle in his own herd, a man may have cows in another man's herd, either those exchanged under the namanyantet contract, which are spoken of as being in *namut,* or those he has loaned to others, which are spoken of as being in *kamanaktay.* (In addition, a wealthy cattle owner may have separate cattle camps in different places, but the herds and the kraals would be considered his own and do not concern us here.) The arrangements can best be understood in terms of the diagram on page 190.

Men of wealth have numerous arrangements, under both namanyantet and kamanakan. It should also be made clear here that the animals he has as namanisyek are not exchanges for those that are in namut, nor are the kamanakanik exchanged for those in kamanaktay. Normally each animal that is in namut or is namanyantet represents a separate exchange contract, though often several cattle are put under loan to the same person at one time. Many men in the area devoted to intensive

Cattle Owned by a Sebei Herdsman

in
kamanaktay
(loan)

in
namut
(exchange)

sikonik
(both tokapsoy and
cattle smeared for
his wives)

kamanakanik
(loan)

namanisyek
(exchange)

Cattle in Kraal(s) of a
Sebei Herdsman

cultivation place all their animals with one person. The details of these contractual arrangements are presented in subsequent sections.

While we are concerned here with the legal aspects of the namanya contract, we should consider briefly why these arrangements are important socially and economically. The Sebei have numerous rationalizations for engaging in such contracts. They consider it bad form to slaughter one's own animal and must therefore exchange it for another. They believe that animals will be more productive if exchanged. They say: "Sweet is the cow of a debt," and "The reason we like namanya exchanges is that if the heifer dies you can go to the owner and he gives you another, but if you buy it outright, you have lost everything." They also say that, because of namanya, "The man who is a slaughterer [of cows] does not lose cattle," and finally, "Do not collect all your outstanding debts; leave some, for if tomorrow you incur an indebtedness, you have a place of supply."

Some of these statements are rationalizations, to be sure; but some express realistic appraisals. Let us examine some of the social and economic realities served by exchange arrangements.

1. A person with few or no cows can, with work, astuteness, and some good fortune, build up his herd. I know one man who claims to have developed a fair herd from some chickens.

2. A person with few or no cows can obtain some, which will provide his family with milk. Furthermore, he has the pleasure that Sebei feel in having cattle around them.

3. A person with many cows spreads the risk on his cattle, for the major calamities that decimate the herds (disease and cattle raids) tend to strike individual kraals or locations.

4. A person with many cows may have more than are convenient for his wives to milk, or for his family to herd.

5. By having cattle belonging to many people in his kraal, a man creates a broader public interest in the welfare of his herd; should enemies take the cattle in a raid, other owners will have a stronger incentive to help him retrieve the animals.

6. Exchange obscures the number of cattle a man owns; the Sebei do not like their riches made public, for fear of jealousy

and hatred and too heavy a demand placed upon them—and, in modern times, the prying eye of the tax collector.

7. Finally, through exchanges one creates a network of quasi-kinship obligations which can be of help in many diverse social contexts, from obtaining free beer to getting assistance in battles.

In sum, then, the entry into namanya arrangements creates advantages of one kind or another for all persons in the society—advantages that are economic and rational in terms of personal wealth and status enhancement, as well as affording sentimental ties.

The Namanya Contract

The prototype for all Sebei contracts (except the marriage contract) is undoubtedly the namanya exchange. The classic namanya contract is as follows: a person who wants to slaughter a bullock asks another for it, offering in exchange a heifer, which is to be born from one of his cows. The person who furnishes the bullock takes the heifer, keeps it until she has produced a heifer, and when that heifer is ready to bear young, returns the original animal to its owner. In short, a man pays a future cow for a present bullock. The etymology of the term was given to me as "to catch the stomach" (*nam*, "catch"; *mo*, "stomach") .[3]

This type of exchange, it seems to me, has all the essential elements of a contract: it is an arrangement freely entered into by both parties; there is a recognized quid pro quo, in which each party seeks something he wants, the purposes of the arrangement being primarily economic considerations; there is a recognized obligation on both parties to perform in accordance with the implicit contractual arrangements; and failure to perform may result in public action in an effort to enforce performance. It must also be recognized, however, that such a contract has extralegal and extraeconomic meaning; that the parties to such a deal acquire, besides the economic connection, a social relationship that requires mutual obligations with respect to

[3] Dr. Montgomery accepts the root form *nam* as relevant but doubts that the stem for stomach is there, as the form is analogous to other verbal nouns of the same type.

their interpersonal behavior. They become *tilyet* (pl., *tilyonu-tek*) to one another, which was glossed as "kin of the cow"; they call one another *tilyeñu*, "my cattle-kin"; [4] they are expected to be hospitable with respect to beer or food; and they are strictly forbidden to sleep with one another's wives. I do not think these social aspects in the least vitiate the concept of contract, but they do mean—as one would expect in a homogeneous and small-scale society—that the economic nexus implicit in the contract becomes translated into a tie of sentiment.

There are variations on this base: exchanges of like kind may be made between goats, sheep, or even chickens; they may be made between chickens and small stock, small stock and cattle, granaries or fields of food and either small stock or cattle, and nowadays money and cattle. Namanya is a standard means of making exchanges. Sebei cattle owners normally have many such exchanges operative at any one time; one man listed thirty-eight in which he was involved on one side or the other.

The namanya exchange is initiated by the person who wants the bullock (or other commodity) and for which he is willing to give a heifer. We might call him the buyer, or as my interpreters did, the borrower, but we shall avoid both these terms (which carry inappropriate legal implications) and call him the *initiator* of the exchange. He may go to any person of his acquaintance to ask an exchange; the man who agrees we shall call the *respondent*. (The Sebei do not have differential words for these parties to the contract; each is tilyet.) There are no social or legal limitations upon those with whom a person may enter into an exchange; I have instances between brothers, between fathers and sons, between a man and his wife's kin, between neighbors, between persons living at a great distance from each other, and between Sebei and members of other tribes (though unless they live nearby or are well acquainted, the last type of exchange may result in difficulties).

The agreement is generally for a specific animal in the respondent's kraal. For one thing, the animal may be "smeared" for one of the respondent's wives, and she would have to agree

---

[4] The term is used in address, but does not override a true kinship such as brother, nephew, and the like.

(and the heifer acquired would be hers, in the same sense).
Again, there is often a need for an animal of a specified color.
But the animal turned over to the respondent by the initiator is
not normally specified. I was told that long ago it was often a yet
unborn animal—the first heifer to be born from a specified cow,
for instance. Nowadays it is normally a heifer about ready to be
serviced, and often the particular animal is indicated if the
respondent so desires, though, as we shall see, this aspect is
really of little consequence. Once the agreement is reached, the
two parties become tilyet to each other; that is, the moral implications of the social relationship are operative.

Protocol demands that the initiator send a kinsman or a
neighbor to fetch the animal, which is normally done at once;
however, the animal remains the property of the respondent
until it is utilized by the initiator, in the sense that the respondent is responsible for replacing it should it die.[5] Protocol also
demands that the respondent send his relatives or friends to
pick up the heifer, though there is no time demand upon his
doing so. He may delay as long as he wishes, but usually he
wants to get the animal as soon as possible; his problem is apt to
be the other way about, for the initiator of such contracts frequently finds means of delaying the fulfillment of his responsibility. We shall return to the matter of enforcement.

The heifer given by the initiator to the respondent remains
(in the sense indicated above) the property of the initiator.
Actually, the initiator has entered into a contract to supply a
productive cow to the respondent at some future date. In the
normal course of events, the heifer is taken by the respondent,
who takes care of it (we must remember that there are no

[5] This occurrence is not frequent, for normally the initiator is seeking
the animal for some immediate purpose and will slaughter it as soon as he
gets it home. It does happen, however, as is indicated in the following case
taken from a funeral kokwet in the highlands area.

Claimant had taken a ram of the deceased which had been killed by hyenas
before it could be slaughtered. The deceased had argued that this was the fault
of the claimant and asked for 5 shillings in addition [about 15 percent of its
value] before he would replace the ram, but this was not done. [Case 143]

Though the case was not resolved, it does indicate that the basic responsibility for delivering the animal intact to the point of use lies with the
respondent.

pasturage costs or stud fees) and enjoys the milk when she is freshened. He keeps the animal and her offspring. If she produces a bullock, that animal belongs to the initiator, and he may (but usually does not) take it to his own kraal after it is weaned. Whether he does so or not, it is recognized as his; if it dies, it is his loss. Ultimately, when the original namanya heifer has herself produced a heifer calf (the calf that "releases" the namanya, in Sebei parlance—the *kotyak,* from *tyac,* "untie") , and when this calf is ready to be serviced, the original animal may be taken back by the initiator, leaving the F_1 calf with the respondent to whom it now belongs. The obligation does not really end there; should the F_1 calf be barren, then there is an obligation on the part of the initiator to supply a substitute. Indeed, the initiator is theoretically seeing to it that the respondent has an additional animal in his herd, and normally a reproductive female. The arrangement may be clarified and better kept in mind by means of the diagram on page 196.

Any circumstance that hampers the performance is essentially the initiator's responsibility, though some fraction of it may be shared by the respondent. Thus, if the original animal dies, if it is barren, if its calves are all bullocks—under any of these circumstances the initiator must replace the animal. The respondent may, however, dissolve the contract by accepting a bullock from the initiator. The animal must be replaced even though it could be shown that negligence on the part of the respondent was responsible for its death; his negligence is not formally relevant to the contract, though a man might hesitate to exchange with a person known to be a poor husbandman or a careless keeper of property. The respondent does have an obligation to preserve evidence that the animal died or was killed, by keeping its skin; presumably neighbors would immediately know if it was taken in a raid. A man with cattle in another's kraal, whether namanya or as kamanaktay (discussed elsewhere) , makes a practice of talking to his tilyet's neighbors when about to visit the tilyet, so he may receive unprompted news of the condition of his cattle. Sebei make a regular practice of being au courant with their neighbors' affairs.

The respondent does share some liability. Just as in the request for a payment of 5 shillings when a ram died (Case 143, p.

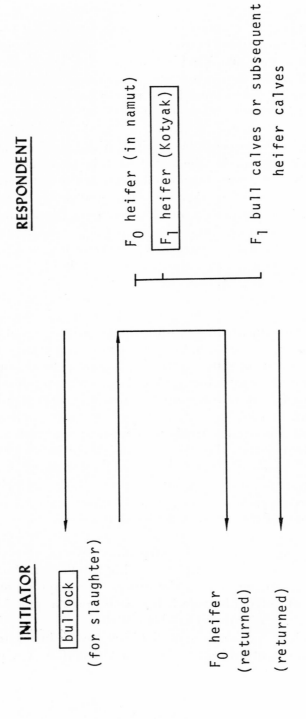

INITIATOR

bullock
(for slaughter)

F_0 heifer
(returned)

(returned)

RESPONDENT

F_0 heifer (in namut)

F_1 heifer (Kotyak)

F_1 bull calves or subsequent
heifer calves

(ultimately the animals exchanged are the bullock received
by the initiator in exchange for the F_1 heifer)

194), when a namanya cow dies the respondent is expected to give a sheep or a goat in order to obtain a replacement—a value of 15–20 percent of the cow.

> The deceased [whose estate was under discussion at the funeral kokwet] had given a namanya cow for a bullock, which he "ate," and she produced a bull. Unfortunately, both the namanya cow and her bullock died, and this fact had been reported to the deceased. The deceased had said that he would have to be given a ewe and would then replace the namanya cow. Claimant has not yet given the ewe, which represents the meat of the two cows that died, but will do so and then will expect to get a namanya cow in exchange. [Case 145]

In one funeral kokwet, a man made a claim that he had given the namanya heifer, which was subsequently stolen in a raid by the Karamojong, and that replacement of the stolen animal became the respondent's responsibility; however, he was decisively overridden by the kokwet (Case 251).

Cases can run on through several animal deaths, though ultimately there is an end. In the following case, the family of the deceased refused to furnish another animal; if the record is correct in detail, the matter had, in fact, been closed. The Sebei feel that some exchange relations are ill-starred and will close them out. In the following instance, Kambuya terminated the relationship by giving a bull rather than a third namanya.

> Kambuya had a bull from Arapkoroyeñ's father, for which he gave him a cow which died, then a second one which gave no milk as its teats were faulty, and when it was returned the man requested a bull to finish the debt and clear off the matter. Kambuya took a bull from me and gave it to him, but it also died. Arapkoroyeñ is now claiming another bull in replacement, but it is being refused as he has been given enough. [Case 254]

The situation with respect to continuance of the obligation was summarized as follows:

> If the namanya doesn't produce calves, or if the calves all die, then you must replace the heifer, but if it produces bulls three or four times, he [the respondent] gives the namanya and bulls back and you give him a heifer outright; that is no longer namanya. [Law Conference]

The following case extends the matter still further, but closes with decisiveness.

Salawi went to Mwoko and asked for a bull, which he slaughtered [for a feast], and gave Mwoko a heifer as namanya. In time she produced a heifer and then a bull. So Salawi came to Mwoko and took the original cow and the bullock. After they came back to Salawi's kraal the original namanya produced a second bull, but unfortunately the Karamojong came and stole them all. Salawi went to Mwoko and said: "My tilyet, I am left without anything." By this time the heifer left with Mwoko had produced three calves—one heifer and two bulls, making a total of four. Salawi was allowed to take the original heifer with two bulls, leaving the other heifer with Mwoko. When Salawi arrived home he paid one of these bulls for bride-price, so that that heifer remained with one bull. Then rinderpest broke out during Ñongki times and killed them both. Salawi went to Mwoko saying that the two animals had died, except for the one paid as bride-price, and asked Mwoko to give him an animal from the same family. Mwoko, who was Ali's grandfather, refused, saying: "You have taken cows two times. How long are we going to go on sharing?" So Salawi took the matter before the kokwet. The kokwet took place at Burgoyem and after hearing both sides of the case, kokwet said that he thought the case should go against Salawi, but asked Mwoko how many animals he had as descendants of the heifer, to which Mwoko answered that he had five. Kokwet said to Mwoko: "Give him just one and that will be the final one." Mwoko gave him a white heifer, and that was the end of the matter. [Case 221]

However, we must not overparticularize; though the contract is a rationally oriented, purposeful, and self-serving action, it also creates a sense of social obligation. In the following instance the respondent felt compelled to replace an animal after the contract had been fulfilled, because the original heifer died soon after it was returned to the initiator's kraal.

My grandfather killed a bull belonging to Bartile, but died before he had paid the namanya. My father, Musani, paid the heifer, and when the cow arrived at Bartile's it produced two heifers, so Musani brought back the cow and her second heifer. After the cow returned home, it died, leaving the heifer. Musani went to Bartile and asked him to give him another heifer, which Bartile did, for the original heifer had multiplied. The grandchildren of the original cow replaced her. [Case 220]

This case was reported at the Law Conference, and the men agreed that "though the request was made politely and it was accepted without difficulty, the matter would have been taken before the kokwet if Bartile had refused, as it was a matter of rule." I am inclined to believe that if one member of the contract has prospered in the exchange while the other has lost, there is a moral obligation upon the former to help the latter.[6] Several cases, including the last two reported, would so indicate. We must not forget that there is not only an established social bond between the contracting parties, but also a continuing interest in further contractual arrangements with members of the community.

While the namanya contract establishes a social bond between the two parties, it remains a contract, and like all contracts is occasionally reneged on. The absence of a time clause makes infractions inevitable and enforcement difficult, for no person need refuse to perform, but must merely find excuses for delay. Furthermore, the social obligations between tilyet often make it difficult for a person to bring action. It might be noted that in some of the cases already cited this action was much delayed; for instance, in Case 220, cited above, the namanya obligation was paid by the son of the man who contracted it.[7] For this reason, a man will use the legal fiction of an obvious theft in order to bring the matter before a kokwet, in cases where etiquette demands he remain silent about the matter.

Both the following cases were offered in the Law Conference. We were discussing the theft of chattels, and the usage was introduced by Ali Musani, who said:

There was no such stealing except in a different way. They used to steal a spear or a shield, but this meant the man wanted to demand compensation. He stole the object without the knowledge of the owner, and when the theft was reported, he spoke out that he had

[6] This obligation need not be relevant to general economic circumstances of the two persons, but only the "family" of the cattle directly involved. The Sebei reckon cattle in terms of progeny in the female line indefinitely, so that, for example, I was shown cows presently in the kraal which "were taken in a raid" perhaps seventy-five years before.

[7] In *Kambuya's Cattle* many old obligations are reported; some of them, indeed, changing circumstances have made practically uncollectable.

indeed stolen the object because the owner owed him a debt. Once the people hear that, the message goes back to the owner, and the matter is brought into the open. When they are in the kokwet, the man who stole will agree that it was because of the debt he claims. In the kokwet there will be witnesses testifying that the owner is indebted, and the people will demand that he pay this compensation and that the thief should return the spear, or whatever he has stolen. This opens the way for a man to demand compensation.

In the foregoing case, it would seem that the man who stole the shield needed the excuse of an insult before he could take the action. Nothing similar, however, is reported in the second case, and it is possible that the insult merely confirmed Mwoko's conviction to press his demand.

Tumwet who lived in Tegeres was a man of Kaptanya clan; he owed a cow to Mwoko, my grandfather. Mwoko kept asking for it over and over again and Tumwet kept saying that he didn't have the cow, until Mwoko became fed up. One time Tumwet brewed beer and Mwoko decided that as his tilyet was having a beer party, he might as well enjoy it. Tumwet saw his tilyet and invited him to a certain pot and they enjoyed beer until it started raining, when they went inside the house and continued drinking. While the beer party was still going on, Mwoko had left the spear and shield outside, but when it started to rain he gave them to Tumwet to put in the place where spears are kept (called *rewet*). When Tumwet got hold of these, he made a special noise (called *koyton*) that goes tsk-tsk, and said: "What kind of tilyet is this man?" and "He had better be eaten by crows."

Mwoko heard this but he kept silent, and later in the evening some of the people left but Mwoko spent the night there. In the middle of the night after everybody was asleep he took his own spear and shield down from the rewet, and also Tumwet's shield, and left. The next morning Tumwet wanted to go out but he saw that his shield was gone and he wondered who might have taken it. He realized that Mwoko had left during the night and might have taken the shield. Tumwet asked his son to go out and visit Mwoko, who lived in Tuban. So the son tracked Mwoko to Tuban and told him that his father's shield had been lost yesterday and did he know who took it. Immediately Mwoko said: "I took it yesterday when I took my shield and spear, because I heard your father say 'What kind of tilyet is this?—he should be taken by crows.' I always demand the cow that he owes me and he keeps putting me off. That is why I stole the shield."

So when Tumwet's son heard this from Mwoko he reported the information back to his father. That meant they wanted a kokwet. Tumwet collected the kirwokik from his side and went to Tuban and held discussions. When the kokwet was held, Tumwet admitted that he had abused his tilyet but that he hadn't intended it, as he had been drunk. He provided Mwoko with beer and accepted that he was guilty and also that he owed a cow to Mwoko. The kokwet asked Mwoko: "If this man had not abused you, would you have taken his shield?" And Mwoko said: "No, only because he abused me." Tumwet was asked: "Do you owe the cow?" Tumwet asked Mwoko to come in the usual manner for demanding the cow. The kokwet took the shield and gave it to Tumwet and told Mwoko to ask for his debt in the proper way.

Mwoko continued to claim his debt but it was not paid even when he died. But my father, Kuryo, a first Ñongki age-set man, inherited the debt and went on claiming it. When Mwoko had stolen the shield, Kuryo had just been circumcised. He continued to demand that cow from Tumwet until he was given it. My brothers and I still have the descendants of that cow. There are six brothers and we all have divided those descendants. We call them *tetapkugo,* cow of grandfather. I was jealous of giving them to my brothers but they nearly fought me, so I divided them. [Case 212]

My father, Psekuton, asked Araptay for a he-goat, but did not give the namanya goat in return. Araptay kept asking Psekuton for that goat for a long time. One day there was a beer party at the home of Chemundwa of Kapyis clan, and Araptay got hold of Psekuton's spear and took it. When Psekuton found his spear was missing, he knew it might have been taken by Araptay. He went home and the next morning took a he-goat to his beer host and asked that it be taken to Araptay. When Chemundwa did this, Araptay said that he had stolen the spear because Psekuton owed him a goat. He accepted the goat and gave back the spear. Psekuton had returned a goat to the man instead of giving him a she-goat namanya [thus ending the tilyet relation entirely]. There was no kokwet over this matter at all. [Case 213]

Contract may be enforced by the use of kankanet sorcery, as indicated in the following case, though here, in fact, the pororyet intervened, and Mwanga did not have to pay compensation.

Mwanga took cattle [as namanya] belonging to Malinga Kamalach and Mwanga refused to return these cattle when Malinga asked for them. So Malinga did kankanet and Mwanga became sick for a long

time, with swarms of lice on his head and other parts of the body.
Malinga asked the pororyet to come together and the pororyet asked
Mwanga what happened to the cows. Mwanga said that he had had
Malinga's cows but they all died of rinderpest and he blamed Malinga for doing kankanet on him. Malinga was ordered by the pororyet to "release" Mwanga, which he had to do. At first Malinga
didn't believe that his cows had died of rinderpest, but it was
"proved," and from that time Mwanga got well and the two men are
friends. Mwanga brewed beer and invited Malinga, who brought
the Kamichagi man who had actually done the kankanet, and they
drank and spit beer on one another.

When I asked why kankanet worked if he was not guilty, Mwanga
said that he had eaten the cows, though they died of rinderpest, and
had drunk the milk and was sleeping on the skins. [Case 191] [8]

The following case does not mention the need for such sub-
terfuge; perhaps the outright refusal of the tilyet makes it unnecessary. The case also demonstrates the fact of appeal from
sangta to pororyet.

Somebody took Muyembe Arapyatya's bull and gave him a heifer
calf, and when it grew up Arapyatya returned the cow. Soon afterward she died, and Arapyatya went back to his tilyet and asked to
share the calf as namanya again (i.e., that it would be treated as the
original namanya cow), but the tilyet refused. The matter was
brought before the kokwet of Kapchewok and members of the sangta
ordered the tilyet to keep the calf as namanya and Arapyatya was ordered to brew beer for his tilyet. This was done. The tilyet did not
agree with the order from the Kapchewok kokwet and he appealed
to Ngeywa, who was the kirwokintet of Chema pororyet. This kirwokintet settled the matter and ordered the tilyet to share the cow.
By this time the heifer produced by the original namanya had in
turn produced a heifer which was old enough, so that first [F_1]
heifer was returned to Arapyatya. [Case 199]

Because contracts are made between persons whose circumstances are well known to each other, patience and timing may
be required. The following case was reported in 1954, nearly
twenty years after the initial exchange; it indicates clearly certain rules and expectations.

In 1936 someone borrowed a bull and gave a heifer in return. In
1939 the heifer had a calf but it died. In 1941 it had a bull. The in-

[8] Both principals were present at the Law Conference (though the case
was not reported by either). Though kankanet is not supposed to work
unless the party is guilty, this did not seem to apply in this instance.

oculation started and the cow died and we returned the bull. The man still owes us. We remember this, but his cattle have all died and he now has none and is an old man. If he dies I have to go to report that he has my cow and the sons will remember. If the sons don't have any cows, I will be patient to wait for a daughter to be married and then I will ask for my cows. The older son inherits the debt, but both of them will be responsible for it. I cannot claim from anyone else in his clan. But if the man had no children, I could claim from whoever inherited his property. [Case 8]

Social pressure appears to be a major means of maintaining and enforcing contracts. It must be remembered that normally a Sebei of substance will want continuing contractual arrangements with many of his fellowmen over the years, and like any modern businessman, will behave in such a way as to preserve his credit rating. The action of such pressure is exemplified in the following two cases.

I asked Chemei for a bull, which he agreed to give me. When I was driving it home, he sent his son to get it back, and I said, "All right. Take your bull back." A long time later he came to me and said that he was wrong and that if I wanted another bull that I should please ask him for it. So I did take the bull, but I took five years to pay him the heifer. People had been blaming him for doing what he had, and that is why he came and offered the bull. Such a man who does not keep a contract is called *sorintet*. [Case 219]

Leleywo went to Chemonges and asked him for a black bull, for which he paid a cream-colored heifer. Later there was a famine and Leleywo asked him for the heifer back, so he could exchange it for a granary of millet, but Chemonges refused: "I am not going to accept that. Remember the other day you took Sayekwo Araputa's bull and gave a heifer as namanya, but later went and took it back without asking, and then when Sayekwo came to you, you said you would give him another bull. But it took you a long time to do even that." Then Leleywo took his small heifer to the man who owned the granary, but that man said to Leleywo: "You are a bad man and I am not going to exchange that granary for a small heifer." So Leleywo did not get the food. [Case 218]

That these pressures exist and are effective is further indicated by negative evidence. In almost every instance (from diverse parts of Sebeiland) when a property conflict with a Mugisu was made public, no mutually satisfactory resolution was achieved.

The operation of contractual obligation rests upon a system of mutual trust and interdependence.

It will be recalled that debts extend through the generations, and numerous cases already cited involve the transfer of a debt from a father to a son. The rules of inheritance have already been dealt with; here we are merely concerned with the fact that these debts are given a public hearing when one member of the contracting party dies. In fact, if a man fails to make a claim against the estate, he forfeits his claim entirely. Similarly, a public statement is made of outstanding debts held by the estate. Apparently often complex and difficult issues are at this time clarified and settled, as in the kokwet at the funeral of Stanley Seswet:

KAMITITAP MBACH: The deceased gave me a namanya she-goat for some hens. It produced a he-goat, which Chepsiker Kapchemoin asked for, but I told him it belonged to Seswet [the deceased]. Seswet said that it was up to me to decide, but when I returned the namanya goat I discovered the he-goat had been stolen by somebody.

CHEPSIKER KAPCHEMOIN: I took the he-goat from that woman's house because the deceased had given it to me and before I took it he had asked me for a she-goat namanya, which I have him and that she-goat produced and I took the mother back, and my debt with the deceased is finished.

Yakobo Maget [brother of the deceased] explained that the family owed the woman a namanya she-goat. [Case 103]

The complications here should be clarified. Kamititap Mbach had been given a she-goat by Seswet in namanya exchange for some hens and this she-goat had produced a male kid. Kamititap had the right to keep the original female until it produced a female kid, but she chose to keep the male instead and returned the original namanyantet she-goat to the owner. Meanwhile, Chepsiker, with permission from Seswet, had taken that he-goat from Kamititap Mbach, for which he gave Seswet a namanya she-goat, which had been released by producing a female for Seswet. Their exchange had thus ended, but Seswet's estate still owed Kamititap Mbach the she-goat she should have received in the first exchange, as his heirs fully recognized.

The initiator may withdraw from his contractual obligation

to provide a cow to his tilyet by taking back the heifer and returning a bullock of the same quality as the original animal he had taken. This was indicated in Cases 218 and 219 already cited; it is specifically at issue in the following:

Siret asked for a bull when he was circumcising his daughters and gave me a heifer which produced three calves which all died. I asked him to take the original namanyantet back and bring me another, but instead his son brought a very small heifer and drove away the cow without my knowledge. That heifer was given me for good. It is not a namanya. [Case 246]

Such instances tend to invoke ill-feeling, which breaks the tilyet relationship.[9] The sentiments and legal involvements are explicit in the following dialogue.

W. GOLDSCHMIDT: If Sikorya [who had taken a bull belonging to Chelakam] said tomorrow that he doesn't want to go along with the arrangement and he gave back the bull, would he still be your tilyet?

CHELAKAM: When I go to Sikorya and he says "I don't have a heifer but here is a bull" and gives no trouble, then we remain friends, but there is no tilyet relationship. If he gives trouble, though, we would no longer be friends.

W. GOLDSCHMIDT: If he does this in a nice way do you just say good-bye and that ends the tilyet?

CHELAKAM: You say "Chematakwey [Good-bye] Tilyet," but you are not happy inside.

ALI MUSANI: If he gave a bull right away and is a good friend, I wouldn't feel bad and if I have beer he can come and drink, and I can drink his beer. [Law Conference]

A man may initiate a contract with a person to whom he has been a previous respondent, for men may have several contracts with the same tilyet. It may happen that each still owes the other a namanya heifer; occasionally such contracts may be canceled out. Several such instances came to light during funeral kokwets. The matter is not so simple as it sounds, how-

---

[9] I was witness to an argument among some Sebei men as to whether the tilyet relationship continues throughout life or is broken when the contract has completed its course. The argument took place in the farming area, where such contracts are relatively rare and unimportant, both economically and socially. Cattle-keeping Sebei, especially men of substance, regard the relationship as very important and enduring.

ever, even though (despite differences in size) the Sebei tend to reckon all bullocks as of generically equivalent value. The complications arise from the fact that the bullock paid may have been held under subsidiary rights by one wife, while the debt owing is for a contract involving another. However:

Naburai took one of our father's bulls and our father took one of his. He hasn't paid and we haven't. If he wants to pay, that is all right; if not, then as each of us took the other's, we will make an end to that. [Case 247]

In some instances that came to light it was recognized that no collection would ever be forthcoming. These cases involved the removal of the person to other areas, frequently outside Sebei territory. Modern courts tend not to apply old Sebei rulings, but have other notions of what is a fair decision—at least that is implicit in comments I received.[10]

It should also be stated that the Sebei engage in outright and direct exchanges, as, for instance, when a man needs a bull of a certain color because it is necessary for ceremonial reasons, and he does not have one. This is implicit in the fact that a person may replace the namanya heifer with a bullock and thus cancel the contract. Outright exchanges are relatively rare and not particularly functional, but they are legally recognized. Similarly, today there is a good deal of exchange of cattle for cash, either with itinerant traders or at the government-sponsored market. In such exchanges there is a tendency to use some of the cash to replace the animal with another one (among those Sebei where stock is important), the replacement being viewed as a continuation of the same line or "family" of the animal that was sold.

Cattle are exchanged for other commodities: for land (in the past, but not today), for crops growing in the field, for granaries of food, and the like. Some of these exchanges are namanya, some are outright; the matter appears to be one of mutual agreement. I deal with this subject more fully in the section on land contracts.

[10] I heard two modern court cases concerning cattle contracts, but none in which a decision was rendered.

Sankanet

Another contractual arrangement is the *sankanet*, which we may call partnership or co-ownership. (The word comes from the verb *sankan*, "to share," and may be applied to ownership in partnership of any piece of property. The only instance I have recorded had to do with cattle. The cow, or whatever is co-owned, is called *sankañantet*.) In sankanet two or more persons purchase or acquire a single animal together and share in its progeny. As many as five, it was said, might share a single cow. The instance I recorded was between a man and his mother's brother's son, a man he calls uncle (i.e., the same term he uses for his mother's brother). Were the two men not related so closely, they would be tilyet to each other, but the tilyet relationship is considered less important than the actual blood tie. Each partner takes a calf in turn. The partner who keeps the animal gets the milk, but "in the old days, we would take turns with the milk, day by day." In this instance the cousin who stood in the uncle relationship took the first calf; I presume it was because of his putative seniority. The sankanet instance occurred in an area of intense cultivation; it is the only one brought to my attention, but it is a recognized, standard practice. I am told it is more frequently used in the Bukwa area than in the west.

The Kamanakan Contract and Hired Herdsmen

Whether to consider kamanakan a hiring of labor or a contract regarding cattle is something of a moot point; it is essentially a simple arrangement in which one man places his cattle in the kraal of another, who receives for his services as herdsman the pleasure of the cattle in his kraal and the use of their milk. The motivations for such an arrangement are similar to those for namanya, though the legal circumstances are different. Normally such an arrangement is entered into because the owner wants to spread his herd or does not have adequate pasture near his domicile. A good deal of it may result today from the fact that certain areas are so densely farmed that only a few cows can be kept, and a man with many animals will have to find a plainsman to take care of the excess, unless he wishes to establish—as some do—a cattle camp away from his house. The

herdsman either has cattle, in which event the added burden is
not very great, or he has none, in which event his need is great.
Men may put one or two or a large number in the hands of
another man, and as in namanya, several arrangements may be
entered into with different people concurrently.

In terms of law, the cattle fully remain the property of the
original owner; the man who is caring for the animals has only
to be sure he can demonstrate, if a cow is missing, that it was in
fact taken by some predator and not consumed by himself.
There is no payment to the herdsman, but if the herd pros-
pers—if in the course of years there is considerable increase
from the original herd—the owner has a moral obligation to
reward the herdsman with one or more animals. He will certainly do so if he wants to keep up the relationship, for it acts as
an incentive to more careful husbandry. It is, however, a moral
obligation, not an enforceable demand right on the part of the
herdsman.

The herdsman is expected to treat the animal entirely as his
own. He may make namanya arrangements with such an animal, but only with permission of the owner.

My grandfather, Mwoko, and a man named Nganya were married
to girls of the same aret. Nganya gave Mwoko cows as kamanakan.
Nganya's cow produced a bull and Mwoko had a visitor and decided
to kill the bull and asked permission from Nganya to kill it, propos-
ing to give a heifer in exchange. He sent this message by a neighbor
but, though the neighbor did not reach Nganya's house, he returned
to Mwoko saying that Nganya had agreed that he could kill the
bull. Mwoko did kill it, thinking that he had been properly author-
ized.

One day Mwoko and Nganya met and the latter asked about his
cattle. Mwoko said that everything was fine except for the bull that
Nganya had given him permission to kill. Nganya said: "I didn't
give a bull to you. When did you ask for it?" They went to the
neighbor, Sayekwo, and asked why Mwoko's message had not
reached Nganya, and the neighbor said that he had stopped on the
way because he had felt hungry and then he returned without seeing
Nganya. Nganya told Mwoko that though the neighbor had given
false information, he would accept the heifer in exchange. [Case
217]

The following case indicates a continuing arrangement that demonstrates the patterns of expectation between men enjoying this relationship, and the breach that may occur as a result of Europeanization. Salimu realized that though the Sebei would recognize the propriety of his claim, it was unenforceable against a man who had left his cultural milieu, since the modern courts would not enforce it.

Kambuya gave a cow to Malinga, his wife's brother. It produced two heifers, which Kambuya sent Salimu to pick up, leaving the original cow. Then it produced four more calves, and thinking that the mother was getting old, Salimu went to get them. Malinga asked him to leave one of the cows which had a calf, which he did. Meanwhile this cow had multiplied to a total of eight when Salimu's mother's brother died. The son sold all eight cows and migrated to Bugisu. The debt is being written off as the man is poor and as no modern court would sustain the case, according to Salimu. "If he had a cow, or if he gets one, I may ask him for just one to cover the whole debt." [Case 260]

The next case, also heard at the kokwet for Kambuya's funeral, likewise expresses some of the modern problems in enforcement.

Kambuya bought four heifers and kept them at Chonkeywa's kraal. Chonkeywa was living in Teso and had no permit to carry cows across the district boundary, so they were left there. In 1948 Salimu went to Chonkeywa's and his son showed him twelve head of cattle descended from these four heifers. When Chonkeywa learned this from his wife he was annoyed with his son and fought him and bewitched him to death for showing the cows. In 1960 Salimu went to Teso District and saw Chonkeywa, who said: "I have no cows of yours here. There are only eleven, but I won't give you those." He said he had some in Sebei but when Salimu inquired he discovered they had been brought back to Teso District. The next time Salimu went, he found Chonkeywa sick and could not ask for the debt. Subsequently he learned that Chonkeywa had died. Although Salimu admits that he cannot identify the cows, he has witnesses to the contract and hopes to recover four cattle through the courts. [Case 261]

This last statement and similar case material suggest that modern courts make debt restitutions only in the amount of the original transfer, in contrast with the Sebei rule that all progeny of the cow transferred belong to her original owner.

Modern courts seem to recognize that the herdsman has some rights in the herd. An illustration is the following complicated case, briefly summarized:

> This is a case of a long history of cattle deals concluding with the fact that a man was holding a cow which had three heifers as kama-nakan but refused to admit that two of the heifers were present. Sa-limu, Kambuya's son, retrieved the three cows through ruses or stealth (the case is not clear on this matter). A court case was then taken against Kambuya by the man who had held the cattle. The court ruled in Kambuya's favor, but ordered him to leave one of the animals with the man who had been herding it. The man had done magic on the cows that were kept by Kambuya so that two of them became barren. These were exchanged for heifers, and the latter have subsequently multiplied. [Case 262]

While the namanya contract is explicit with respect to the rights and obligations of the two parties, and furthermore gives substance to them by creating a formal social bond, the kamana-kan relationship is loose and poorly defined. The following case suggests this fluidity. The man who made the arrangement had sent his young son to engage in the negotiations rather than go himself—perhaps to play on community sympathy or to avoid personal embarrassment in making a dubious claim. Nevertheless, it exemplifies the absence of adequate "documentation" in such contracts (nothing similar is found among my namanya cases unless a non-Sebei is involved).

> In this case apparently Kambuya had given Koroyeñ an animal at the time he was marrying because he was poor, and subsequently Koroyeñ returned the animal. Koroyeñ's son claims that this re-turned animal was given to Kambuya as kamanaktay, but the peo-ple in general, remembering the instance, felt that this was the re-payment of a debt for the earlier assistance in bride-price. [Case 256]

The Sebei also hire herdsmen simply as laborers; during the early colonial period these were largely Bahima tribesmen from western Uganda. The arrangement, according to the one in-stance of which I have any record, is an agreement that the herdsman shall have the right to milk certain cows in the herd. In this instance the herdsman lived in the compound with the family, which retained the right to milk some of the cattle for their own use. Some of the milk the herdsman gets is converted into ghee and sold at the local market; otherwise there are no wages.[11] The pattern appears to be an adaptation of a yet older system of indenture of poor persons to a rich family. This explanation was given at the Law Conference: "Slaves were people who lost their parents; they would find a rich man and stay with him so they could be fed. Such a man may be one whose wife died and he had no cattle with which to buy another wife, so he attached himself to a rich man. Such a person is called *mutworintet*." But "slave" is an inaccurate gloss; the man is not sold or inherited (unless mutually desired) nor is he prevented from leaving; and should he have clansmen, compensation would be demanded if the householder killed the mutworintet.

Moyket and Kwoloyit

Another contractual arrangement by which one person obtains the services of another is the *moyket* and its variant, *kwoloyit*. Whenever a man wants to build a house, a woman wants to prepare her fields, or anyone has any large-scale enterprise for which he needs the assistance of a number of persons, he arranges a moyket, or work party. The essence of the arrangement is an afternoon's beer drink in exchange for a morning's work. Though there is no previous discussion of the matter, though there need not be and usually is not any specific invitation or request to individuals in the matter, nevertheless the moyket may essentially be considered a dyadic contract (though not enforceable in law) between the man who holds the moyket and the individual who shows up to engage in the labor. It is under-

---

[11] A colloquy between the owner and his herdsman is reported in *Kambuya's Cattle* (chap. ii) in which the herdsman is demanding some wages, which were summarily refused. It was not the tradition to make any standard payment; I would assume that some food in addition to milk might have been given to the herdsman, but have no information on this point.

stood that the latter has explicit obligations to perform a clearly defined task for which he gets a more or less specific quantum of beer.[12]

The preparation of beer takes several days; by the time it is ready, the neighbors know when the moyket is to be held and what work is to be done. The amount of beer brewed is apparently consistent with the expectations for the task. For preparation of a field, the owner appoints a person, preferably not related, who marks off the plots that each woman will cultivate with her hoe, and for this service he also is rewarded with beer. At a moyket I observed near Binyinyi in 1954, the unit of work was eleven by six long paces, about 800 square feet of land that had been cultivated the preceding year, or ten by five paces, about 600 square feet of land that had not been previously cultivated and was therefore harder to work. This was apparently a kind of standard; there was some quarrel over amounts of work and sizes of plot. Each woman works when she wishes; she may share the task (and her share of beer) with a relative. The person who brews the beer has the right to invite specified nonworking guests. The evidence is somewhat conflicting as to whether the person who gives the moyket can deny the right of others to work. I was told that he could, but in a case described earlier (see pp. 123–128), Maria was not allowed to prevent her co-wife from participating despite their enmity.

To the outsider, the moyket looks like a cooperative work party ending in a social gathering, an informal "bee" such as those of our own pioneer days. To the participants, while it performs precisely that function, it is a carefully planned quid pro quo of work for satisfaction, and any failure to perform his obligations by either party results in recriminations, abuse, and social pressure. Nor is the fact that pay is in beer something to be taken lightly. Enjoying beer is the major social activity of the ordinary Sebei citizen, and older persons regularly and younger

---

[12] Sebei beer is of various kinds; the most common variety is a maize mash brewed with sprouted millet as the malting agent. It is served in large pots around which individuals congregate with their long filtered straws. As the thick beer is consumed, it is replenished by the addition of warm water.

ones usually feel that a day without beer is a wasted one.[13] Beer is undoubtedly also a major source of nourishment.

On the other hand, the contract is enforceable only in the court of public opinion; it is not a matter for formal action. There is no dearth of gossip about the quality or quantity of beer provided, and no woman would want adverse comment on her performance; nor could she afford to alienate her neighbors, for there is always more work to be done. It was said that if a woman failed to finish her plot, her host would do likewise when she was the worker and the woman the host.

If a person requires such service from his neighbors at a time when for some reason he cannot provide beer, as may happen, he promises to give beer to the group in the future. Under this system, called *kwoloyit,* the person hiring the labor agrees to furnish, in addition to beer, a slaughtered sheep or goat for the workers to eat. Also, under this plan the work is contracted for by a kind of middleman *(kwoloyintet)* who is responsible for arranging to get workers and seeing to it that the owner meets his obligations at a later date.

One group of younger Sebei men formed a kind of work society, in which they performed work either for one another or for Sebei who had governmental jobs and could pay them in shillings. This arrangement seems to be a new adaptation of the old moyket system, but whether it will grow into a regular Sebei institution cannot yet be determined.

What should be emphasized with respect to both the moyket and the kwoloyit is that while the arrangements are standardized and informal, while very nearly the same persons will be collaborating on the work of each member of a village, and while disputes do not reach the level of any formal court action, nevertheless each party to the arrangement sees it in terms of an obligation and a right; he sees it as a dyadic relation between the owner and the worker; he jealously protects his rights

---

[13] Beer may now be purchased, and served in the same way—that is, the privilege of participating in a pot. It costs 2 shillings, the price of common labor for a day lasting from about 8 A.M. to 2 P.M. (I do not have a measure of the amount of beer made available, but the Sebei know the amount expected and insist on the proper quantity.)

against unfair practice on the part of the other; and he would
punish by informal means or by personal abuse any instance in
which he felt he had been unfairly treated. It is not simply a
cooperative domestic group.[14] The moyket is in effect a number
of contracts between the person who gets the assistance and each
individual who gives it, just as in our basic hiring arrangements.

The Sale of Land and Crops

Sales and exchanges of land, as well as rental arrangements, all
are made today among the Sebei, and have been for some time.
Contractual arrangements are not so clear in matters relating to
land as they are with respect to livestock. Both the nature and
the importance of land use have changed over the past century
or more in Sebeiland, and vary regionally, as I have shown. Let
us first consider land acquisition in the period a generation or
so prior to direct European contact. At that time, the central
region was sparsely populated by people engaged chiefly in the
herding of cattle, and farmland was not at a premium. There
were three means by which land could be obtained. The first of
these was extralegal—the use of superior force to push out
people who were already occupying the area.

The Kapserot people were living in Ragon and the Kapchay clan
below the cliff. The latter came above the cliff and started cultivating the land. The Kapserot people objected; they started a fight and
killed a Kapchay man. The Kapchay called an alarm and brought
together all their people, and two men of Kapserot were then killed.
The Kapchay still have this debt and no compensation was paid. I
think the Kapserot people have forgotten it now. They tried to kill
more Kapchay people, but we walked in groups and stopped walking at night. The Kapchay people stopped cultivating the land of
the Kapserot people. [Case 150]

Though this effort was not successful, we did note one that was
(Case 83, p. 105), an instance referred to by another informant
as "chasing off the earlier clan."

The second means of acquiring land was adoption of a man
into the pororyet. The process seems to have required a sponsor
and usually involved a marriage, either the taking of a daughter

---

[14] It was a Sebei who brought up the kwoloyit arrangement when the
topic of contracts was under discussion at the Law Conference.

from the pororyet or a giving of one to it. This means of land acquisition, which relates to affiliation and inheritance patterns, is discussed in chapter 2, as it seems to be subsidiary to the social relationships established by a change of residence. There is a formal acceptance into the pororyet.

The third means of acquiring land was negotiation with the present landowner. There were three methods: borrowing the land, making an exchange comparable to the namanya, or making an outright exchange. No separate terms for these arrangements exist, though the Sebei analogize this way of acquiring land to the namanya and use the appropriate namanya terms. The first method was a matter of friendship and nothing was paid; it was a favor. The second was followed with land devoted to plantains. The person who borrowed the land paid a namanya heifer, and used the land for a delimited period of time. The data here are not precise; one informant suggested the borrower used it "until the plantains were finished, as long as he can take care of it" (plantains continue to produce for as long as fifty or more years when properly cultivated). Another described the procedure somewhat differently, referring to it as *kanam tengek* (*tengek* = land). "If a man has given me land, then when I brew beer for the moyket to cultivate that land, I give him one pot of beer because he is my tilyet. It can be a 20-shilling pot if there is not much beer, and 10 shillings paid to him in addition; but if I have enough beer, I feed him beer through the day and that evening I kill a goat or a hen and feed him a good meal and that encourages him to let me use the land for more than a year. I may offer him beer more than twice. He may belong to any clan or any village, provided he has enough land." I have no case evidence for such a use of land. It is, perhaps, not entirely different from the purchase of crops, to which we turn next.

The third method of negotiation was outright purchase from an individual seller. For this I have a number of old instances.[15]

---

[15] All instances but one (Case 66) took place either in Chema or kapeywa pororyet. This is the area into which population was moving during the last half of the nineteenth century, under pressure from the Gisu, and which has long been densely settled and heavily planted. Case 66 took place in Tulel, an area less densely populated.

The earliest of these must have taken place at the close of the nineteenth century, for my informant, who was in his seventies in 1962, was a small boy at the time. His father paid three goats for one piece of land and a bull for another. At about the same time, another transaction took place farther to the east.

One day when my father Kwirit was still alive, he went to Malinga and borrowed a bushy place and cleared that and planted an area that was two senchen,[16] which was enough for a bullock. When they were about to get bananas (i.e., when the crop had developed into a potentiality), Kwirit died. Afterward Malinga's father came and told about this, and demanded his bullock. We paid a brown bullock with a white face. So we went on using that, and those two senchen are still mine, but the rest of the land belongs to Aloni's clan. But now the plantains have died. [Case 66]

An outright purchase for cash was made in 1910–1915, a man paying 80 rupees (160 shillings) for a piece of bushland of unspecified size (Case 69, pp. 67 ff.). Another sale took place in the same area and at the same time; five goats were paid for a piece of land partly in plantains and partly in bush. The same man also bought another piece of land in 1927—again for five small stock—from a man of his own clan. For this transaction and for the cash sale, formal witnesses were used.

It seems certain that such land purchase was not a part of old Sebei tradition, and at the Law Conference I was specifically told that "in the old days" land was never used as security, but was given freely. It may be that this mode of transaction was simply adopted from Europeans, though it appears very early in the history of contact for this explanation to seem adequate. Again, it may have evolved from the earlier custom, described above, of acquiring land by attaining pororyet membership through slaughtering an animal for the host population. The latter, however, is economically, legally, and socially different from purchase, which is clearly a contract between two individuals, and not an agreement between an individual and a group.

[16] A senchen is a measure of land based upon the more or less standard distance at which the senchontet boundary-marking plant is put. It is a plot about 10 by 30 paces. The value at that time was placed as follows by modern informants: 1 senchen = 1 ewe or she-goat; 2 senchen = 1 bullock; 4 senchen = 1 heifer.

It seems most likely that it developed from the pattern of the purchase of crops growing in the field, which is an old Sebei custom.

My father went to Arapchesyewa to ask him to exchange *masapek* [17] for a he-goat and Arapchesyewa agreed, but it was only one year's crop that was purchased. [Case 223]

A man named Sagadya went to buy Stanley's mother's masapek. I was asked to go and measure the field he had bought. I dug out to see if there was masapek and then demarcated the field. I found there was food in the ground. He dug it all out and then went away. He exchanged a she-goat for that masapek. [Case 224]

These instances exemplify the exchange of animals for food-stuffs, which served the important economic functions of allaying local famines and equalizing the distribution of food resources. They represent another example of contractual arrangement. The second instance may be a case of namanya exchange, though this was not specified.

Nowadays land may be sold, mortgaged, rented, borrowed, or taken under a kind of namanya contract. There does not seem to be a standard pattern of behavior, a fact attested to by the tendency, when engaging in a land contract, both to have witnesses present and to record the matter in writing.

I observed two land sales, in both instances for cash. Each time the first point of concern was to determine the existing boundaries of the plot to be sold, and in one instance there was evidence that the boundary plants had been moved. This act did not hamper the sale; it was understood that the seller had the responsibility for any court action to establish the validity of his asserted boundaries, though what sanctions were available to the buyer was not indicated. The principals to the transaction, together with their witnesses, a court clerk, and an assortment of neighbors, were present. The price in each instance was bargained, but the negotiations were carried out, not by the buyer and seller, but by their respective witnesses, after neutral persons had expressed themselves as to a proper price. I was told that if boundary plants had to be set, this would be done at a later date in the presence of the seller, at least two witnesses,

[17] *Masapek* is a local tuber cultivated by the Sebei.

and the neighbor or neighbors along whose land the boundary
followed.

Nowadays land is frequently used as security for loans. One
old man in Sasur (our village of residence in the intensively
farmed area of Sebei) was making a practice of lending money
to poorer and less provident persons who needed cash for taxes.
One of the sales mentioned above was made to him by a man
who had taken such a loan. There seems to be no explicit
foreclosure system, however; in this instance the borrower was
in need of further cash and went to the man who had originally
loaned him money. In another instance (Case 130) it was announced at a funeral that such a loan had been made, secured by
a piece of land that had already been sold to another person.
The debt was recognized, but there was no penalty. Action for
restitution against the person who had thus falsely used nonex-
istent collateral would have to be taken either to the modern
court or through the use of sorcery.

Maunia had a brother named Chepsegoi who died and Maunia
inherited his land. Before he died, his brother had taken a cow from
my father under contract, but he failed to pay the cow back. The
land was offered to my father in place of the cow. This is the base
for my father's claim on the land. Chepsegoi's wife is still alive, and
proved that she ate the bull taken from my father and says the land
was given to him.

According to the informant, the local councillors ordered Maunia
to quit the strip of land between the road and the path leading to
the home of Maunia's wife. Though Maunia was forced to quit the
land, his son George has refused to do so and there will be a case before the court. [Case 97]

The Sebei also recognize the right of option. Option is called
kotiñet (from the verb *tiñ*, "to hold something down") , and the
concept is taken from the marital contract.[18] "If there is a
[uncircumcised] girl you love very much, you give her parents a
cow with calf to produce milk for your future bride, and that is
kotiñet, and is to be a part of the bride-price." In one instance of
land sale, a person had paid 80 shillings on a piece of land,
which gave her the right to use it and could be applied to the

---

[18] The term is also said to be used for rape, which by definition involves
holding the woman down.

purchase; however, the option was not being taken up by its holder, who wanted the money back. Unlike option arrangements in Western law, the holder does not forfeit the advance payment in such an instance. I could get no information as to whether the option holder could insist on getting the land; presumably not, as the option was not based upon a pre-established sale price. The lack of prearranged price is consistent with the use of kotiñet in obtaining a bride.

A Perspective on Contract Law

The data on contractual arrangements in Sebei support two general theses that have run through our discussion of Sebei legal institutions. First, inasmuch as contracts are regularly made between competent individuals, the data reinforce our understanding that property is privately and personally held, and is not a right held by any corporate group. These contracts involve the major capital assets of Sebeiland, cattle (and lesser stock) and land. They also involve the use of labor, and this arrangement, even when groups of men are working together, has the character of a dyadic contract between the employer and the individual worker.

Second, the contractual arrangements involving sales and use of land are less precise and less clearly conceptualized than those for either cattle exchanges or labor (or, for that matter, marriage) ; they seem to have been an adaptation of other, preexisting institutions. Some of the practices may have been adapted from old forms of pororyet affiliation, some from cattle exchanges, and one, at least, from the marriage contract.

We know from other sources, as I have already indicated, that the intensive cultivation of land in Sebei is relatively recent; that Sebei institutions must be seen as having been developed originally by a cattle-keeping people for whom farming was of but secondary importance and whose land was not fully used. Under such circumstances, it would not be necessary to have elaborate regulations concerning rights to land and land exchanges, though it would be necessary to have regulations governing the exchange of commodities and the rights to the improvements resulting from human effort. I think it is reasonable to see the pattern of legal institutions filling, so to speak, an institutional vacuum when, through the increased concentration of population, new regulations and procedures become requisite. I find it interesting that this development should take place by the syncretization of preexisting contractual forms applied to other aspects of Sebei life.

It is relevant in this context to stress that the incidence of land disputes in the cattle-dominated plains area is very low when compared with that in the intensively cultivated area in the western region of the escarpment. Only two cases involving land on the plains appear in my records, while there are very many from the farming sector. Indeed, when mapping the landholdings of a few selected persons in the latter area I came upon numerous instances of localized boundary disputes that were not entered into our case file; none was recorded during similar work on the plains. I witnessed and recorded the disputes in four funeral kokwet. Two of these were in the area of intense land use; here, of the sixteen cases brought forward, six had to do with land, four with cattle. The kokwet on the plains involved sixteen publicly made claims, none of which dealt with land and fifteen with cattle. In the highland kokwet, where farming is also unimportant, there were again no land claims but only stock disputes among the five cases recorded.

Sebei law is weak in techniques for forcing performance under contract, while redress and punishment for fraudulent action are entirely wanting. The primary court for action in modern Sebei is the funeral hearing, where under the sanction of bereavement and before a community of elders, the parties to a contract can reassert their demands and express their grievances. It is my observation that this is a forceful sanction (though one that can be long delayed) for performance under contract. It applies both to matters involving land and those involving cattle. Behind this sanction lies the modern court, and it is far more readily resorted to in land cases than in cases involving cattle. This difference could be an expression of the fact that European and Baganda jurists are better able to understand land law than they are the elaborate details of the cattle contract, though I think it also expresses the relative indecisiveness of Sebei law regarding land, an indecisiveness that creates a stronger potential for dispute.

In old Sebei, prior to the advent of Europeanized courts, the law of contract appears to have been chiefly concerned with spelling out the implicit rights and obligations under the specific form of exchange. Performance under contract, though it might long be delayed, was not normally a matter of litigation; it was neither the province of the clan nor of the pororyet. It was, rather, ensured by mutual interdependence, by the operation of a market in which each party to the contract had an ultimate interest in preserving his public reputation; his very survival in the community, and certainly his social and economic advancement, depended upon his fulfilling the legitimate obligations he had incurred. This process is no different from the major sanctions supporting contractual performance in commercial societies.

PART FOUR: Conclusions

CHAPTER 12

The Metaphysical Infrastructure of Sebei Legal Behavior

The Conceptual Framework

When we examine the cases of interpersonal conflict and draw together the diverse data on the rights and duties of, and the restraints on the behavior of, the individual citizens as expressed by informants, we uncover a pattern and a unity which we may call Sebei jurisprudence. It is not a body of doctrine consciously formulated by Sebei jurists, nor is it even the work of a particular institutional machinery, for there are no jurists and there is no truly separate social institution of courts. Nevertheless, the society recognizes a body of rights and certain sets of obligations, as well as transgressions of such rights and failures to meet the obligations; it affords means by which individuals or the community may act so as to enforce performance and punish transgression. These considerations are the subject of this book, and I now want to draw them together.

Permit me to digress and personalize for a moment. I find myself surprised at the degree of internal consistency displayed by the data on Sebei law. I am, of course, aware that anthropologists have, at least since Malinowski and Benedict, taken for granted that cultures are integrated and patterned wholes. But the Sebei actions, followed closely from day to day, and the Sebei legal cases drawn from a variety of sources, along with the limited degree to which Sebei verbalize and intellectualize their own behavior, had led me to doubt the applicability of this generalization to the Sebei. Furthermore, as I have indicated throughout the text and shall again discuss later, the Sebei have had to make a dual adaptation to diverse economic circumstances: first to their own sedentarization, and next to the acculturative influence of Baganda-British institutions. This need for adaptation, and the regional diversity of Sebei economics, led me to feel that any consistent patterns would have been shattered and obscured. To be sure, the pattern becomes discernible only when we recognize these dynamic temporal elements. In this chapter I want to develop the understanding of the unity and pattern of Sebei legal practices in terms of underlying assumptions and attitudes shared by the Sebei. In chapter 13 I discuss the dynamic adaptation of Sebei law to changing economic circumstances.

In order to reach an appreciation of what I here call Sebei jurisprudence, it is first necessary to discuss the several levels on which cultural behavior operates, for the uniformity of manifest behavior can be understood only in terms of the forces at work on the deeper levels of psychological orientation.

1. *The action level: law cases.*—The first level is that of the day-to-day actions of individual members of the community as they relate to one another and as they perform functions for self-maintenance and personal satisfactions. Taking the cattle to graze, going to the fields to plant or harvest, finding and participating in beer among neighbors are all aspects of this level of action. The instances of interpersonal conflict and their resolution, which I have called law cases, are examples of such behavior within the realm of law.

2. *The formal level: jural rules.*—Underlying these actions of everyday life are the accepted codes of behavior, the formalized rules and regulations the Sebei accept as proper conduct, and upon which they base their actions and anticipate the behavior of others. Theoretically, it would be possible to deduce this coda from actual behavior, but such deduction is, in fact, nearly impossible to do. First, it would take a very large number of cases given in great detail. Second, not all instances of conflict are, in fact, decided in a way that is consistent with the terms of the coda, so that without having the rules formulated in advance, it would require statistically reliable numbers of cases to establish what was regular and what was deviant. Fortunately, the detailed study of numerous cases is not necessary, because people everywhere formulate their expectations; they can

verbalize them and do so regularly, both among themselves and to the ethnographer. It is therefore not only possible to discover what the rules and regulations are, but to learn when an instance deviates from such regularity. Perhaps it should be made explicit that so formal a level does not apply merely to the realm of law, but to all aspects of culture—the right time for planting a particular crop, or the proper performance of a ceremonial. It is when such rules and regulations apply to rights and obligations of a serious nature, and when the community enforces them (or allows an injured party to enforce them with impunity) that we consider the matter to be one of law, rather than morality per se, propriety, custom, or etiquette. This statement is, of course, *our* definition of the realm of law, though the Sebei (nowadays at least) seem to recognize a similar realm demarcated in more or less the same way. The formal level can thus be discovered directly through statements by informants as well as adduced from the actual resolution of cases. Because of the possibility of variant interpretations and understandings, as well as the likelihood of change, it has seemed of great importance to me to substantiate as much as possible the formal rules by actual cases in order to arrive at an accurate picture of what these rules are. It is, of course, these rules that form the substantive part of this book.

3. *Ideational level: metaphysical presuppositions.*—What I here call the ideational level is the pattern of covert assumptions and orientations that characterize a particular culture, in the context of which individual motivations are set. Such assumptions and orientations are not overtly expressed as such, though their expression is implicit in the statements and actions of individuals within a culture and can be reconstructed from the consistencies that appear in such data. I consider the reconstruction of this level essential to an understanding of the formal level of Sebei law, to which I shall return shortly. Meanwhile, the ideational level may be illustrated by examples from Western culture: the concept of the Protestant ethic as formulated by Max Weber, for example; or the assumption that men of sound mind act of their own free will; or the assumption that children (as legally defined) are not responsible agents. In our

society, with its long history of jurisprudential and theological writing, many of these assumptions have become explicit—though probably not all of them, and not necessarily to the ordinary layman.

4. *Psychological level.*—A still deeper level of behavior, not normally in the awareness of the people themselves but still a part of the cultural sphere, I here call the psychological level. It embraces the sentiments of anxiety, hostility, dependency, desire, and the like, as they are induced in the normal member of the community and reinforced by the continuing social environment in which he lives. It is the level of personality characteristics upon which psychologically oriented anthropologists have focused their attention. Consideration of these elements takes us out of the realm of law, except insofar as the law jobs requisite to any social situation depend upon the psychological set induced in its members. Thus a culture that induces status anxiety and interpersonal hostility may have need for more stringent law enforcement techniques than one that, by whatever means, reduces status anxiety and hostility. But these considerations, though they underlie the phenomena in our purview, take us beyond the realm of law, which is our concern here.

A word is necessary regarding the notion of level itself. It is used in terms of psychological depth, of manifest action (at the top) and unconscious motivation (at the bottom). These levels may also be seen as levels of generalization. They are not used in a causative sense. That is, I assume that the psychological sets induced are the result of the cumulative acts of behavior and the reinforcement of the moral order to which each individual is subject, just as his behavior on the manifest level is influenced by the psychological set he has acquired. This circularity in culture is taken for granted, and these levels do not represent successively pervasive causes in an ultimate sense. When we try to appreciate the laws of Sebei as a legal system, however, it is the ideational level that must be understood as giving the formal laws their consistency and meaning. An individual act—such as any of those represented in the cases used—takes place in the context of more or less clearly perceived rules, and is motivated

Level of Analysis	Realm of behavior		
	Economic	Legal	Supernatural
1. Action	Individual transaction; acts of production or husbandry, etc.	Instances of interpersonal conflict or interaction: law cases	Initiation rituals, other ceremonies, acts of witchcraft
2. Formal	Rules of good husbandry; patterned expectations of the work round, etc.	Jural rules, recognized rights and obligations of persons to things and to one another	Standardized ceremonial patterns; correct performance, even when of an improper act, such as witchcraft
3. Ideational	Control of goods in relation to individual's welfare; spread of risk over time and space	Agnatic affiliation, with its rights and its obligations; adult male competence, etc.	Spiritual identification; post-mortem influences
4. Psychological	Culturally induced attitudes of hostility, aggression, anxiety, etc.		

in part by those deeper meanings on the ideational and psychological levels.

The accompanying tabulation gives a representation of this cultural topography with the content of the several levels in terms of Sebei institutions. The several realms are analytical constructs, not Sebei categories. An act of sorcery undertaken as legalized retribution for failure to perform on contract crosscuts the three realms. We could also add different realms such as morality, etiquette, education, procreation, and child care. On the psychological level, it is impossible to distinguish the several realms of action at all. For purposes of anthropological study, for the elucidation of cultures, for cross-cultural examination, it is necessary to work within delimited categories, and we have here consistently been concerned with the realm of law.

A legal system thus operates within a framework of generic notions of time, space, and causality, and the daily affairs and the regulations that govern them can be seen only in terms of this deeper set of presuppositions. These presuppositions are not set forth as such, but must be reconstructed in terms of the logical postulates that make both rules and behavior meaningful and systematic.

Supernatural Forces and Sebei Justice

The Sebei recognize the existence of supernatural forces that work upon man. These forces are neither the automatic retribution of the wicked or the wrongdoer, nor are they the postmortem rewards and punishments of the kind that are more familiar to the cosmologic ideas of the West. Rather, they are a set of forces that man can bring into play through certain actions of his own. This is the essential character of all black magic, I believe, and certainly it is of Sebei witchcraft. These forces can be drawn upon as a system of sanctions to Sebei legal disputes, and, what is more important, they are regularly so drawn upon.

Thus it is that if all else fails in finding satisfaction in a legal action—if matters cannot be resolved in terms of manifest behavior—then the Sebei will invoke these latent forces. To do so is dangerous, for if a man forswears himself, or if, having evoked these forces, he does not use them with appropriate circumspection and compassion, they may turn upon him. A sorcerous act will also, if not stopped, ultimately have reflexive action against the person perpetrating it. Above all, testimony and accusations operate under oath, and the oath is an act that calls forth forces of retribution, but these forces will turn upon the person giving false testimony or making false accusations. These supernatural phenomena may thus not be treated casually; they may not be invoked with complete impunity.

It is not difficult to psychologize on these basic notions, to recognize in these supernatural phenomena the workings of guilt feelings and suppressed wishes. We cannot examine the case of Maria without recognizing her own guilt as responsible for the oyik that were plaguing her; we cannot escape the conclusion that she burned her own house or that she bore a heavy burden of hatred and guilt. These are the ultimate sources, if you will, for the working out of justice, though the strong at heart—the callous with respect to the sensibilities of others—may escape the working of such manifestations of justice. But such psychologizing is not relevant to our task; what we are concerned with is the existence of a set of metaphysical assumptions about the supernatural world in its relation to the everyday life of human beings.

It is an essential element in Sebei cosmology that the workings of such supernatural forces know no limitations of time or space. The record is replete with instances where this supernatural justice was delayed at least two generations. With such an assumption it is fitting that time not be the essence of legal obligations; there is no statute of limitations, a debt never rots. Though the Sebei live in a world where nature provides the basis for calculating interest (in the form of natural increase of livestock), and though the namanyantet contracts suggest a notion of interest-rate recognition in that a present bullock is worth a future heifer, but only worth half a present heifer, this principle never operates in the working out of retributive justice. I think the more deeply rooted concept of temporal irrelevance is the reason.

These forces may be tapped by all Sebei under appropriate conditions—even by children—though some men have greater control over them than others. Significantly, it is not immoral to use them for legitimate purposes; it is a wrong only to use them without justification. For this reason, it is not illegal in Sebei eyes to have magical power or to be in possession of magical materials. Indeed, Sebei law would not function in the form it has without such a system of sanctions. It is not illegal, but it is dangerous. In this context, kankanet, which works only upon those who are guilty and has no reflexive action when misused, is an exception. It is tempting to think of it as a recent innovation, as appears to be the case with the ntarastit, but for this there is no evidence except its limited distribution. It is a powerful tool and gives status to its practitioners, creating something more akin to hereditary offices than is elsewhere the case in the Sebei social system.

The Sebei recognize forces in the supernatural which act without human will, but merely on humans as agents—the evil

eye, the "bad birds," and the like. These forces exist; undoubtedly they "explain" events to the Sebei, but they are not significant in the realm of law. They are not significant because they
do not punish offenders or create offenses against which sanctions may be taken. (One protects against the evil eye, but one
does not condemn the man who possesses it.) What this empha-
sizes is that in Sebei cosmology, supernatural forces do not of
themselves render order among men—there is no judgmental
God—but men utilize the supernatural in seeking retribution
and enforcing "justice" in an imperfect world. Man remains the
actor, the initiator.

The Sebei do not let this other world take over the affairs of
men; they endeavor to settle matters by direct action and economic pressures, and by the use of regular processes. Yet we
cannot understand these processes without a recognition of the
underlying forces in Sebei cosmology.

Agnatic Affiliation and Identity

If we are to understand Sebei law, we must appreciate the strong
force of agnatic identification. Let us examine this phenome-
non, by way of summary, as it affects the legal behavior of the
Sebei.

1. Clan identity is established "genetically," that is, by the
presumed biological father of the child. It is theoretically [1] un-
changeable, except as a whole lineage can break away from the
clan. Adoptions do occur, but they are manifestly tension-
producing and are discouraged, and under stress may be disen-
gaged. No individual can either join the clan of another or
dissociate himself from his clan obligations. There is theoretically no spatial or temporal limitation to the clan association,
though in practice distance does have an effect. Within the clan
the lineage affiliations are similar, and the ties more immediate
and demanding, the difference being one of intensity rather
than of kind of relationship. The woman's affiliations remain
ambiguous, practically, operationally, and theoretically. In view

[1] In this discussion, "theoretically" has reference to the Sebei ideas as to
what is, not to my theory. Exceptions may be known to exist (or not), but
they are then viewed as such.

of the woman's lack of competence in public affairs—those affairs in which the clan takes a major part—the matter is not considered very important by the Sebei.

2. Clan ties are reinforced through the religious belief in the role of ancestral spirits (oyik) who are concerned with the welfare of the clan and the behavior of its members. These spirits can harm only members of their own clan, except that the spirits of the mother's clan may also affect the welfare of a person.

3. All witchcraft and sorcery act between clans. To be sure, the individual normally initiates such an act as an individual against another individual; however, the effect of the sorcerous act may fall upon any member of his clan. Furthermore, when it has a reflexive action against the perpetrator, any clansman may suffer. Thus sorcery, curses, and oaths are clan matters.

4. Any act of violence or any act of witchcraft which may lead to the death of a man is seen as an act against the clan by the clansmen of the initiator. Each clansman is thus equally vulnerable in retaliation, and each is induced to seek revenge. The basic concept is that of clan weakening and the evening of the score, rather than punishment for a criminal act.

5. The vulnerability of each person to the acts of his clansmen makes for a strong sense of mutual dependence, and clansmen act in terms of such mutuality. This interdependence is all the more poignant in that the Sebei do not display strong ties of sentiment among clansmen, nor do they have ceremonial reinforcements of the clan except those that are prophylactic in character, that is, those to eliminate an external threat against the clan. This mutual vulnerability, both on the overt and on the spiritual level, forces the clansmen into cooperative action when the clan's welfare is threatened.

6. Despite the absence of clan sentiment, but because of the mutual protection that is the product of mutual vulnerability, the individual's material welfare is directly related to the strength of the clan. He therefore acts in such a way as to increase the strength of the clan, and sees any weakening of it as a threat to his security.

7. Matters internal to the clan are handled in terms of max-

imizing clan strength. Thus, on the one hand, fratricide may go
unpunished for fear of further weakening of the clan, whereas a
recidivist thief will be killed by his clansmen to avoid retaliation
by outsiders which might be taken against any clansman, without elimination of the source of trouble.

*The first underlying ideational premise of Sebei, against
which the legal machinery of retribution, justice, and legal
process must be seen, is the clan as a metaphysical entity.* It is
not sufficient merely to recognize the clan as a corporate group;
indeed its corporate activities are limited and defensive rather
than far-reaching and positive. Nor is it quite correct to say that
the clan is a group based upon sentimental ties, as noted above.
Rather, the pervasive element lies in the metaphysical presupposition of the inescapable unity of clanship.

Property as an Individual Right

The next central premise that is essential to Sebei jurisprudence
is the concept of the individual right to property. If property is
defined as the things an individual (or a group) may use as he
sees fit (so long as he does not infringe the rights of others),
the use to which he may exclude or limit, and the rights to
which he may transfer, then the material world of the Sebei may
be divided into things that are property and things that are not.
The former category includes the things that have been created,
or in some measure improved, by man for his own use; the latter
comprises things that remain in their natural state. Domestic
animals, cultivated land, plants that are harvested, animals that
are captured, or minerals that are collected belong to the former
category. Of these items, domestic animals and cultivated land
are by far the most important, and our attention will be focused
upon them. Women have chattel possessions used exclusively by
them; otherwise property ownership is limited to adult men.

Ownership properly has reference to the rights held in
things—by an individual, by a group, or by the community at
large. When the community as a whole shares property, or a
category of property, it may be said to be communally owned;
when the rights inhere in an individual or a group (as, for
instance, a clan or corporation) we may speak of it as being

privately owned. In Sebeiland, unimproved land and other resources are communally owned; all other things are privately
and individually owned, and with the few exceptions already
noted, by the adult male. The rights inherent in the concept of
ownership are also subject to definition in the law of any society; a community may put limitations upon such private
rights, as we do in our zoning ordinances. Among the Sebei, the
private rights to property include not only the right to consume
or to use, but also to sell, exchange, give away, or destroy. There
are only two significant limitations upon this freedom of action.
First, a man may have allocated to another person, usually his
wife or son, a secondary right to livestock or land, and once he
has done so this subsidiary right is inalienable (without consent) but persists as long as either the wife or any of her sons are
alive. This limitation has been self-imposed, however, even
though it cannot be revoked. Second, the clan and community
may express an interest in his use, and if its interests are threatened, may place a limitation on his action.

The regulations inherent in ownership may also involve obligations as well as rights. Liability laws in our society express the
obligation of the owner to protect others from the destructive
potential of his property. The Sebei regulations in this regard
are limited, but they do apply to the responsibility of the cattle
owner for damage his stock does to crops. He has a further
responsibility to use his cattle in support of his clan—a matter
of great importance (though not very clearly defined), as we
shall see.

The private and individual nature of property ownership is
essential to laws regarding theft. Whereas delicts involving bod-
ily injury, if they enter into the realm of law at all, are seen as
action between two clans, delicts involving property are normally private matters between two individuals. It is the owner,
not his clan, who is seen to be harmed, and the thief is regarded
as an individual against whom retribution is taken. Yet there
are important exceptions to this generalization, but they apply
only when the matter of theft threatens to escalate into a feud
because of its repetitive and unconstrained character. Even
when community sentiment has been sufficiently provoked to

demand the slaying of a recidivist thief, this action cannot be taken until the community has demanded that the thief's clansmen restrain or kill him. Also, the community can punish a thief under ntarastit, but this subject is discussed later.

The private and individual nature of property ownership also underlies the law of contract among the Sebei. Exchanges and contractual obligations are freely engaged in by individuals with respect to property they own. No outsider intervenes in these matters, except that a wife may have an allocated secondary right to animals. The clan, lineage, or community cannot intervene except when an action clearly threatens its integrity, but such an action would be against the person, rather than the property.

There is an ancillary aspect of property law. As property consists of goods whose value has been enhanced through human effort, it is logical that contracts for labor are recognized, just as are contracts respecting property. In such contractual obligations women as well as men take part, and the product of a woman's labor is hers rather than her husband's. She also has the right to sell or exchange the products of her field labor, either to sell the commodity directly or to sell beer, or (nowadays) waragi distilled from it. In fact, however, the commerce in such commodities tends to be local and contained within the women's world; it does not relate to clan or broader community matters.

The second metaphysical presupposition in Sebei law is that the individual has an inalienable and essentially unimpaired right to the humanized things he has created, or which have come to him in accordance with customary procedures of transfer. While this principle may seem obvious, inasmuch as it is a principle in all Western law, anthropologists do not have to be reminded that the cultural attitude embodied in this principle is far from universal.

Social Ties and Pecuniary Relationships

With a nice sense of etymological propriety, we may say that the Sebei translate social relationships into pecuniary terms, and conversely, pecuniary ones into social terms. These ties are essentially calculated in cattle, other property having only secondary social value, and in this section only livestock are considered. (The situation with respect to land is reserved for the next chapter.)

1. The filiation of the son to the clan has its parallel in the legal recognition that the son has a right to a portion of his father's livestock. There is no expressed maxim that the father merely holds cattle in trust for future generations (as is the way some peasant societies view the role of "landowner"), but there is a legal compulsion to supply the son with cattle when he is ready to establish an independent household. Furthermore, a man is urged to husband his cattle and maintain the integrity and continuity of the herd, so that while cattle are not owned by clan or lineage, they nonetheless express and symbolize the continuity of the agnatic kindred. This principle is reinforced by the use of clan earmarks.

2. The distribution of a herd within the household, precisely paralleling the distribution of people, reflects the character of their social relationships, with allocation of rights to the several wives, these rights being transmitted to her sons when they reach their majority. These ceremonial "gifts" are expressions of the established mutuality between a man and his wives.

3. The custom of bride-price establishes an equivalence between an economic bond and a social tie, and in so doing translates into specific pecuniary terms the worth of a human being. I do not mean to suggest that her "price" represents a "sale," but rather to assert that between the woman and that which has been given for her there is a psychological equivalence which is reinforced at every proper marriage, which becomes a consideration with every contemplated divorce, and which is validated by the woman as she produces sons who will continue and strengthen the agnatic group.

4. The custom of wergild has the same force with respect to males, for each man has a value in cattle to his clansmen.

5. The ties of clanship are also ties of an economic kind. It has already been shown that the son acquires an interest in his father's cattle, which relates him economically to his agnatic kindred. The clan, however, has a claim on him for economic

support at such times as it needs animals, either for a ceremonial or as payment for a killing. This claim does not impair the individual's ownership, but rather expresses the pecuniary nexus inherent in all social obligations.

6. Conversely, a pecuniary relationship is translated into a tie of kinship, for each cattle exchange also establishes a bond of sentiment between the principals which is treated as a kinship bond and which ideally leads to such a bond through a future marriage.

The third major principle in Sebei law, then, is that all social relations may be translated into pecuniary terms; that there is a pecuniary counterpart to the model for the significant social relations of the community.

Structural Integrity in Sebei Principles of Interrelationship

The three major premises here enumerated form a triad that gives a basic unity to the structure of Sebei legal action. The first two would appear to be contradictory, for if each individual is inexorably tied to his clan, to which he must inevitably demonstrate allegiance in time of crisis, and if this allegiance must be affirmed in terms of property, then it would appear that the clan has an established and prior right to the property. If I read ethnographic literature correctly, I believe that clans frequently do have such rights; yet clearly they do not among the Sebei. However, the third principle, that ties of kinship and sentiment—interpersonal relationships—are translatable into property, brings the first two apparently contradictory principles into full conformity. We can reduce these three propositions to a unity by the assumption that the Sebei, in the psychological sense, make an identification between the individual and his property. This assumption is supported among the Sebei (as elsewhere among East African cattle-keepers) by the many positive expressions of Sebei identification with their animals. The basic unity in the Sebei legal structure may be summarized as follows: (1) *the individual is bound by an indissoluble bond to his agnatic kindred through the spiritual forces that are seen to exist;* (2) *the individual has independent control of his property (particularly cattle) and has a close psychological identi-*

fication with this property; (3) *the inherent contradiction apparent in these two statements is resolved by the fact that the Sebei recognize a ready translation so that each may be resolved into the other.* Put another way: *an individual is his property, so that relations between individuals are also relations of property.*

Bride-Price and Kin Relationships in the Context of Sebei Legal Theory

The importance of the above considerations to the understanding of Sebei law may be illustrated in their relation to bride-price and family attitudes; indeed, such an understanding eliminates the confusion that is found in most discussions regarding this custom.

Each man is born of a marriage in which he forms a part of the return on an investment made by the father in the mother. The marriage relationship is validated through the payment of a bride-price for which he is the essential quid pro quo. As in any society where the law of wergild obtains, he has a pecuniary value. His mother has also had a price; his wife comes to him with the payment of property, and he will in due course receive like consideration for the daughters she bears.

It is important to pause a moment over the matter of daughters. An improper understanding of the character of the economic relationships will lead us into grave error in our efforts to understand the basic motivations and attitudes of the Sebei. Westerners may be divided into two camps with respect to the operation of bride-price as a means of establishing the marital relation: either they feel that the marriage is "really" a tie of sentiment, and the goods exchanged are nothing more than an elaboration of our own prestations; or they turn to the other extreme and see the economic nexus as a capital investment in which the payoff is in daughters, and thus a return on capital. Both are wrong. The former does violence not only to the analogy (the diamond is given to the bride, but the cattle are paid to her father), but also to the evidence with respect to attitudes and behavior. The latter view psychologizes the situation in terms of a profit-motive economy in which capital gain and individual advancement are the expected goals of each economic transaction. The logic of that position suggests that a man should hope for many daughters and no sons, which is manifestly not true of either the Sebei or, so far as I know, of any other peoples with bride-price customs. The economic nexus is not capital investment for capital return, and the reward for the cattle paid to the father-in-law is not a full kraal a generation later. The reward is a houseful of sons, an expansion of the kin group, a strengthened clan, increased personal protection, and greater individual and group influence. For these desiderata it is sons that are needed, though daughters, because they make it possible to attain bridewealth for the sons, and because through these exchanges social bonds of great practical value are created, are likewise desirable. But clearly they are but instrumentalities to other goals, and these goals are the strengthening of the kin group. It is important to appreciate that the pecuniary nexus is essential in all social relationships, both intimate and remote; but it is equally important not to read into this the profit motives that derive from our own market economy. Unless this distinction is understood, the operations of Sebei law—and Sebei attitudes in general—will remain enigmatic.

The individual is tied to a kindred, to an agnatic corporate group, which for all the centrifugal forces working toward its destruction is the essential spiritual unity underlying social interaction. He is thus tied as son and brother and father and ever more remote kin. It is a tie that, as we have seen in discussing the law of violence, is of deepest concern to him for his own personal welfare. But the clan is also tied together by pecuniary considerations. The relation between father and son, like that between husband and wife, is a pecuniary tie. We have seen that a man's herd is structured as a replica of the family itself; indeed, it is coterminous with the structure of that family, so that the relationship between brothers, between half brothers, between mother and son, are all defined (or redefined, if you prefer) in terms of rights in cattle. And the ties of kinship are ties that have this involvement with cattle, for any matter of clan welfare—whether it be the payment of blood money or the performance of a ceremony—also is translated into cattle.

Conversely, as illustrated by the law on contracts, a pecuniary transaction becomes a tie of kinship. It is so considered, and the obligations to kindred are an important part of that exchange. A good tilyet is said ultimately to lead to a happy marriage, thus making the fiction of kinship a reality. More immediately, a tilyet relationship, whether it is good or indifferent, creates an economic bond that further strengthens one's social position and personal influence.

Though these contractual relationships, like ties of marriage, are a means for widening a man's connections, strengthening his social ties, and thus furthering his influence, they are not the man's basic strength. That strength lies in the clan, whose unity is perduring, with deep-seated psychological ties expressed by the behavior projected onto the oyik, with an identity implied by the clanwide operation of witchcraft; and that unity is further expressed through the expansion of economic relations from the individual into ever-widening circles until it embraces the kota and the clan. Though property is privately and individually owned, it serves the clan as a whole; the economic relationship is perhaps a template for the ultimate social nexus.

The Absence of Authority Roles

An important counterpart to Sebei ties to the agnatic kindred and identification with their cattle is the denial of all authority roles. No person in Sebeiland is empowered to command the action of another. No person is a chief. No person has the established right to render a judgment that is binding on a pair of disputants and will be enforced. The kirwokik are not really judges. This situation is not unique; it is characteristic of truly acephalous societies. The existence of such situations has led to numerous and, in my opinion, fruitless debates as to whether law exists.

Let us examine roles in which some decision-making is inherent, in order to explore the limits of the flat statements made in the preceding paragraph. Such overall governance of Sebeiland as existed aboriginally rested with the prophets. These were men with the supernatural capacity to foretell events; their judgments were sought and their counsel was followed, but except for the determination as to when a ceremonial was to be performed, they did not express themselves in terms of command. Furthermore, when their predictions proved false, or were found undesirable, they were killed. They were men of great influence and often wise leadership, but they were not men of authority.

The kirwokik were not empowered to render decisions and had no means of enforcing their opinions. Instead, they were individuals who had the capacity for articulating community sentiment and thus bringing public pressure to bear upon disputants to accept a settlement of their affairs. It is most significant that they were individuals who emerged, that they were acclaimed for their manifest behavior rather than appointed to a position. Military leaders, incidentally, similarly achieved their position from the demonstration of their natural endowments, and were accepted rather than empowered. Every cooperative work party was essentially a dyadic contract between the individual wanting the work done and those willing to help for a consideration. Hunting in the forest was similarly led; it is in this context that the anarchy of the plains hunting party takes on significance.

Nor is there any evidence that clan and kota heads had any power over individual members; rather, they were simply foci for action in matters requiring clan unity. Their position derived from their genealogical relation to the presumed founder, built upon considerations of relative age. They were expected to serve an organizing and leadership function, but they could not enforce compliance.

The only exception to this general rule is that men could force women, and initiates could enforce noninitiates, into compliance. This means merely that it is the men who are the free and independent agencies here described, that women and children are not viewed as being independent parts of the social system. Yet even here, the actuality was far less than the legal fiction holds to be the case, for women had their own sources of influence and certainly their rights, as did sons.

It is in this context that the role of magic in law, discussed earlier in this chapter, takes on particular saliency. The use of the supernatural was available to all men; it was an expression of individual psychic strength, just as much as a full kraal was an expression of individual pecuniary strength, or a strong body or a large clan was an expression of physical strength. The individual with courage could tap this resource, and all men feared it; sorcery was the great leveler. Only the special inherited right to kankanet, with its self-limiting power of affecting only the guilty, was a partial exception. Clearly such a system had no place for a theology of a controlling deity, nor for a fatalistic, nondeterminate philosophy.

The absence of authoritative roles does not mean the absence of compliance. Pressures of the marketplace, pressure of an informal kind, social pressures, and the recognition of mutual obligation—not to mention the pressures of potential sorcery—all serve to make persons willing to do what they do not want to do. Leadership exists, and leaders can and do galvanize community or clan sentiment so as to gain compliance to an imposed program of action. But the action is never enforced by a neutral, superior third party to a dispute; it is not coerced. Only under ntarastit do we find an exception, and that I want to discuss in the next chapter.

Summary

The central character of Sebei jurisprudence is as follows: law is primarily direct action between clans when treating with matters of violence, not between individuals. Cattle, however, are privately owned, and there is an identification between the individual and his stock; thus all personal relations are translatable into property relationships, and all contracts regarding cattle create a personal bond. Though property delicts are personal delicts, when these involve cattle they threaten to escalate into violence and thus potentially invoke retaliation from the threatened clan. The prime motivation is toward maximization of the clan, which means it is desirable to have many sons and many cattle (which through bride-price ultimately translate into sons), for it is through the clan that an individual's welfare is maximized. The whole pattern is substantiated by the workings of supernatural forces, as viewed by the Sebei, which give spiritual unity to the clans and the sanctions that enforce the law. Such a system is eminently suited to an economy of cattle-keeping people.

CHAPTER 13

The Dynamic Adaptation
of Sebei Law

The legal institutions of the Sebei have their roots in the past; they are fundamentally attuned to the social demands of a cattle-keeping economy, and the attitudes and orientations thus implied. But the Sebei had acquired, in the century or so prior to European contact, an increasing dependence upon hoe-farming, and particularly the intensive use of land associated with the cultivation of plantains. It is the burden of this chapter to demonstrate that important institutional adjustments in the realm of law accompanied this economic shift; that is to say, the legal institutions of the Sebei underwent a process of adaptation to meet the new needs and circumstances that arose as a consequence of the new economy. It is therefore an example of institutional adaptation.

Economic Change and Its Sociological Involvements

In the historical summary (chap. 1) I pointed out that the Sebei arrived on Mount Elgon as a primarily pastoral people, cultivating only small plots of millet and sorghum on a shifting basis. Their population was sparse; land was freely available to stock except for the cultivated plots. They subsequently learned the cultivation of plantains from their Bantu neighbors to the west, and brought this new mode of economy onto the northern escarpment in the mid-nineteenth century. They also acquired maize. As a result, the population density increased, arable land was increasingly brought under cultivation, good land became scarce, and permanent land use became possible. Cattle never lost their economic usefulness (though cattle-keeping declined in importance), and the social and psychological meaning of the livestock continued. These changes did not occur with the same intensity in different parts of Sebeiland, farming being more intensive in the west and less so in the central, more arid part of the escarpment and on the plains.

The research program of which the general study of Sebei culture was a part (and of which the present book is an ancillary product) was directed to the understanding of ecological adaptation. In the broader investigation, a team of scholars analyzed four separate tribes, each characterized by spatial differentiation in economic activities between pastoral and farming emphases. The details of the theoretical assumption, the methods and techniques employed, and some of the data have been set forth elsewhere.[1] Most simply stated, it is an effort to examine the spatial variation in institutions and attitudes in order to determine whether a common process of adaptation took place among them, in accord with a general ecological theory of culture. In this chapter I am concerned with the theoretical problems, but am dealing directly with temporal change rather than spatial variation.

The theory may be briefly stated: Institutions are instrumentalities for the maintenance and coordination of group activities; the nature of such group actions is significantly related to the means by which a people gets its livelihood; when the form of economic exploitation changes, the institutional requirements also change; hence, with a shift in economy, certain institutions become dysfunctional and tend to disappear, while other functions become requisite, and institutional machinery will develop to meet these needs.

Cattle-keeping and hoe-farming are economic activities that make very different demands upon man, and offer different circumstances; indeed, they represent as wide a differential as any that can readily be found in preindustrial societies. These differences relate to matters of annual and daily life cycle, to the kinds of work activities, to the needs for movement, to the

[1] Walter Goldschmidt, Philip W. Porter, Symmes C. Oliver, Francis P. Conant, Edgar V. Winans, and Robert B. Edgerton, "Variation and Adaptability of Culture: A Symposium," *American Anthropologist*, 67 (April, 1965), 400–447.

character of social rewards, to the density and permanence of settlement. When the differences are very nearly absolute as, say, between the Masai and the Chagga, the differential in life modes is sharp. When, as often happens—and did happen with the Sebei—the difference is one of emphasis rather than being absolute, the evidence of social differential is less obvious, but it is nevertheless there.

Let us briefly review some of the areas where we may reasonably expect differences that will have relevance to law, on the basis of our general knowledge of the problem, and taking the extreme contrasts as our first point of approach.

1. The most obvious differential between the two economies lies in their relationships to land. Cattle-keeping people almost universally recognize the right of any stockowner to pasture, water, and salt; they make no restrictions other than a broad territoriality because anything else would quickly destroy the herds. One might make the proposition: if cattle-herding is to remain the paramount economic activity, then land and water will be freely accessible to all animals (and their owners). Conversely, a farming people (where land is permanently usable) must protect the farmer's right to continuous use; therefore private rights to land will be found.

2. Pastoral people must be free to move around to meet the requirements of water and pasturage; they cannot be tied to a locus. Farmers, on the other hand, must be tied to the land, which is their sustenance; they cannot freely move about, however much they might want to.

3. As a direct corollary, social units must develop around spatially defined areas in a farming society, while narrowly defined spatial units are dysfunctional for pastoralists.

4. Farmers must therefore develop institutions for the preservation of spatially defined communities, both those necessary to protect them against the predations of other peoples, and those required to maintain internal harmony.

5. The reward system of a cattle-keeping people is more closely tied to the individual fortunes of a person, is dependent upon the efficacy of his personal decisions, and assigns greater importance to individuated action. It is also more given to wide

changes of individual fortunes, as raids, diseases, famines, and good husbandry decimate or multiply a man's herds. By contrast, a farmer's rewards are steadier, if not surer; his circumstance is less closely tied to his personal decisions and achievements than to the circumstances of his birth. He is more dependent.

Such contrasts as these, which can be substantiated in the comparative literature but have been put forward here in terms of general observations, apply to the broad spectrum of social institutions and cultural attitudes. For purposes of this study of law, however, it is sufficient to deal with those in which a demonstrable adjustment in legal institutions has been made. We will deal (1) with matters pertaining to land, (2) with matters pertaining to military organization as a control system, and (3) with the development of a kind of community law under ntarastit.

The Development of Landownership and Contracts

The distinction the Sebei make between things that may be privately owned and things that are a public good is so consistent and far-reaching that there is no reason to assume it is not an ancient Sebei tradition. Furthermore, there is every reason to believe that this distinction was operative with respect to cultivated lands, that is, plots that were sown to millet and sorghum. Even though, according to ethnographic description, women went down in work groups to prepare land on the plains as a matter of mutual protection, each woman, it was said, had her own plot, and if they returned to the same area each reclaimed the same parcel. The rights to individual cultivated parcels, therefore, goes as far back as ethnographic memory can reach. But when the Sebei were predominantly pastoralists there was no dearth of land, and it is unlikely that severe disputes arose over this resource, or that any legal machinery was needed to attend to such rights as did exist. As farming supplants cattle-keeping, however, and land fills up, the need to delineate ownership (both physically on the ground and legally as a set of rights) develops, and the provision for transfers of such rights becomes requisite.

Fee-simple private property ownership is not necessarily the solution of choice for a society engaged in hoe-farming, especially where there is a long-fallowing rotation or constant movement to new land. More frequently we find some kind of kin-based corporate group either with basic ownership or with some kind of administrative prerogative over the land. There apparently was some tendency among the Sebei, after they had adopted intensive farming in the west and then pushed (with their plantains) into the central sector, to settle into clan-communities and exert some influence over clan holdings. But, as the discussion of landownership shows, this tendency never developed into corporate property control. The reason seems clear to me: Sebei property concepts applicable to livestock were precise; they were based upon deep psychological orientations, and they were reinforced by many social situations. Rather than adopt some communal solution to land, the Sebei adapted their notions of livestock ownership to landownership. It would seem that the individuation in Sebei behavior and the close identification between the individual and what he owned were attitudes too deep-seated to change, and it was easier ultimately to adapt landholding to the attitudes than to change the attitudes themselves.

The system of legal rights which was operative with respect to livestock came to be applied to land, though the social uses of cattle were not so applied. Ownership is universally in the hands of the men, despite the fact that most of the cultivation is actually done by women. The man allocates land to his wives in a manner similar to the allocation of cattle, even keeping some back "for his own use" if he wishes. There seems to be more freedom for the man to retrieve these allocated rights when he remarries (and this is a subject of no little dispute between co-wives and between a father and his sons) , but the pattern is essentially the same. The land is inherited by sons, so that it remains within the clan; and like anointed cattle, it is inherited by the son whose mother cultivated that particular plot. A man has an obligation to supply his wife with land and to provide his sons with land.

On the other hand, the social uses and meaning of cattle were not, as already stated, applied to landholdings. Land does not figure either in bride-price or in wergild. We have the occasional instance of a matrilocal residence and of land given by a father to his daughter, but none of these were expressed in terms of marital regulations and seem rather to be but instances where an atypical behavior suited mutual convenience; nowhere is there a case of a man giving to his father-in-law a piece of land in lieu of cattle as part of the bride-price. And while we do have instances where land was taken over in lieu of wergild, these seem to be deficiency adjustments. They reiterate the value placed upon land in these agricultural sectors, but do not suggest even the beginnings of an institutionalized change, or a psychological identification. There is no land equivalent of cattle praise songs, nor is there any ceremonial expression of the allocation of land to a wife, as there is with cattle.

It does not follow, however, that land is disregarded as a mark of social status, or that Sebei do not jealously regard their holdings. The Sebei have boundary markers and fear land encroachment, and even in areas of relatively sparse settlement they dispute over land rights. Some Sebei have built up large personal holdings. In the farming village subjected to intensive study, one old man was busily engaged in increasing his holdings by purchasing plots from more impecunious neighbors. The modern practice is in part an acceptance of Western legal patterns, but it also has its roots in old Sebei custom.

In the discussion of contracts regarding land it was pointed out that the Sebei apply the namanyantet exchange in the purchase of field crops. There is no reason to believe that this is not an old practice in Sebeiland, for it would fit well a pattern of exchange under a system of pastoralism with secondary cultivation. Yet it is difficult to escape the feeling that even namanyantet exchange was an adaptation of the standard cattle contract to the uses of agriculture. Everything the Sebei said supports such a notion, though they did not specifically say that it was an adaptation. The evidence for such a thesis is that (1) the Sebei etymologized the word *namut* as "catch stomach," with the implication that it refers to the pregnancy of the heifer, and though the etymology is doubtful, the attitude implicit in the folk-etymologizing is itself suggestive; (2) the Sebei regularly and frequently use the contract in animal exchanges, but instances of its use for crops is rare; (3) the exchange creates a quasi-kinship, associated with strong psychological identification with the cattle, which does not fit attitudes respecting the land, let alone the food crops of the land; (4) this kin term was glossed by interpreters as "kin of the cow"; (5) there is a close delineation of contractual obligations under diverse contingencies when the contract is related to cattle, but no such clear detailing of obligations was found in exchanges involving crops; indeed, in one or two of the instances there was a suggestion of freedom to maneuver for advantage; (6) the pattern of cattle exchanges has been reported widely among cattle-keeping peoples in East Africa, but no similar report of exchanges for crops is to be found; and finally, (7) there are animal-for-animal exchanges and animal-for-land/crop exchanges, but none solely within the agricultural realm. None of these reasons is compelling alone, but taken together (and with the known increase in the importance of agriculture) they form a syndrome of circumstances that make it a reasonable assumption that the namanyantet contractual arrangement was an adaptation of a pastoral legal institution to the uses of farming.

A second adaptation appears also to have taken place, more in keeping with the sale of land than with the sale of crops or with limited use to the land. In obtaining clan histories in the area of intensive cultivation I learned that a number of clans had moved from the area now belonging to the Bagisu. Some had merely expropriated the land, but others, according to their grandsons who were my elderly informants, had "purchased" the land for one or a few animals. These events took place in the nineteenth century. But as we have seen in the discussion of pororyet affiliation, at a still earlier date there was the custom of slaughtering an animal and giving a feast to establish membership in one's adopted homeland. By the turn of the century, outright land purchases were made with livestock, and for the period when the rupee was currency in Uganda (ca. 1910) I have an instance of cash sale. Nowadays, there is a fairly active market in real estate.

This sale of land, which would have been entirely meaningless in an earlier epoch of Sebei economy, I view as a syncretic development, first out of diverse Sebei customs and later with European land practices. The Sebei practices that went into this development are (1) the furnishing of animals as a means of affiliating with the new area of residence, (2) the custom of namanyantet exchange, and (3) the practice of outright purchase of crops for livestock.

There is one further adaptation of the legal system of the past to the uses of commercial transaction in land: the use of options. Sebei told me that this was an old practice in marriage arrangements; a man might want to marry a young girl after she matured and would make a payment "to hold her down." Such a payment was an earnest of intent, and while under prevailing regulations it did not—and does not now—force ultimate performance, it was an effective instrument in a closed community. This practice has been adapted to the acquisition of land.

All in all, it seems entirely reasonable to assume that the institutional apparatus for ownership and exchange which had applied to the control of livestock came to relate to matters of land, and the assumption is supported by a good deal of internal evidence. At the same time, it is worthwhile noting that not all the elements of stock ownership transferred. The people in the densely farmed area today are quite absorbed in landholdings, as the prevalence of land cases testifies, and individuals gain status through their control of land; yet the strong psychological identification—or at least the institutional expression of such identification—is not found. There is no equivalent to praise songs, "bull of the herd," wergild, or bride-price which makes it possible to say that the individual and his land are psychologically one, or that social relations are translatable into land relations. If the shift to farming had reached so far into the substratum of Sebei culture, so deep into the psychological attitudes as that, it had still not been given any social expression.

The individuated attitudes, the personal independence of each adult male, had, I think, the effect of preventing the development of cooperative or communal holding of land, despite the fact that territories were taken over by clans, and despite the patterns of collaborative work parties. The contractual work arrangement may be seen as an institutional mode of circumventing the need for communal activity, and it fits the individuated basis of Sebei life.

In sum, the adaptation of ownership and contractual patterns from livestock to land represents a shift in the rules, the formal level of culture, as presented in the tabulation in chapter 12 (see p. 229) ; it does not represent a shift on the ideational level to any significant, or at least visible, degree.

The Age-Set in Sebei Legal Structure

Early in this analysis of Sebei legal institutions it is stated categorically that the age-set system had no role to play in Sebei juridical procedures or (with a minor exception) in the substantive aspects of Sebei law. This is most surprising, for the initiation by which a man enters his age-set is a focal element in ritual life, and furthermore, age-set membership is an important dimension of the social system in its nonlegal aspects. Every man and most women know their age-set; they greet in special ways their fellow age-set members; they are under obligation to entertain them specially; they utilize this bond in asking favors, and the like.

The age-set system in Sebeiland is a local variant of a widespread institutional pattern in East Africa, and in most instances these units play a major role in tribal governance. This role may have either or both of two aspects: (1) there is an internal control system within the age-set which coordinates its activities and gives the unit some aspects of a corporate group, and (2) the several age-sets play explicit social roles in the community at large—warriors, elders, and the like. When these operate together, they actually form an institutional structure for governance and hence for matters of law. There is every reason to believe that the Sebei, who share this institutional system (even sharing age-set names with some tribes) , must once have utilized it in legal action. If my informants were correct in saying that the Sebei once lived in age-graded manyattas, then certainly they would have had to have an important governing role.

Of such a role, the only aspects touching upon authority which remain are the regular recognition of seniority, the generic pattern of age deference, and the control of initiates over the behavior of preinitiated children. None of these is a matter reaching into the realm of law. It is fair to ask why so radical a change has taken place.

The age-set organization is functionally relevant to its two major and closely interrelated pastoral roles: herding cattle and military activity. Among such peoples as the Masai, who are perhaps the world's most devoted pastoralists, the cattle were in the charge of a junior age-set, young men in the full vigor of their youth. They were thus charged not because their livestock required such strength and agility—East African cattle are generally very docile and can normally be handled by a child—but because they were under constant threat of an enemy raid, and less importantly, of quadrupedal predators. Thus the age-set was prepared to fight, and inevitably also to retaliate. The age-set was the corporate structure that took over the military role and therefore had to have systematic internal control. The ceremonial and social supports for internal harmony were far-reaching. Under the inexorable pressure of time, the members of such a unity lose their youthful vigor while a later generation reaches it, and the role of warrior must be transferred. The older generation, however, does not lose its long-established sense of identity, nor would its members readily relinquish power. The corporate group remains a unity of elders and preserves a power derivative of seniority, thus performing functions of governance.

As cattle decline in importance, the economic and military roles of youth wane. It is true that some herding continues, but now it is near houses. Furthermore, the caves and escarpments of Mount Elgon make it possible to endeavor to hide from the raiders. While as a matter of fact the Sebei were repeatedly subject to attack and frequently lost both cattle and lives, they did utilize hiding as a regular tactic. The age-set was largely deprived of its useful role through the diminution of cattle, and to have preserved their strong unity would have created a potential for disruption—youthful gangs are not notoriously constructive social groups—while depriving the economy of their services to agriculture, slight as these were.

In addition to this negative influence, a positive force was at work making for a change of behavior. A sedentary farming people must be organized to defend a territory; hearth and property must be protected. Sebei military activity was organized on a territorial basis, each pororyet being responsible for its own defense. Military pressures were so severe that it made no sense to have a separate cadre of warriors; all able-bodied men were expected to help defend their territory. Military organization, therefore, appears to have been restructured from an age-set warrior band enterprise to a vertically integrated, spatially delimited operation. At the same time, military prowess lost much of its cachet (youths in the farming area today view it as simply foolishness) as well as many of its rewards. The Sebei did (and in the pastoral area still do) mount raids, but they tend to be retaliatory rather than initiatory, and not very profitable.

A contributory factor to this development may have been internecine strife among the Sebei. Bagisu pressure, as already indicated, pushed Sebei of the populous western region onto the north escarpment, where they in turn used their superior force against their fellow Sebei in a manner hardly calculated to preserve the lateral sense of harmony that would have made age-set military organization effective.

In this account there is perforce a good deal of conjecture over the causes for and the course of events with respect to the declining importance of the age-set. But comparisons with close neighbors of the Sebei and statements made by Sebei render it virtually certain that the pinta was once an important institution for social control; manifestly it is not so now. This basic change must certainly have deprived the Sebei of an orderly means of social control.

Ntarastit as a Transfer of Authority to the Community

The sedentarization of Sebei life in response to the development of agriculture, the concentration of population, and the conse-quent formation of permanent geographically based communities created a condition that required social restraints of a new kind. This need arose at the very period when (for the same basic ecologic reason) the juridical authority that we must assume once resided in the age-sets disappeared. I believe it is entirely reasonable to assume that the development of the unusual, not to say peculiar, custom of ntarastit was the Sebei means of seeking a sanction for community control of individual behavior, and in this section I want to examine it in that light.

It will be recalled that ntarastit was a Sebei-wide ceremony, initiated by the prophet and performed sequentially by the men of each pororyet, starting from the east and progressing to the west. Informants were in disagreement as to the frequency with which the ntarastit ceremony was held, but the general import of their statements indicates that it was at no regular interval, but was undertaken when the prophet felt the level of its moral force had so reduced itself as to require reaffirmation. Thus: "The time we punish in this manner is when we insist that the laws be obeyed and the time that we don't do this is when the law is not in effect. . . . In the third year, laws become weak and are forgotten and if the pororyet tries to take this kind of action, there will be a war."

The ntarastit ceremony consisted chiefly of an oath by all adult men of the pororyet, who swore a kind of fealty of acceptance on the pain of supernatural death. All circumcised men gather naked at the specified location, and before an altar of implanted branches of certain specified plants of ceremonial significance, swear as follows: "Anybody who kills anybody passing by (or who takes things belonging to others, etc.) , may the earth eat him." They thrust their spears at the altar in unison each time they recite this formula, naming a different kind of offense.

This oath has the same basic form as the oath of accusation normally performed between clans when an accusation was made. There, too, the men gathered naked around an altar of specified plants and thrust their spears toward it in unison, the clansmen of the injured party and of the accused party expressing their accusation or their innocence respectively in turn. Such a ceremonial oath was a means by which the supernatural forces of retribution would ultimately bring reprisal against the clan of the wrongdoer.

Ntarastit in its formal aspects is so like the sorcery that serves as underlying sanction for legal clan law that it is difficult to doubt that the two are related, that the one derived from the other. Ntarastit is, in effect, an invocation of supernatural authority for the maintenance of peace in the community. It differs from the sorcery underlying clan law on four counts:

1) Unlike the curse that follows a delict and seeks out the doer of an evil act, ntarastit precedes the act and stands in readiness as a retaliation against some future misdeed. It is thus a public affirmation of the law.

2) The oath is a community affair; it involves all the men of a pororyet and thus unites a geographic entity into a bond, without respect to age-set or clan, without respect to economic status—a bond that asserts a public right in the behavior of each individual and the personal obligation of each individual to maintain peace in the community.

3) Its sanction does not rest upon mystical forces, but in the action of the community; it asserts the right of the community to try, convict, and punish the offender, and to engage in such punishment free of either personal or supernatural retaliation.

4) It may also be viewed as significant that the oath refers to the fact that the *earth* will "eat" the person guilty of the delict. I believe oaths generally refer to the specific things involved. I do not mean to emphasize the use of earth here as being relevant to its agricultural productivity, but rather in its implication of locality or place—though both aspects may well be relevant.

I have already presented cases involving, and described the nature of community action under, ntarastit rule, but will summarize its operation here. The ritual brings any delict into the jurisdiction of the pororyet, which can then punish the responsible party. The punishment takes the form of destruction of his property—killing his livestock, slashing his plantains, destroying his crops, seizing his stored grain, and even burning down his house.

Before action is taken, apparently there is an informal hearing to decide that the punishment is proper. Once embarked upon, however, such retaliation appears to have been more a wild mob scene. While the ntarastit justifies the action of the community, it is always possible that the man they seek (and his clansmen) will resist the action. As one informant said, "Women and children don't go—it is a little like a war." Presumably the similarity to war varies to the degree that the moral imperative of the ceremonial act has been dissipated by the passage of time. Punishment does not legally eliminate the demand for compensation by the injured clan, though in none of the cases I collected was compensation obtained. One participant said: "You can punish the murderer's clan by taking property because they broke the law—still, the murder is not forgotten. The clan of the deceased must take revenge by killing a member of the murderer's clan or can accept compensation paid by that clan."

Ntarastit punishment is meted out both for murder and for theft. The punishment is the same, except that (appropriately enough) retaliation against a murder involves the destruction of property of the whole clan—or significantly that segment that resides in the pororyet—while in cases of theft the action is directed only at the household of the thief. This practice is in accord with the basic principle of Sebei law that violence is a matter of clan law and action is always against the clan, while the law of property is individual law and is always directed at the individual. The punishment in cases of theft, however, is severe in the extreme: one man was literally ruined by the destruction, during a famine, of his resources in retaliation for the theft of a bushel or two of millet. Another person suffered heavily for the theft of a single stem of plantains. One case indicates that several pororisyek took concerted action, which in view of general attitudes is surprising.

Some informants believed that ntarastit was an invention of the prophet Matui, others that he reinstituted it. It is not possible to reconstruct the history of the development of the institution. In addition to the above suggestion that ntarastit was a recent innovation, however, two important relevant facts must be borne in mind. First, it is nowhere reported among other Kalenjin or neighboring tribes, so far as I can discover, and thus must be a Sebei development. Second, it is clearly associated with the prophet Matui, who operated in the western, heavily cultivated region of Sebeiland.

The ntarastit, then, creates a kind of loose citizenship. This citizenship has two levels of applicability. It is quite explicitly pororyet-oriented, which is to say it reinforces the very social unity that is the military protective unit: it holds together the very people who have to stay together for protection against the constant marauding of neighbors. Secondarily, by coordination of the several pororyet ceremonies under the guidance of a single prophet, it also reinforces a sense of commonality and harmony among the Sebei as a whole. One case cited suggests that the ntarastit sanctions the punishment of individuals across pororyet lines, and informants spoke of the amity among all Sebei developed under the influence of the prophet Matui.

From this examination of ntarastit it is difficult not to think of it as an effort on the part of Sebei leadership, and particularly on the part of the prophet, to reorder the basic character of interpersonal relationships. Though even among pastoralists no man is an island unto himself alone, the need for community action is far less compelling. It is not merely because the population is more sparsely scattered over the land, but rather because of the freedom of movement that cattle-keeping permits. As Spencer writes regarding the Samburu, "In theory any stock owner has the right to live . . . where he pleases," and ". . . if two people quarrelled then they generally moved apart and kept apart." [2] This privilege is not, as I have already stated, readily available to a farmer.

As a solution, the ntarastit left much to be desired. Indeed, its very crudity—one might almost say it was only semi-institutionalized—suggests the recency of its development. It did not offer precise procedures, it did not adjust the level of punishment to the seriousness of the offense, and above all it did not demonstrate those staying powers that would make it a

[2] Paul Spencer, *The Samburu: A Study of Gerontocracy in a Nomadic Tribe* (Berkeley and Los Angeles: University of California Press, 1965), pp. 5, xxiv.

reliable instrument for the maintenance of order. Yet one cannot help but feel that at about the time Sir Henry Maine was analyzing ancient law and discussing its evolutionary development, Sebei leaders were taking a first tentative step away from the law of status to the law of contract.

Adaptation of Law and Cultural Evolution

The evolution of culture is not the progressive rise to higher levels of social existence; it is the adaptation of instrumental institutions to novel circumstances. It is in the detailed changes of explicit situations, changes made possible or requisite by shifts in technology, environment, or exploitative opportunities, that an understanding of the evolutionary process is to be found. The Sebei had made a major economic shift in their productive techniques not long before their mode of life was overwhelmed by the impact of Europeanization, and this economic development had important consequences for demography, settlement pattern, military needs and potentials, and the meaning of natural resources. It is not surprising that these changes should, in turn, render old institutions obsolete and new ones desirable. In short, they had an influence on the character of Sebei law.

I have shown in this chapter that in at least three areas the Sebei legal system did make adaptations to the new situation. As should be expected, the changes that were made involved the adaptation of existing institutions to new needs and the elimination of useless functions from continuing institutions. In cultural evolution, as in biological evolution, the essential process does not pose an opposition between adaptation and continuity; rather it sees continuity in adaptation.

Appendixes

Listed below is a glossary of all native terms used in the text. I have chosen to provide a simplified orthography in the text, both for economy and for ease of reading. A phonemic spelling follows each entry, together with a brief definition and index reference to major usages of the word. Native words used throughout the text are here printed in boldface (e.g., **aret, pinta**). The page reference to the definition in text or to major discussion of a concept is likewise in boldface. I have included place-names and a few names of important personages (but not clan names) in the list, together with a few Swahili or Luganda words, when appropriate.

I am indebted to Dr. Christine Montgomery for the phonemic analysis and other assistance relative to this glossary. She is currently preparing the first phonemic and grammatical analysis of Sebei.

The orthography used in this glossary is a phonemic one.

1. Consonants

stops	p	t	c	k
fricatives		s		
nasals	m	n	ñ	ŋ
laterals		l		
medians	w		y	
flaps		r		
trills		r̄		

In Sebei, the distinction between voiced and voiceless stops is not phonemic. All stops are voiced when preceded by nasals; /p/, /c/, and /k/ are also voiced intervocalically and following /l/, /y/, and /r/:

/sencɔntet/ is pronounced "senjɔndet"
/küparkɔr/ is pronounced "kübargɔr"

/c/ represents the palatal stop—characteristically heard t^y—which is rendered by literate Sebei (and in the text) as *ch*. The palatal nasal /ñ/ is similar to the *ni* sound in "*onion*"; it is not a separate articulation of *n* and *y*. /r/ is a flap and /r̄/ a series of flaps (or a trill), as in Spanish. These sounds contrast only in medial position.

2. Vowels

	front	central		back
high	i		u	
		ï	ü	
median	e	ë	ö	o
		ä	ɔ̈	
low	a		ɔ	

Two vowel lengths are distinguished: short vowels, which are marked with a diaeresis, and long vowels, which are unmarked. Although the long vowels may be reduced to the quantity of short ones in rapid speech, their quality remains distinct. Differences in quality among the short vowels, however, are often difficult to distinguish, since they are all articulated at points close to a mid-central tongue position.

The allophones of /i/ vary from a height approaching the French /i/ (as in *lit*) almost to the English *i* in "bit"; allophones of /u/ vary similarly, from some point near French *ou* (as in *fou*) to that of English *oo* in "book." In the case of /e/, the scope of variation in tongue height appears to be somewhat more limited; the distinction between the [e] and [ɛ] allophones is never so clear-cut as in the French *épée/paix* distinction. The pronunciation of the remaining vowels is less varied.

a as in f*a*ther
ɔ as in t*o*ss
ï as in b*u*ses
ë as in b*u*ses
ü as in p*u*t
ö, ɔ̈, and ä are reduced versions of their long equivalents, a distinction not made by all speakers.

3. Tone.

There are three phonemically significant tones in Sebei. The high tone has been marked with an acute accent; the midtone remains unmarked; the low tone is marked with a grave accent.

aletarion (Military leader; a Masai word adopted by Sebei.) 12

ankurwet /ànkúrwet/ (A bush widely used for "breaking sticks" in wife-bargaining.) 42n

aret, arosyek /aret, arosyek/ (Agnatic kin group or clan.) 11, 27, 35–39, 40, 148

aryemput /aryemput/ (A special horn for making announcements.) 101

Baganda (A Bantu people. The Baganda, under General Kakunguru, conquered the region of which Sebei was a part, and ruled it for several years. Singular, *Muganda*. The country of the Baganda is Buganda; their language, Luganda. The root form *Ganda* is often used for the people collectively.) 1, 15, 20, 24, 85, 92, 99, 106, 109, 160, 179, 181, 182, 220, 226, 274, 289

Bagisu (Bantu-speaking tribe living on the southwestern slope of Mount Elgon. Prefixing of the root-*gisu* is as with *Baganda*, above.) 8, 9, 13, 14, 15, 91, 94, 105, 123, 147, 149, 251, 255, 289

Binyinyi /piñíñ/ (A Sebei village, site of our 1954 fieldwork.) 58, 176, 181, 212

Bok /pɔk/ (A Kalenjin tribe, speaking a language that is mutually intelligible with Sebei, living south of Mount Elgon.) 32, 91

Bongom (A small Kalenjin tribe, speaking a language mutually intelligible with Sebei, living south of Mount Elgon.) 32

Budadiri (Village in Gisu country, formerly Sebei territory; a saza headquarters.) 63, 176

Bukwa (The eastern region of Sebei, near the Kenya border.) 9, 10, 15, 144, 148, 207

Chebonet /ceponét/ (A market village on the escarpment, east of Sipi.) 160, 175

Chema /cema/ (A pororyet in the Mbai territory.) 34, 86, 130, 202, 215n

chematakwey /cemëtapwéy/ (Good-bye) 205

chemorunyontet /cèmɔrũnyɔntet/ (A married woman who chases after men.) 55

Chepelat /cepelat/ (An age-set, subdivision of Maina.) 99

chepkerkayantet /cèpkërkáyàntet/ (Term for woman who uses women's magic, ntoyenik.) 114

cheporir /cepɔrír/ (The "cow of mourning" given to man who buries the deceased.) 61, 95

chepsokeyontet /cepsɔkéyɔntet/ (Diviner.) 83, 117

Kamnyerer /kamñèrer/ (A pororyet in Sapiñ area.) 33

kanam tengek /kanäm teŋek/ (Land contract.) 215

kankanet /kànkànet/ (A form of sorcery known to two clans only.) 49, 114, 117, **177**, 182, **201–202**, 231

Kapcheptemkoñ /kapceptemkɔ́ñ/ (A pororyet in Sapiñ area.) 33, 54, 86, 165, 175, 182, 183

Kapchorwa /kàpcɔrwa/ (The community in which the central offices of Sebei District are located.) 18, 106, 136, 178, 286

Kapeywa /kapeywá/ (A pororyet of Sapiñ.) 86, 215n

Kaproron /kaprɔ́rɔ̀n/ (A market village and gombolola headquarters in the central escarpment area.) 160, 177

Kaptui (A clan, also an area in Sipi.) 83, 99, 110, 180

Karamoja (The territory to the north of Sebeiland, occupied by the Karamojong.) 9

Karamojong (A "Nilo-Hamitic" tribe living to the north.) 9, 32, 91, 179, 180, 197, 198

kasaña /kàsàñà, kàsàñantet/ (Term of reference to clan of mother, or of mother's mother's mother. A man may not marry into these clans.) 56

Kaserem (A pororyet of the Sapiñ.) 54, 150, 174

katokyi /kàtɔkyi/ (Murder; purposeful killing.) **89**

kechiryet ap kamama /kecìryèt ap kamàmà/ (Sheep given to bride's mother's brother in marriage payment.) **45n**

kelil /kèlíl/ ("Sweet death"; death from old age.) 82, 94

kichepchuyta /kicepcuytá/ (Establishing the independence of a son by giving him his share of the stock. Glossed as "chasing him out of the house." The term is derived from the verb *pcuwu,* "to serve food from a dish," plus the suffix *-te,* denoting motion away; thus, "handed out or distributed.") **60**

kimngonget /kimŋɔ̀ŋèt/ (Stealing by force.) **163**, 168, 171, 172n, **181–183**

kintet /kíntet/ ("Bull of the herd," a special animal each man has in his kraal.) **61**

kiriketik ap koyeyto /kirikètìk ap kɔyèytɔ/ (Literally "breaking sticks of bride-price"; i.e., wife-bargaining session.) **42**

kiroroyek /kirɔrɔyék/ (Medicine made from crushed seeds, used for trial by ordeal.) **116, 118**

kirwokintet, kirwokik /kìrwɔ̀kìntét, kirwɔ̀kïk/ (An elder whose judgment in council is respected; loosely, a judge. Derived from the verb rwɔ̀c, "discuss.") 12, 18, 33, 34, 85, 101, **163–169**, 170, 202, 241, 242

kirwokintet ñe mining /kìrwɔ̀kìntét nye mínïŋ/ (Lesser kirwokintet.) **167**

kirwokintet nye wo /kìrwɔ̀kìntét nye wó/ (Major kirwokintet.) **167**

kwoloyit /kwòlòyít/ (A contractual arrangement for work service where payment is delayed.) 211, 213

lakanek /lakanék/ ("Evil eyes.") 115
latyet /latyét/ (Neighbor.) 44, 164
Luganda *See* Baganda. 15, 263, 290–291
luket /lukét/ (Raiding party.) 163

Maina /maynà/ (An age-set, initiated *circa* 1886–1906; by extension, that period of Sebei history.) 24, 55, 104, 107, 111, 172, 174, 180, 274, 276, 280–285
manyatta (Masai term for enclosed village, usually all men of same age-set.) 8, 30, 40, 149, 253
Masai (A Nilo-Hamitic tribe living in Kenya and Tanzania.) 9, 91, 151, 247, 254
masapek /mäsapék/ (A native root crop.) 217, 217n
masop /müsɔp/ (Upward on the mountain; particularly the area above the forest line.) 157
Matui (The last major prophet, resident of Kaptyai in western Sebei.) 32, 87, 94, 103, 106, 108, 156–157, 182, 183, 258, 259
Mbai /mpay (ék) / (The westernmost tribe of the group that formed Sebei.) 34, 74, 91, 106, 148, 149, 183
miruka (A minor civil division in modern government, roughly equivalent to the native sangta.) 290
morontoyit /mɔrɔntɔyít/ (Spear with point that disengages so as to remain in animal in order that poison can operate more effectively; used for hunting elephants.) 132
mowet /mɔwet/ (A fig tree.) 110
moyket /mɔykét/ (A work party.) 126, 131, 137, 157, 211–214
moykutwet /mɔykútwet/ (A plant whose roots are chewed and spit upon objects as a blessing.) 111
Muganda *See* Baganda. 15, 183
Mugisu *See* Bagisu. 91, 119, 122, 203
mumek /mumek/ (A public curse against an offender, not necessarily known.) 109, 111, 112, 160, 171, 177, 180
Murkutwa (A pororyet.) 165, 166, 184
mutisyet /mùtìsyet/ (Circumcision, both male and female, referring both to the operation and the ceremonial cycle.) 29
mutongole (A chief of a subdivision of a gombolola; also the subdivision. A Luganda term.) 177, 290
mutworintet /mùtwɔrintét/ (A person indentured to a rich man because of poverty.) 211
mwengket, mwengkonik /mweŋkét, mweŋkɔnïk/ (Beehive.) 158
mwongintet /mwɔŋìntét/ (Person who takes by force.) 181

namanet, namanisyek /nämanet, nämànĭsyèk/ (Cow held in one's kraal under namanyantet contract.) 66, **189–190**

namanya /nằmàñà/ (Thematic or "short" form of namanyantet used here adjectivally to refer to the contract.) 66, 67, 176, 191, **192–206,** 208, 215, 217

namanyantet, namanisyek /nằmànyantet, nằmànïsyek/ (Contract in which a bullock, or other consideration, is given in exchange for a heifer, which is returned after she has produced a heifer, which is kept.) **189,** 204, 205, 231, **250–251**

namut /nämút/ (Cows held in another person's kraal under namanyantet exchange contract which will return to owner when contract is fulfilled.) **189–190,** 196, 250

Nandi (A Nilo-Hamitic [Kalenjin] tribe living in Kenya.) 7, **9,** 30, 91, 163

nkokok ap kamama /nkokòk àp kamàmà/ (Chickens given to bride's mother's brother in marriage payment.) **45n**

ngokisto /ŋokïstɔ/ (False claim.) **163,** 168, 171, **178–180**

Ñongki /ñɔŋki/ (An age-set, initiated *circa* 1866–1885; by extension that period in Sebei history.) 24, 34, 104, 198, 201, 276–284 *passim*

ntarastit /ntàràstít/ (Ceremonial affirmation of community law.) 32, 34, **85–87, 106–107,** 162, 166, 170, 172, 173, 183, 184, 185, 236, 243, **255–260**

ntoyenik /ntɔyenïk/ (Magic done by women against men.) **55, 114, 121**

onantet, oyik /ɔnantét, ɔyík/ (Spirit of the dead.) 14, 36, 37, 76, 95, 113, 122–128, 230, 233, 241

panet /panét/ (A completed act of witchcraft; also the objects associated with witchcraft.) 114

paswet /paswét/ (A cut of meat from an animal's back.) **156**

piko che kikese /piko ce kikése/ (Witnesses; people who were watching.) **164**

piko che kimi cheto /piko ce kimí yétɔ/ (Witnesses; people who are present.) **164**

pinta /pïnta/ (Age-set.) 11, **27–31,** 42, 138, 255

pitet /pìtèt/ (A ceremony to remove a curse.) 111

Pokot (Kalenjin tribe living to northeast, formerly known as Suk.) **9,** 32, 91, 111

ponintet /pɔnìntét/ (A witch.) 113, 114, 115, 118, 119

ponisyet /pɔnìsyet/ (Witchcraft in the process of action.) 114

pororyet, pororisyek /pɔrɔryét, pɔrɔrïsyek/ (Basic territorial unit; subdivision of tribe.) 11, 13, 27, **32–34,** 40, 54, **85–87, 106–107,** 144, 146, 151, 162, 163–167, 171–174, 201, 202, 214–215, 255, 256–259 puronet /pürɔnét/ (Laziness, as basis for divorce.) 54 ff.

puswok /pùswɔ̀k/ (A negligent or incompetent person; one who is left behind.) 164

put /pùt/ (Literally, to pinch or pinch off; a payment made to close off an indebtedness.) 47, 166

Ragon (A village near Sasur on the western part of the escarpment.) 49, 214

rewet /rewet/ (The place in the house where spears are kept.) 200

ropsyet /rɔpsyét/ (A fine levied against a person; also, specifically, a penalty for past acts against the bride's family, claimed in bargaining for a bride.) 47

Sabaot (Modern term for closely related group of Kalenjin-speaking tribes; Sebei, Koin, Bok, Boŋom. They share the greeting *subay*.) 91, 144

sankañantet /sànkàñàntet/ An object that is shared by persons.) 207

sankanet /sankanét/ (Partnership, particularly in purchase of a cow.) 207

sangta, songmwek /sàŋtà, sɔŋmwëk/ (Minor delimited territorial unit; village.) 11, 27, 34, 40, 57, 144, 146, 150, 162, 163–167, 168–169, 171, 173n, 202

Sapiñ /sàpiñ/ (One of the Sebei tribes. The modern term *Sebei* is a Luganda corruption of *Sapiñ*.) 7, 91, 183

Sasur (A village of plantain-growing Sebei on the western section of the escarpment; one of the two villages in which the research camps were established.) 64, 218

saza (The Luganda term for major administrative district; county.) 15, 18, 63, 288, 289–290

sekutet /sèkùtet/ (A curse made privately against a suspect.) 109, 111, 159

senchen /sencèn/ (A measure of land.) 216, 216n

senchontet /sencɔ̀ntet/ (A plant used to mark boundaries between fields.) 149, 180, 216n

setet /sètet/ (Cattle raid.) 163

sikonet, sikonik /sïkɔnet, sïkɔnïk/ (The cattle in the herd belonging to the owner, whether or not allocated to a wife, but exclusive of those held under contract.) 189

sinantet (A vine used in many ceremonials as a sign of friendship.) 111

Sipi (The market village and gombolola headquarters on the western edge of the escarpment. Also a stream at that location.) 14, 58, 67, 120, 180

sokoran/sokɔ́ran/ (A sinful act.) 133–140

The specific events described to me or observed (in part) by me constitute both a source and a substantiation of the text. I drew 264 such instances from my notes, covering diverse legal matters and a period of about a century in time. This appendix offers three tabulations, the first indicating the source of information by type of offense for all cases, the second indicating the period of time to which the case may be allocated, and the third being an index of all cases referenced, listing their primary classification, source, time reference, and a brief notation. These tabulations are offered to give the reader a better appreciation of the range and types of data upon which the analysis is based. It should be emphatically clear that they in no sense reflect prevalence rates for types of offense; the mode of collection precludes their use for such purpose.

The legal encounters I have used as cases cannot always be neatly categorized; often they involve more than one offense. I have here classed them according to the delict (or the issue) that appears to have initiated the conflict.

Table 1.—The cases heard in the government-sponsored court, with few exceptions, were observed in 1954. As indicated in the text, rarely were such cases observed in full, but the major issues could be discerned and they offer us insight into present uses in legal matters. Most of the miscellaneous items (contempt of court, peculation, administration of governmental rulings with respect to health measures, etc.) are from this source. It is clear that certain offenses are not importantly represented: matters involving death are automatically excluded; witchcraft disputants generally avoid the courts (the single case was a man arrested for divination) ; contractual obligations, inheritance, and family matters (other than divorce proceedings) seem to be rare.

Most of the fifty-two cases observed in part were in connection with funeral moots and therefore deal heavily with contractual obligations. This category includes other observational data: disputes arising at wife-bargaining sessions, family hearings other than funeral moots, and ceremonies for the removal of sorcerous actions.

Of the ninety-five cases obtained directly from informants, fourteen were presented by groups of two or more men together.

Table 2.—I have tried to indicate the period of occurrence of the original delict or conflict in table 2 by type of case (see also Introduction, pp. 23–24). The categorization requires some explanation. The first two columns refer to the age-sets that were the last before the conquest of the Sebei by Kakunguru's men which took place about 1905. Ñongki refers roughly to the 1870's and 1880's; Maina to the period from the late 1880's to 1905, or thereabout. The next period has reference to what informants often often call Baganda times, that is, the period before the British administration was effective. I have expanded this period to cover the whole of the Chumo circumcision cycle, which closed in 1920. The fourth column has reference to the period of British control, but prior to my first visit to the Sebei; the fifth column refers chiefly to cases recorded during that visit (including most of the thirty-two court cases recorded). The last column includes those cases observed in 1961–62, including nearly all the moots.

Table 3.—This tabulation (and index) lists the cases cited or referenced in numerical order, indicating source, estimated time, type of case, and notation. It may be helpful to note that the numerical order is the order in which cases were recorded, that Cases 1–77 were recorded in 1954 and the remainder in 1961–62, and that the Law Conference cases include eighty-five entries running from no. 152 through 236.

TABLE 1

LAW CASES BY TYPE ACCORDING TO SOURCE OF INFORMATION

Category of case		Observation		Description		Total
		Govt. court	Moots	Informants	Law Conference	
PART ONE I. Affiliation				1	2	3
II. Family matters: Bride-price			1	8	3	12
Divorce and separation		5			7	12
Other			2	3		5
III. Inheritance: Livestock			1	3	3	7
Land				4	1	5
Wives			1			1
Other					1	1
PART TWO I. Violence leading to death: Murder				21	9	30
Other			1	4	16	21
II. Assault and injury Physical		3		1	3	7
Verbal					1	1
III. Sexual offenses: Rape		1			1	2
Other			1		3	4
IV. Witchcraft: Death				2	4	6
Illness				4		4
Sexual			1	4		5
Other		1	1	4	1	7
PART THREE I. Property offenses: Encroachment		1	2	5		8
Other land disputes		8		12	1	21
Chattels		1	1	6	8	16
Livestock		2	1	2	5	10
Other		1	6	4	4	15
II. Contract: Livestock		2	23	2	7	34
Land			3	3	2	8
Money			5			5
Other			1	1	2	4
Miscellaneous		8		1	1	10
Total		33	51	95	85	264

TABLE 2
LAW CASES BY TYPE ACCORDING TO TIME OF OCCURRENCE

	Category of case		Ñongki	Maina	1907–1919	1920–1949	1950–1959	1960–1962	Unknown	Total
PART ONE	I. Affiliation		1	1		1				3
	II. Family matters:	Bride-price		1	1	3	1	6		12
		Divorce and separation		3	1	3	5			12
		Other			1	1		3		5
	III. Inheritance:	Livestock		4	2	1		1		8
		Land	3	2						5
		Wives						1		1
		Other		1						1
PART TWO	I. Violence leading to death:	Murder	3	20	5	1	1			30
		Other	1	6	2	8	1	1	2	21
	II. Assault and injury:	Physical			2	1	3	1		7
		Verbal		1						1
	III. Sexual offenses:	Rape		1			1			2
		Other		1		2		1		4
	IV. Witchcraft:	Death		5	1					6
		Illness		2		1		1		4
		Sexual	1					4		5
		Other	1	1		3	1	1		7
PART THREE	I. Property	Encroachment		2		1	2	3		8
		Other land disputes	1	3		3	9	5		21
		Chattels	1	13	1		1			16
		Livestock		5	2		2	1		10
		Other		2	1	4	1	6		15
	II. Contracts:	Livestock	2	2	2	3	1	24		34
		Land		3	1	1		3		8
		Money						5		5
		Other		3				1		4
	Miscellaneous					1	8	1		10
	Total		14	82	22	38	37	69	2	264

TABLE 3
INDEX OF SEBEI LEGAL CASES
(Letter *r* = reference only.)

No.	Source	Time reference	Classification	Notation	Page reference
1	Gombolola Court	1954	Contract: livestock	Brother vs. brother	66, 291r
2	"	"	Marriage: divorce	Cruelty charge	50r, 56
4	"	"	Marriage: divorce	Claims desertion: denied	76r
7	Informant	1907–1920	Murder	Surupik performed to remove curse	103r, 110r
8	"	1936	Contract: livestock	Unpaid claim vs. father of informant	202
9	"	1929	Marriage: bride-price	Unpaid; responsibility of brother	46, 60r
10	"	1907–1920	Inheritance: livestock		64r, 66, 70r
11	"	Ñongki	Death: other	Brother killed for wizardry [also involved wife inheritance]	70
12	Gombolola Court	1954	Marriage: divorce	Bride-price returned	58
16	Group informants	Ñongki	Land dispute: other	Boundary dispute between brothers	170r
17	"	Maina	Murder	Land transfer in compensation	104
18	"	"	Murder	Compensation paid by clan	95r, 101, 165r
19	"	Ñongki	Witchcraft: sexual	Woman forced out for use of love magic	55r, 121
21	Gombolola Court	1954	Property dispute: other	Damages by livestock in field	151
25	"	"	Sexual offense: rape	Two men took woman by force	136r
27	Informant	Maina	Encroachment	Oath ceremony enforcement	180
32	"	"	Witchcraft: illness	Punishment under ntarastit after use of ordeal	118
33	2 informants	"	Witchcraft: illness	Ordeal did not "catch" either party	118
34	"	1907–1920	Witchcraft: death	Ordeal "caught" accused; he was killed [same as Case 187]	118

277

No.	Source	Time reference	Classification	Notation	Page reference
35	Informant	Maina	Death: other	Prophet killed for prophecies of doom [same as Case 177]	32r
37	"	"	Theft: livestock	Intraclan theft of cattle	169
38	"	"	Murder	Man killed for suspected witchcraft, but clan pays compensation	103
39	"	1907–1920	Murder	Compensation negotiated	103r
44	Saza court	1954	Theft: livestock		163r
46	"	"	Miscellaneous	Abuse against chief; 2months in prison	132r
52	"	"	Theft: livestock	Man claims brother failed to share bride-price	64
53	Informant	Maina	Murder	Avenged	107
54	"	"	Murder	Avenged	99
55	"	"	Murder	Avenged by killing man of equal standing with victim	97r
56	"	"	Theft: chattels	Destruction under ntarastit	107r
57	"	"	Murder	Settlement of 50 cattle, 10 sheep	103r
58	"	"	Theft: chattel	Man took elephant tusk; payment demanded by clan	157r, 179
61	"	"	Inheritance: livestock	Division of cattle	63
64	"	"	Land dispute: other	Dispute between half brothers	170r
66	"	"	Contract: land	Payment of bullock for land	215r, 216
67	"	Maina(?)	Theft: chattel	Interpororyet raiding	183

68	"	Maina	Theft: chattel	Punishment under ntarastit	107r
69	"	Ñongki to present	Inheritance: land	Allocation of land through generations	67r, 216r
72	"	Maina	Encroachment	Thief claims action in response to earlier assault; both punished under ntarastit	170
73	"	"	Theft: chattel		
78	"	1907–1920	Marriage: other	An instance of wife capture	172, 180r
81	"	Maina	Inheritance: land	Transmitting land to daughter's son	43r
82	"	Ñongki	Inheritance: land	Transmitting land to mother's brother	53
83	"	"	Murder	Land compensation for murder	53
84	"	Maina	Murder	Intraclan; use of surupik	97r, 105, 214r
86	"	"	Murder	Punishment under ntarastit	93r, 110
87	"	"	Murder	Punishment under ntarastit	106
89	2 informants	1961	Miscellaneous	Clan helps in restitution for man who has made false accusation	106
90	Informant	1920–1953	Witchcraft: other	Causing man to cry during initiation	133r
93	"	1961	Witchcraft: sexual	Witchcraft not effective	120
96	"	Maina	Murder	Vengeance and settlement	121
97	"	1962	Land dispute: other	Refusal to quit land after sale	90r, 99
98	"	Maina	Theft: chattel	Retaliation through blacksmith's witchcraft [same as Case 190]	218
99	"	1962	Marriage: bride-price	Use of kankanet to obtain payment	178
103	Funeral moot	1962	Contract: livestock		49 204

TABLE 3—*Continued*

INDEX OF SEBEI LEGAL CASES

(Letter *r* = reference only.)

No.	Source	Time reference	Classification	Notation	Page reference
113	Informant	Maina	Witchcraft: death	"Caught" by oath but escapes	119r
115	"	1907–1920	Murder	Compensation in cattle [same as Case 148]	103r
117	"	Maina	Death: other	Witnesses agreed killing accidental	89, 97r
118	"	"	Encroachment	Only case of record from plains area	144r
120	Observation	1953	Contract: land		54r
122	"	1962	Encroachment	Between co-wives	153r, 170r
127	Funeral moot	"	Family matters: other	Funeral rites held for missing man	76
130	"	"	Land dispute: other	Man sold land he didn't own	218r
136	2 informants	1950	Land dispute: other	Son takes land against father's will	168r, 169
138	"	"	Land dispute: other	Sons claim father took land of their mother	153r
139	Informant and observation	1962	Marriage: other	Court demands man give up unwilling bride	132r
141	Informant	1943	Property offense: other	Encroachment on right to use tree for beehives	158
143	Funeral moot	1962	Contract: livestock	Hyenas got ram; must be replaced	194, 195r
145	"	"	Contract: livestock	[Same as Case 115]	197
148	Informant	Maina	Murder	Over woman, vengeance	103r, 105r
149	"	Ñongki	Murder	Vengeance; cause, land dispute	99, 104r
150	"	"	Murder	Kota "expelled" from clan	214
151	"	"	Affiliation		93r, 107
152	Law Conference	Maina(?)	Death: other	Man "causes" wife's death; must pay bride-price	60r, 94

153	"	1920–1953	Death: other	Wife's death in childbirth requires compensation	94r, 95
154	"	1952	Death: other	Man must pay bride-price for woman who died in childbirth	60r, 94
155	"	Maina	Witchcraft: death	Use of ordeal	118
156	"	"	Murder	Vengeance: person of similar status	99
157	"	Maina(?)	Murder	Troublemaker's death unavenged	107
158	"	1952	Murder	Murderer committed suicide; cattle divided among family of two victims	103r
159	"	1920–1953	Death: other	Jail sentence; ceremonial payment only	89, 97r
160	"	Maina	Death: other	Ceremonial payment	89
161	"	1920–1953(?)	Murder	Between brothers; land given to victim's family	92,104r
162	"	1920–1953	Death: other	Fratricide; no compensation	91
163	"	Maina	Death: other	Clan brothers; no compensation	91r, 92
164	"	"	Murder	Brothers kill a mad killer	108
165	"	"	Murder	Property destroyed under ntarastit	86 106r, 173r
166	"	1907–1920	Murder	Killing of wife demands compensation to her family	91r, 94, 103r
168	"	"	Death: other	No action in killing own son	92
170	"	1920–1953	Death: other	Fraticide; no action	91

TABLE 3—*Continued*

INDEX OF SEBEI LEGAL CASES

(Letter *r* = reference only.)

No.	Source	Time reference	Classification	Notation	Page reference
172	Law Conference	"	Death: other	No action	95
173	"	"	Death: other	No action to person inciting suicide	96
175	"	?	Death: other	No action to person inciting suicide	96
178	"	1907–1920	Assault: physical	No compensation	130
179	"	1920–1953	Assault: physical	Payment of goat	129
180	"	1907–1920	Assault: physical	Payment of goat	130
181	"	1920–1953(?)	Sexual offense: other	Despised by people	133
182	"	"	Sexual offense: other	Replacement of cow	138
183	"	Maina(?)	Sexual offense: other	No action	137
184	"	"	Sexual offense: rape	Speared to death for repeated rape	136
185	"	"	Assault: verbal	Man killed for spreading rumor of witchcraft	132
186	"	Maina	Witchcraft: death	Killed by victim's relatives without ordeal	117, 119r
187	"	"	Witchcraft: death	[Same as Case 34]	118
188	"	"	Witchcraft: death	Avenged by witchcraft (tortayet)	119
189	"	1907–1920	Theft: other	Kankanet used to kill thief	182
191	"	"	Contract: livestock	Kankanet works, but fails to force repayment	201
192	"	1920–1953	Theft: other	Kankanet forces return of money	177
194	"	Maina	Affiliation	Method of joining pororyet	34r, 54
195	"	"	Contract: land sale	Clan refuses to allow sale to suspected witch	150
196	"	"	Property offense: other	Right to bee trees sustained	138

No.		Period	Name	Offense	Disposition	Pages
198	"	1907–1920		Contract: land	Clan won't allow sale to outside clan	149
199	"	"		Contract: livestock	Appeal of ruling to pororyet	165r, 202
200	"	"	Maina	Property offense: other	Disallow cultivation of kok	146
201	"	"	"	Marriage: bride-price	Animal returned to groom's family	47r, 62r, 166, 168r
202	"	"	"	Theft: chattel	Fine of two goats imposed	171
203	"	"	"	Theft: chattel	Fine of two goats imposed	107r, 171
204	"	"	"	Theft: chattel	Punishment under ntarastit	93r, 107r, 172
205	"	"	"	Murder	No action against woman-killer	94r
206	"	"	"	Murder	No action; no clan, and ntarastit not in effect	86
207	"	"	"	Theft: chattel	Matter ultimately resolved through sorcery	157r, 178
208	"	"	"	Theft: chattel	From father; ultimately settled by mumek	160, 169r
209	"	"	1910–1920	Theft: livestock	From father; restoration demanded	160, 168r
210	"	"	Maina	Land dispute: other	Land taken from father	160, 168r
211	"	"	"	Theft: livestock	Supported by force, but ultimate justice through surupik	180, 184r
212	"	"	Ñongki	Theft: chattel	To force contract into court	183r, 200
213	"	"	Maina	Theft: chattel	To force contract into court	183r, 201
214	"	"	"	Theft: livestock	Clan kills recidivist thief	90r, 176
215	"	"	"	Theft: livestock	Clan kills recidivist thief	172r, 174
216	"	"	"	Theft: livestock	Clan kills recidivist thief	107r, 172r, 174

TABLE 3—*Continued*

INDEX OF SEBEI LEGAL CASES

(Letter *r* = reference only.)

No.	Source	Time reference	Classification	Notation	Page reference
217	Law Conference	"	Contract: livestock	Man must get permission to kill namanya animal	208
218	"	Ñongki	Contract: livestock	Difficulty in making contract for man with poor performance record	203, 205r
219	"	1920–1953	Contract: livestock	Delay of payment as retaliatory sanction	203, 205r
220	"	Maina	Contract: livestock	Continuity of liability under contract	198,199r
221	"	Ñongki	Contract: livestock	Continuity of liability under contract	198
223	"	Maina	Contract: other	Purchase of crop with goats	217
224	"	"	Contract: other	Purchase of crop with goats	217
225	"	1910–1920	Marriage: divorce	Annulment because of "bad birds"	48
226	"	Maina	Marriage: divorce	Annulment because of "bad birds"	56
227	"	1920–1953	Marriage: divorce	Incompatability	58
228	"	"	Marriage: divorce	Woman leaves husband	59
229	"	1920–1953(?)	Marriage: divorce	Woman leaves husband	59
230	"	Maina	Marriage: divorce	Man divorces wife for laziness	54
233	"	"	Inheritance: land	Man inherits land from wife's father	53
234	"	1907–1920	Inheritance: livestock	Stepson inherits cattle	36, 75r
235	"	Maina	Inheritance: livestock	Man vs. guardian who used up his inheritance	74
236	"	"	Inheritance: other	Disinherited son	75
238	Informant	1962	Land dispute: other	Woman demands land from husband; refused	59r, 69, 153r
240	"	Maina	Murder	Small compensation for killing old man	103r

284

241	"	Contract: other	"Purchase" of elephant poison	157
242	1962	Marriage: bride-price	Problems in failure to negotiate	50r
246	Funeral moot	Contract: livestock	Abrogation of agreement	205
247	"	Contract: livestock	Cancellation of debts	206
248	"	Theft: money	Son steals from father	169r
249	"	Sexual offense: other	Use of oath to deny intercourse with father's wife	133r
251	"	Contract: livestock		197r
254	"	Contract: livestock	Kamanaktay	197
256	"	Contract: livestock		210
260	"	Contract: livestock	Impossible to collect debt from man who left area	209
261	"	Contract: livestock	Impossible to collect debt from man who left area	209
262	"	Contract: livestock	Kamanakan arrangement	210
263	1920–1953	Inheritance: livestock	Sharing of cattle between brothers	63

A Special Note on the Law Conference

The Law Conference, a meeting held at my request at Kapchorwa, was attended by some dozen elderly members of the Sebei tribe; they were mostly of the Chumo age-set, persons circumcised between 1910 and 1920 and therefore in their late sixties or seventies. I presided over the conference; Gale Goldschmidt served as recorder, and either Fleming or Hunt was present at each session. Y. Chemtai did most of the interpretation, aided by R. Bomet. At most sessions there were younger officials present who entered freely into the discussion. (The regular participants are listed at the end of this appendix.) Sessions convened at about nine o'clock in the morning, and in accordance with Sebei practice continued until one or two in the afternoon. The citizens were given expense money as compensation; the general level of interest among them was quite high.

We followed an agenda that was not made available to the participants, taking up legal problems as recognized in modern law, but taking into account such knowledge of native rules as I had acquired in the course of my work with the Sebei, and formulated with the help of Fleming. Participants were asked to give supporting cases for generalizations, although sometimes they could not find a case for a rule they insisted on, and occasionally their case did not support the matter at hand. Disagreements, which were rare, arose from misunderstanding rather than from different interpretations of the law. Native terms were sought and their semantic limits explored, but not in the detail currently in vogue among those engaged in componential analysis.

It seems unnecessary to give the detailed agenda, which ran to five single-spaced pages, but the order of discussion may be summarized.

1. *Murder and physical violence resulting in death.*—The discussion was opened by exploring Sebei ideas of the cause of death and proceeded to the factors defining death as a murder; the concept of accessory and other factors affecting ideas of responsibility; apprehension; determination of guilt; and assessment of penalty.

2. *Other forms of violence.*—This discussion pertained chiefly to what modern law calls assault and battery, but a discussion of verbal abuse, slander, and rumor was included.

3. *Sexual offenses.*—Marriage prohibitions, definitions and treatment of rape, adultery, fornication, and "unnatural" sexual acts were discussed.

4. *Witchcraft.*—This included the use of oaths.

5. *Ownership.*—The kinds of goods that could be owned and the nature of the owning agent were the first foci of discussion, followed by the nature of the rights and obligations attendant on ownership.

6. *Offenses against property.*—Encroachment, theft, misrepresentation, and destruction of property were discussed, together with mode of apprehension and nature of punishment. Arson was inadvertently omitted.

7. *Contracts.*—Discussion covered competence to contract; ingredients of contracts, such as time, consideration, witnesses; penalties for broken contracts; detailed elements of normal contractual obligations; and enforcement.

8. *Marriage and divorce.*—The nature of the marriage contract, obligations of the parties, and the grounds for divorce of both men and women, together with matters of settlement and custody, as well as adoption, were taken up.

9. *Inheritance.*—Inheritance rules for property and for wives, and disinheritance, were discussed.

Affiliation.—This topic included obligations of membership in clan, sangta, pororyet, and tribe, and the selection, rights, and duties of kirwokik and other special roles.

The citizen participants in the Law Conference were the following (the last two are women) :

Richard Bomet   Kapchemoikin   Mwanga Muganga
Kapsilut   Psiwa Kapchekutwo   Chemawo Kiteywo
Juma Malinga   Ali Musani   Yapchemisto
Manguso Aramusani   Erika Chelakam   Samari

Officials present at most of the sessions were:

Aloni Muzungyu, Saza Chief
Stanley Salimu, Saza Judge
Paulo Salimu, member of District Council

A Note on Present Legal Behavior

Since Kakunguru's organization established a modicum of authority over the people of Sebei, about the year 1905, there has been external influence on court procedures and the judgment of disputes. The Baganda administration was, by modern accounts, an extremely harsh one. It was soon replaced by the British Colonial Service, which gradually exerted more and more authority over Sebei affairs until 1962, when Uganda was established as an independent nation. During the last decade or so of British rule there was an increasing devolution of authority. During my 1961–62 visit, there was considerable shift in personnel. At the same time, the Sebei were establishing themselves as an independent district, thus freeing themselves of domination in political and legal matters from the Bagisu, their Bantu neighbors to the west who resided at the center of government in the Eastern Province of Uganda and had achieved a higher level of education and a greater degree of acculturation. In 1962, also, the Uganda government was undertaking to separate the judiciary from the administrative arm of government and endeavoring to train a cadre of special magistrates to hear cases in the local courts.

By 1954 there was already a Saza (county) judge, but local courts were presided over by the local chief, assisted by a group of assessors. Uganda has long been divided into a series of provinces; Sebei is in the Eastern Province, whose headquarters were established at Mbale about 1954. Each province was divided into districts, and as indicated, Sebei was a part of Bagisu district until 1962. At that time Sebei constituted a saza, the boundaries conforming with reasonable accuracy to the present distribution of population. (The term *saza* is of Luganda origin; it and the other political divisions are referred to by their Luganda equivalents.) The saza was divided into several gombololas—the number has varied—and these in turn into mutongole and miruka. Each unit had a chief, but the miruka had no formal court. The chief, together with the appointed council of the subdivision, heard cases within the jurisdiction of the subdivision, which meant not only those that fell within the community, but also those within its established area of competence as delineated under the Native Courts Ordinance. Certain cases were initiated at diverse levels, and the ordinance laid down with precision the punishment that could be awarded. Certain cases could be appealed from the native courts to the "subordinate courts" presided over by the district commissioners and the resident magistrates. The native courts were commonly rendered incompetent to deal with any offense involving loss of life or (prior to independence, at least) with any matter involving a non-African. They were often specifically empowered to enforce colonial legislation, as for example the Waragi Ordinance and certain sections of the Witchcraft Ordinance.

The courts were enjoined by the ordinance governing them to try their cases in accordance with "local law and custom" except when in "conflict with natural justice and fundamental morality."

Court was normally held in the saza or gombolola headquarters, though occasionally the saza court acted as a circuit court to ease the burden of the citizenry, and to enable the assessors to examine the evidence of land boundaries and the like. It was presided over by the chief of jurisdiction, and heard by him and a group of appointed assessors. A clerk recorded the gist of each statement and read his summaries back to the litigants or the witness; these statements were signed—by a thumbprint if the person was not literate. Each party to a civil complaint, or the police officer in a criminal complaint, presented his case. Witnesses were then called. The procedure usually devolved itself to a single issue drawn by the president of the court. Assessors were then asked to express their views with respect to guilt and determination of punishment or action, after which the chief rendered a decision that was binding, though subject to appeal.

The chief's decision did not always conform to those of the assessors, but it usually did, and the punishment meted out was within the range of their evaluations. No vote was ever taken. Some indication of the nature of the colloquy may be had from the presentation of Case 1, page 66.

It can readily be seen that these procedures conform to little in Western law and to considerably less in that of the Sebei. Significantly, Baganda and British overrule quickly eliminated the major sanctions of Sebei law: the use of the oath (including ntarastit) and the resort to feud. The elimination of the oath and its replacement with sworn testimony of witnesses altered the basic "rules of evidence" as well.

When we turn to substantive matters, the situation is different. Within their area of jurisdiction the Sebei native courts reflected more often than not old Sebei attitudes, even when the latter were in conflict with the moral (and I believe judicial) precepts of the current government. As we have seen in chapter 3, on family law, the Sebei consider it the prerogative of the father to determine whom his daughter shall marry. The Sebei native courts did not always protect the role of the father (or of the husband, in divorce cases), but its operation clearly reflected the basic presumption of their rights and acted against them only when these rights were demonstrably and flagrantly abused. From remarks made in passing, I am persuaded that the native court did not appreciate the niceties of Sebei contracts regarding cattle; the implication was that the native court would award an owner only a number of cattle equivalent to what he had lost, whereas Sebei regularly expect that the original animal *and all its progeny* would be a legitimate claim.

It is quite clear from the record that this formal court system is not the only arena currently available for the resolution of conflicts of interests among modern Sebei. Sorcery is formally interdicted, but clearly its use remains and is functionally effective. Family moots and other local gatherings are used with varying degrees of formality to determine matters of contract, inheritance, family relations, witchcraft, and theft. As much of this informal litigation is surreptitious, it is impossible to assess the relative importance of such older procedures—nor would statistics be meaningful. It is quite clear that the Sebei readily move from one system to another in an endeavor to arrive at a satisfactory settlement: behind a funeral moot claim stands the threat of a native court action, and surely behind the action of that court there still remains the possibility of sorcery. This interplay between old procedures and modern courts has made for greater continuity in the underlying attitudes and patterns of legal behavior than appears on the surface.

Index

Index

(Cross-references to native terms indexed on pages 265–272 of the Glossary are indicated by italics.)